THE
HAUNTING
OF
WILLINGTON
MILL

THE
HAUNTING
OF
WILLINGTON
MILL

The Truth Behind England's
Most Enigmatic Ghost Story

MICHAEL J. HALLOWELL
& DARREN W. RITSON
FOREWORD BY COLIN WILSON

Dedicated to the memory of Catherine Crowe

First published 2011

The History Press
The Mill, Brimscombe Port
Stroud, Gloucestershire, GL5 2QG
www.thehistorypress.co.uk

British Library Cataloguing in Publication Data.
A catalogue record for this book is available from the British Library.

ISBN 978 0 7524 5878 6

Typesetting and origination by The History Press
Printed in Great Britain
Manufacturing managed by Jellyfish Print Solutions Ltd

CONTENTS

ACKNOWLEDGEMENTS

Our thanks must go to: Beth Amphlett of The History Press, for her tenacity and support. Colin Pratt, Operations Manager, and Ray Summerson from Bridon Ropes at Willington Quay, for their incredible co-operation. Colin Wilson, author and researcher, for kindly writing the foreword to this book. Dr Melvyn Willin, the Honorary Archive Officer for the Society for Psychical Research, and Peter Johnson, its secretary, for helping the authors access material crucial to their research. Durham County Libraries, for kindly supplying information regarding Dr John Trotter and 'Jane'. Guy Lyon Playfair, for his well-received advice. Ionela Flood from the Romanca Society, for helping to resolve the enigma of the mysterious *Umanian Magazine*. Professor Katie Wales, Special Professor in English, University of Nottingham, for her advice regarding the use of English language in the nineteenth century and, in particular, the Procter Diary and other documents. Newcastle-upon-Tyne Central Library, for their help in tracking down *The True Story of the Willington Ghost* and other archived materials. North Tyneside Reference Library, for supplying much information regarding the history of Willington Quay and Willington Mill. North Tyneside Borough Council Planning Department, for information relating to Willington Quay in past times. North Tyneside Borough Council Housing Department, for information regarding the modern-day street layout of Willington. Peter Meadows, archivist at the Society for Psychical Research, for helping the authors ascertain the existence (or otherwise) of archived materials from the file on the Willington Mill enigma held at Cambridge University. Philip Solomon, clairvoyant medium, for his much-valued assistance and astounding abilities. Richard Freeman, Zoological Director of the Centre for Fortean Zoology, for his advice regarding the mysterious moonrat and for his contribution towards the discussion on 'Window Areas'. South Tyneside Local Studies Library, for helping the authors track down rare pieces of archived information regarding Thomas Hudson. The Society for Psychical Research, for allowing us to quote liberally from their publications and for their valued assistance in so many other ways. Tony Stockwell, clairvoyant medium, for his much-valued assistance and astounding abilities.

FOREWORD

In my introduction to Catherine Crowe's advertisements at the back of old Victorian novels, I experience a certain melancholy. It is sad to realise how many of the great and famous of the previous century are now totally forgotten. The once-celebrated Bertha H. Buxton can be found next to Honoré de Balzac, whilst Mrs Gore, Theodore Hook and Amelia B. Edwards seem to be as highly regarded as Walter Scott, Alexandre Dumas and Victor Hugo. And, to judge from the advertisements in the back of Routledge's Railway Library, Mrs Catherine Crowe was as famous as Dickens and Thackeray.

Who was Catherine Crowe? Among other things, she was the narrator of one of the oddest ghost stories of all time, the haunting of Willington Mill in North Tyneside, to which this book is devoted.

Other well-known contemporaries, like W.T. Stead and William Howitt, were just as baffled by the procession of bizarre phenomena which occurred in the mill situated on a river called Willington Gut.

I also noted that, 'to judge by her novels Mrs Crowe was a highly intelligent and imaginative woman, with a good ear for dialogue and a certain flair for languages'. But for all her qualifications, this gifted lady was as puzzled by the haunting of Willington Mill as we are today.

Not that Mrs Crowe was uncritical; on the contrary, *The Night Side of Nature*[1] is the first sustained attempt to treat paranormal phenomena in the scientific spirit which would later characterise the Society for Psychical Research. In that respect, her presentation of the case of the haunted mill is a classic.

The problem faced by Crowe and others was not so much collecting the data – they were in touch with many of the eyewitnesses – but in interpreting it. That is our problem too. Over the passing decades the Willington Mill story has become confused by myth and folklore, so our perception of events is distorted, as if we were looking back at the mid-nineteenth century through a prism.

To unravel the truth behind the case is no easy task, as Henry Sidgwick, the founder of the Society for Psychical Research, discovered when he applied his mind to it in the 1890s. He also noted the involvement of several apparitions – such as a woman in a grey shawl, a boy in a 'drab hat' and a bare-headed priest in a clerical surplice, seen by various witnesses at the mill; not to mention a confusing menagerie of bizarre animals, such as an odd-looking donkey, a cat-like creature with a long snout, and a mischievous monkey, all of which appeared – and just as suddenly disappeared – without trace.

The authors of this book make no claim to have solved all the mysteries of Willington Mill, but they have certainly solved many of them, and for others offer some plausible and intriguing hypotheses. It is also worth adding that, if they are correct, they may also have gone far towards proving the reality of life after death.

In this book, for the first time, the full truth about what occurred at that sleepy Tyneside village has been laid bare for all to see. The strength of *The Haunting of Willington Mill* lies in the fact that the writers have, also, for the first time, drawn together almost all of the available historical material relating to the case under one literary roof.

In my own opinion, the authors have remained faithful to the high standards set by Catherine Crowe.

In my introduction to her book I stated 'that Mrs Crowe ... attempted to establish psychical research on a rational, scientific basis'. In another work, *The Supernatural: Unlock the Earth's Hidden Mysteries*[2], I also noted that, 'with the wisdom of hindsight, we can see that the most interesting and significant pages of *The Night Side of Nature* are those that concern the haunting of a house owned by an industrialist named Joseph Procter. Here Mrs Crowe presents the kind of carefully documented account that would be the aim of the later investigators of the Society for Psychical Research'.

Also with the wisdom of hindsight, we can say that it is strange indeed that no one has hitherto attempted to write the definitive work on the Willington Mill mystery. The case has been detailed in numerous books, journals, articles and newspapers, but no one has penned an exhaustive, detailed work devoted exclusively to unravelling the truth behind this, one of the world's most enduring paranormal mysteries. Michael J. Hallowell and Darren W. Ritson have decided to set matters straight, and you now hold in your hands the fascinating results of their handiwork.

Colin Wilson

Notes

1. Crowe, Catherine, *The Night Side of Nature* [ed. Colin Wilson, fr. The Colin Wilson Library of the Paranormal] (Aquarian Press, 1986)

2. Wilson, Colin, *The Supernatural: Unlock the Earth's Hidden Mysteries* (Parragon, 1995)

INTRODUCTION

Ghost stories have an almost unique ability to marry the past with the present. A ghost may be the spirit of someone who lived then, but may well be seen by witnesses who live now. Hauntings are timeless – a fact which only serves to enhance their mystique. The allure of a true ghost story depends, of course, on what one wishes to draw from it. For some, it is the deep feeling of unease that permeates the senses combined with the soothing knowledge that one is not an eyewitness, but merely a reader. A colleague of ours once described this as 'being scared at a distance'. Reading about truly frightening hauntings may rack up the tension, but is unlikely to cause blind panic. It's a bit like going on a roller-coaster ride; you get scared, but all the time you know deep down that you're really pretty safe.

For some, though, the allure is different. It is not so much the horror that attracts, but the ambience; the setting of the tale is, to many, of equal importance to the events. Hence, the ghost of a lady dressed in grey who walks the parapets of an old castle will act as a much stronger magnet than that of a spectral teenager seen riding a bicycle down the street. Some true ghost stories are fortunate enough to possess both qualities. Some researchers may instinctively shy away from accounts that are set in an environment rich in history. It is as if the ambience may in some way detract from the tale, making it sound more like a novel by Charles Dickens that an account of a real-life haunting. The authors would venture that to take such a stance would be to throw the metaphorical baby out with the bath water; if the setting of a true ghost story is rich in history and romance, then so be it. We should enjoy it without in the least feeling that our pleasure in some way diminishes the value of the facts.

This book is about one of Britain's most notorious hauntings. For several decades in the mid-nineteenth century, a series of seemingly inexplicable events occurred in an old flour mill at Willington Quay,

North Tyneside. To this day there have been no satisfactory explanations offered as to its cause. The story of the Willington Quay haunting is steeped in local history, and speaks of a bygone era divorced from our own in a multitude of respects. We live in a different world now, but what happened at Willington Quay all those years ago may – if you'll excuse the pun – still come back to haunt us.

When the authors began their research into the case the story was not new to them. Indeed, both authors have made reference to the case in their previous publications. Mike's attention to the case began when, in July 1999, he was researching material for another book project. He visited the Local Studies Library at South Shields and, quite by accident, stumbled across a yellowing newspaper cutting which detailed the death of a local character called Thomas Hudson. Much of the lengthy obituary was taken up with a discussion of the Willington affair and the part that Hudson played in it. On a whim, Mike photocopied the cutting and stored it away in his archives. Then, in February 2004, Alan Tedder – a first-class researcher and author from Sunderland – gave Mike another cutting from an undated, unsourced newspaper which also recounted the story. Both sources were filed away and forgotten about until, in February 2009, Darren suggested to Mike that they collaborate together on a book about the incident.

Darren first heard about the Willington Mill poltergeist as a youngster. He would often cycle past 'Willington Gut', and his father regularly recited stories to him about the ghosts which were said to have haunted an old mill that once stood there. In later years, he heard other tales of hauntings in the same area, including the spectre called 'Kitty, the Ghost of Haggies' Mill', which will be elaborated upon later in this volume. After he moved into the area, in 2002, he began to visit the site regularly and would often walk along the bank of the dene in the hope of seeing the spectre of Kitty. Unfortunately, he never did.

One of the sad aspects of paranormal research – and in particular the investigation of hauntings – is that so many times the facts are distorted and twisted before being written down. The end result may be fascinating and make for a good read, but bear little or no relationship to the truth. The authors of this book have tried to avoid falling into this trap as much as they can. There may be mistakes in their work – no authors are perfect – but they endeavour to make as few as is humanly possible.

Like all supernatural stories, the haunting of Willington Mill has suffered from the effects of sloppy research and the making of too many assumptions. When seen in its true light, the affair is as fascinating – and troubling – as any of the romanticised versions.

There have been relatively few attempts to explain the Willington Mill haunting, despite the fact that, at the time, it received considerable media attention and was investigated by the Society for Psychical Research, which holds a file in their archives about the affair to this day. The authors have been given access to some little-used material held in private collections and have also uncovered documentary evidence which was previously thought lost or not even known to have existed. As with all their investigations, the authors went in with a completely open mind, neither believing nor disbelieving the accounts they had been made privy to. Approaching a case from the perspective of either a believer or a sceptic is hopeless and makes it virtually impossible to weigh the evidence objectively.

To the authors' knowledge, this is the first book dedicated entirely to the haunting of Willington Mill. It is one of a handful of true supernatural stories that seriously challenges the sceptic. The authors make no apology for that, and are happy to present the facts to those who are open-minded enough to acknowledge that 'believing only what you can see' is a flawed philosophy. Sometimes we may see things that are truly hard to believe. Something very strange did indeed happen in that old mill house all those years ago, and we are still bereft of many answers. If this book goes some way to rectifying the situation, then the authors will rest content.

At first, the authors viewed their investigation as purely an historical enigma with distinctly paranormal overtones; a story about a fascinating haunting in an old mill which positively begged to be told. But then they uncovered a number of disturbing facts, little known or completely ignored by other researchers, which forced them to concede that there was far, far more to the case than met the eye and drew them to a conclusion that was nothing short of explosive. If they were right, then the haunting of Willington Mill provided them with an opportunity to answer a question that has plagued mankind since the beginning of time: is there really life after death?

The authors believe that they were privileged to be allowed to take part in the culmination of a drama that stretched over several centuries and has baffled a number of great intellects. The story begins with an old woman who lived in a cottage in the seventeenth century, and ends with two modern-day psychic mediums attempting to unlock the past. The haunting of Willington Mill is a story that touches every one of us, for the lessons learned from it indicate most powerfully that nothing can be hidden forever. The sands of time may ebb away from us, but they also flow back.

The ghosts of Willington Mill have waited long enough for their tale to be told, and this is it.

Michael J. Hallowell & Darren W. Ritson

Note

Unless otherwise stated, all quotations from the diary of Joseph Procter, and/ or the introduction to and commentary upon it by his son Edmund Procter, are taken from the manuscript held by the Society for Psychical Research which was given to the society by Edmund Procter in 1892.

One

THE WILLINGTON WITCH

One of the difficulties surrounding investigations into cases like Willington Mill is that some aspects of the story that have been passed down are essentially unverifiable. This places authors in an unenviable position, for if they do not at least detail unverifiable legends in their writings they can be accused of overlooking what might be essential material. On the other hand, if they do detail them but are unable to furnish hard evidence in support, they will almost certainly be accused of playing fast and loose with the truth and placing too much stock in 'old wives' tales'.

The authors of this book thought long and hard about the problem, and decided quite simply to publish and be damned. If some of the old tales are true, then the haunting of Willington Mill had its origins long before the mill was even built.

For whatever reason, Willington Quay seems to have acted as a magnet for discarnate spirits. Although the village was relatively small, it managed to rack up an impressive array of spectres over the years. The earliest paranormal phenomena linked to the site of the mill itself now only exist almost exclusively within oral legends passed down from generation to generation.

One of the most controversial subjects in British history, stretching from the nineteenth century as far back as it is possible to go, is that of witchcraft. The north east of England, like everywhere else, saw the terrible persecution of those who clung to 'the Old Path', as it was sometimes called. For those who doubt that witchcraft really held much influence in the region in times past, a perusal of *Dancing With the Devil*[1] by Jo Bath and *More Ghost Trails of Northumbria*[2] by Clive Kristen should prove enlightening.

There have been times in our history when pretty much anything could get you accused of witchcraft. Witchfinders, like the infamous

Matthew Hopkins, would be delighted to find you guilty for such obvious signs of devilment as not brushing your hair, refusing to drink milk from a cow that has walked through a churchyard or allowing fingernail clippings to fall to the floor in your kitchen.

That a witch once lived on the site where Willington Mill would later be built is generally accepted, although details are scant. The Catholic priest Montague Summers, in his book *The Geography of Witchcraft*[3], made a brief but telling reference to the Willington Witch, saying that she lived in a cottage and was 'notorious'.

We need to be careful when embracing the opinions of Summers regarding witchcraft, though. Although he wrote extensively on the subject, he was stridently opposed to 'the craft'. His Catholicism, although not orthodox, still precipitated within him a dislike of the occult practices with which, ironically, he was so fascinated.

The Willington Witch lived in the village in the early part of the eighteenth century, when witchcraft was still shunned by all who believed themselves to be God-fearing – in such a social climate, the woman couldn't have helped but be anything other than notorious.

Still, the fact that she earned such opprobrium and even came to Summers' attention indicates that she was perhaps more notorious than most. What exactly she was supposed to be guilty of we may never know, although some hypotheses will be made later and at least one author[4] has suggested that, shortly before her passing, a priest refused to hear her deathbed confession. After her demise, her humble dwelling and the land around it seem to have developed a reputation for being cursed and locals avoided the place.

Researcher Catherine Crowe[5] stated, 'We have lately heard that Mr [Joseph] Procter [a subsequent owner of the mill house] has discovered an old book, which makes it appear that the very same "hauntings" took place in an old house, on the very same spot, at least two hundred years ago'. While Liddell[6] stated that the old house had actually been subjected to hauntings for a period of 200 years, to the authors' knowledge no other researcher has made this claim.

When going through the mill-owner Joseph Procter's diary, after his death, his son Edmund noted:

> … *in my father's handwriting, is the following memorandum below the above recital; there is a line drawn through them, however, whether by himself I am unable to say, and the sentence is apparently unfinished:—*
> *'An infirm old woman, the mother-in-law of R. Oxon, the builder of the*

premises, lived and died in the house, and after her death the haunting was attributed-----'.

I have heard my father speak of this circumstance, but the evidence appeared to be of a slight and hearsay character.

As time passed, the reputation of the Willington Witch faded, but it never did disappear. We can, however, make a number of tentative suggestions regarding the Willington Witch. First, it may be that Summers had a particular dislike of her due to his Roman Catholicism. Could it be that the witch was someone who, peculiarly, practised both Roman Catholicism and witchcraft at the same time? Could this also be why she allegedly asked for a priest to give her confession when she was lying on her deathbed? Also, could her 'notorious' reputation identify her as someone who had drawn the attention of the authorities to her activities? These are questions the authors will attempt to answer later in this book.

There are reports – almost certainly true – that a small mill was built on the site, but later demolished. This building was also allegedly haunted – although this may have been due, at least in part, to the site's chequered history.

When the Willington Mill proper was built there later, it was almost inevitable that it would inherit the spooky reputation of its architectural predecessors.

Notes

1. Bath, Jo, *Dancing With the Devil and Other True Tales of Northern Witchcraft* (Tyne Bridge Publishing, 2002)
2. Kristen, Clive, *More Ghost Trails of Northumbria* (Casdec, 1993)
3. Summers, Montague, *The Geography of Witchcraft* (London, 1926)
4. Anon, *The World's Greatest Unsolved Mysteries* (Chancellor Press, 2001) pp 502-3
5. Crowe, Catherine, *The Night Side of Nature, or, Ghosts and Ghost Seers, Vol. II* (T.C. Newby, 1848)
6. Liddell, Tony, *Otherworld North East: Ghosts and Hauntings Explored* (Tyne Bridge Publishing, 2004)

Two

WILLINGTON
AND ITS MILL

Flour mills were a common sight in the north east of England in the mid-nineteenth century as the Industrial Revolution began to take hold.

Willington Quay was a relatively small, picturesque village on the north bank of the River Tyne which mirrored much of what took place elsewhere along the banks of the region's most famous waterway. Shipbuilding was already thriving, providing employment for carpenters, moulders and other tradespersons. The adjacent town of North Shields also played host to a number of busy chandler's stores, where ship owners, captains and ordinary sailors could equip themselves with pretty much anything they required. Fishing, too, was a much-needed and valued profession. Indeed, the name North Shields is actually a bastardisation of the name North Sheels, a sheel being a small fishing boat used by many of the locals. In the mid-nineteenth century, communities like that found at Willington Quay were much more closely-knit than in our own time. It was quite possible to be born, raised and die within a small community without ever leaving it. Everything needed for survival was available on the doorstep, including a dairy, a bakery, a butcher (sometimes called a flescher), a cobbler and a fishmonger, and, of course, a miller.

Perhaps Willington's most famous son was the engineer George Stephenson (1781–1848), who, although not born there, resided in a small cottage in the village after his marriage to Frances Henderson.

Willington also had within its precincts a rope factory, which was opened in the year 1843 by the firm Robert Hood, Haggie, and in 1900 became Messrs Robert Hood, Haggie & Son Ltd. This factory will figure in our story to some considerable degree in a later chapter.

Willington Mill was supposedly built around the year 1800[1] or 1806[2], and, as previously stated, there is some evidence that it may have been constructed on the site of an earlier mill. The bulk of the testimony strongly suggests that the mill itself may have opened for business in

The original mill house with the factory buildings in the background. (Courtesy Bridon Ropes)

The site of the mill house today, now a car park for employees. (Thunderbird Craft & Media)

1800, but that the mill house itself was not built – or at least occupied – until 1806. This, the authors assert, is simply not the truth, as we shall see.

According to legend, the construction of Willington Mill got off to a bad start. A dark aura seemed to hang over the place and few locals, although they were happy to purchase their flour there, had a good word to speak about it.

What precipitated this negative view of the mill and the adjacent mill house is difficult to say, although there is an unsubstantiated rumour that during the construction a local person murdered someone and subsequently buried the body in the foundations. The anonymous writer of *Ghosts and Legends of Northumbria* may be alluding to this when he says, 'There were various rumours of evil-doing by workers engaged

Left: *Willington village as it is today. (Thunderbird Craft & Media)*

Right: *A digital reconstruction of the mill house, as it would look today on the original site if it was still standing. (Thunderbird Craft & Media)*

in the building of the house, and that it was haunted by the ghost of someone who had been "most foully murdered"[3]. Of course, the fact that a 'notorious' witch had once lived on the site didn't help either.

Although a number of murders did take place in the North Tyneside area between 1798 and 1806, in all cases the body was found at the crime scene. Neither were there any reports of missing persons subsequently being found buried at the mill by the authorities. If that had been the case, then it would surely have been written up in the local newspapers. This leads us to conclude that if someone was murdered and buried at the mill then the crime did not come to the attention of the authorities. Perhaps the victim was an itinerant worker or even a homeless individual.

When the mill house was later demolished, no skeletons seem to have been found when the foundations were disturbed. Of course, that doesn't mean that they weren't there.

Notes

1. Poole, Keith B., *Britain's Haunted Heritage* (Guild Publishing, 1988), p. 92
2. Tegner, Henry, *Ghosts of the North Country* (Butler Publishing, 1991), p. 67
3. Anon, *Ghosts and Legends of Northumbria* (Sandhill Press, 1996), p. 45

Three

IN THE BEGINNING

According to some researchers, Willington Mill was built at the behest of (or at least first occupied by) George Unthank and his family. The enterprise was a successful venture from the outset, being the first steam-powered mill in the north east of England. When the mill house was constructed in 1800, so the story goes, the Unthanks moved in straight away, occupying the three-storey dwelling that was adjacent to the mill itself.

There is a problem with this scenario, though. In 1829, George Unthank formally entered into a business partnership with his cousin Joseph Procter (in some accounts wrongly called Proctor). In his diaries, Joseph says that the Unthanks 'entered it [the mill house] in 1806' and enjoyed an 'occupancy of 25 years', indicating that the Unthanks left the mill house in 1831. However, if, as some researchers have suggested, the Unthanks moved into the mill house as soon as it was built (1800) their twenty-five-year occupancy would have ended in 1825. Further confusion is added by the fact that there is almost unanimous agreement amongst historians that the Unthanks left the mill house in the year 1829.

The belief that the Unthanks left the house in 1829 is probably a misinterpretation of facts. Records state that Joseph Procter entered into a renewed formal business relationship with George Unthank in 1829 and, almost immediately, took up residence on the mill site, and this is assumed by many to be the mill house. However, the mill complex included a number of residences that had been built for managers and employees, and it is perfectly possible that Joseph Procter initially lived in one of these whilst the Unthanks were still ensconced in the mill house itself. Two years later, in 1831, Joseph Procter married Elizabeth Carr from Kendal, and it is presumably then that the couple moved into the mill house and the Unthanks vacated it. This version of events would agree with the testimony of historians that their occupancy began in 1806, and also with the testimony of Joseph Procter that the Unthanks lived in the house for precisely twenty-five years. For a period of two years, then, between 1829 and 1831, Joseph Procter was living at the mill site but not in the mill house.

Having solved one conundrum we are immediately faced with another: if the mill complex was built in 1800, but the Unthanks did not move in to the house until 1806, who occupied the building during those first few years? The *Monthly Chronicle*[1] states that Joseph Procter's 'relatives appear to have bought the building in 1806', which would indicate that another owner, perhaps completely unrelated to the Unthanks, was the first occupant. Either that, or, for the first few years, they initially only rented the house and merely purchased it in 1806.

Some researchers seem to suggest that the conventional story – that the Unthanks moved into the mill house immediately after it was constructed – is the correct one. Poole, for example, says, 'It was first occupied by Joseph's cousin named Unthank'[2], although Poole may simply have meant that Unthank was the first occupant connected with the case to live at the mill house, and not the first person to live in it after it was constructed.

There was (and still is), for instance, a generally held belief amongst North Tyneside's mill cognoscenti that it was someone attached to the Unthank family who, at least in part, commissioned its building. If this is the case – and it does seem likely – then the first occupants were either called Unthank or were in some way connected to them.

What we do know is that almost from the day the mill was erected it gained a terrible reputation for being haunted. Poole[3] relates how Mr Unthank was warned that the mill house was haunted even before he moved in, whilst another author[4] points out that, later, the Procters knew of the rumours about the haunting before they moved in but chose to disregard them. If the mill house was already enjoying a reputation for being haunted before the Unthanks moved in, then it is obvious that they could not have been the first to reside within its walls. Who could have warned Mr Unthank about the building's reputation? It seems likely that the previous residents were close enough to the Unthanks to be able to confide in them regarding this matter. This may indicate, albeit circumstantially, that the first occupants of the mill were related to the Unthanks in some way or intrinsically connected to them.

As readers will have gathered by now, when one reads books dealing with the history of Willington Mill confusion reigns supreme. However, by careful research and investigation, the authors believe that they have managed to cut through the miasma of conflicting theories and 'facts', and uncovered the truth about what really happened during the first few years of its existence.

In the late nineteenth century there lived at Yarm a draper by the name of Joseph Procter. Procter, a Quaker, married a woman, also of good Quaker stock, called Elizabeth Richardson. Elizabeth was the son of John Richardson, and had an elder sister named Margaret. Margaret subsequently married a man called Joseph Unthank in 1791. Joseph Procter and Joseph Unthank thus became brothers-in-law.

Margaret was originally from the area of North Shields known as the Low Lights, named after a beacon situated near the river to help shipping navigate safely. Joseph and his new wife went to live in Whitby, but Margaret just couldn't settle. Joseph Unthank could see that his wife was pining for her home and mentioned this to his brother-in-law. Between the two of them they hatched an idea. They decided to purchase the old mill situated at a village called Willington Quay, North Shields. They were confident that the business would provide them with a good living and, of course, it would allow Margaret to return to her beloved Tyneside.

The original mill at Willington seems to have been owned by a man called William Brown, who later became related to both the Unthanks and the Procters by virtue of his marriage to one Mary Richardson. Between Brown, Unthank and Procter, Brown was the only one with any milling experience. Joseph Unthank, on the other hand, was the oldest of the trio and had a good deal of business acumen. Procter, still only a young man, had experience in neither business nor milling, but did have a large amount of capital. Unthank and Procter approached Brown and suggested that the three became partners in Brown's mill. The men then came up with a radical plan; why not demolish the old mill completely and replace it with one of the new steam mills that were becoming more fashionable? Steam mills could churn out flour at an unbelievable rate, and there were huge profits to be had. Shortly afterwards, the firm of Brown, Unthank & Procter came into being, and the three partners commissioned the building of the grandiose new mill.

As soon as the new mill house was finished, the Brown family moved into it. However, at this time rumours of a murder began to circulate and the premises gained a reputation for being haunted. Sometime between the years 1801 and 1806, the Browns left the mill house, but whether this was because of the alleged haunting we cannot say. Then, in 1806, Joseph Unthank and his family moved in. In 1807, Brown sold his share in the business to the other two partners and opened up two mills of his own; one in North Shields and the other in Sunderland.

What precipitated this dissolving of the partnership we do not know, but it was odd to say the least. The new mill at Willington was thriving, so why pull out of a business that was making money hand over fist? It is possible, although it cannot be proved, that it may have had something to do with the alleged murder.

Despite later denials, from the outset the Unthanks began to see and hear strange things in the house. Robert Davidson, in his book *The True Story of the Willington Mill Ghost*[5], relates the following incident:

> *Mr Unthank … did not at all believe in the existence of the ghost. Shortly after his arrival at Willington he enquired of the housekeeper if there was a mangle in the house. On being answered in the negative he replied, 'Dear me, that is strange; I have heard a mangle going all night'; and never after was he heard to deny the existence of things mysterious.*

By the time Joseph Unthank and his family had moved into the mill house, his wife had already given birth to several children, including a son whom they named George. George must have been aware of the supernatural occurrences at the house and very probably experienced some of them himself. This piece of information will prove to be of crucial importance later in this book.

We know that the mill house consisted of three storeys, but as far as we can tell the Unthank family only ever occupied the ground floor and the first floor. The second floor – and specifically one room within it – was never regularly inhabited or, it seems, even utilised for storage purposes. This was odd, for one would think that a reasonably wealthy family like the Unthanks would have made use of every available part of the building. Even stranger was the fact that at least one of the rooms on the top floor was permanently locked, and, as Keith B. Poole relates[6], even had the windows bricked up.

Prosaic explanations for such a circumstance are not easy to come by. It is possible that after they moved in Joseph Unthank might have decided to use the upper floor for storage purposes for the company and had the windows bricked up to reduce the likelihood of the premises being robbed. Although not impossible, this explanation is extremely unlikely, particularly as the storage facilities at the mill itself were extensive and he had the financial wherewithal to extend these facilities if necessary.

The alternative explanation is that the upper floor of the dwelling was left unused because it was the epicentre of some extraordinary paranormal activity that, being so intense, rendered it uninhabitable and unusable.

Both the Unthank and Procter families were members of the Society of Friends, commonly called Quakers, and were held in high regard by their neighbours. However, that 'locked room' on the top floor of the mill house gives us just the faintest clue that something in that mansion was wrong.

In 1813, Joseph Procter died. Legally, Joseph Unthank and his son George, who had by then purchased a stake in the business, could simply have seized control. However, they magnanimously made Joseph's thirteen-year-old son, also called Joseph, a partner in the firm. This meant that the mill now had two partners; Joseph Unthank and Joseph Procter Jr. George Unthank was a financial stakeholder, but not a partner, although he was eventually made a full partner in the year 1829[7].

TO BAKERS, FLOUR DEALERS, AND OTHERS.

THE Executors of the late GEORGE UNTHANK, have DISPOSED of their interest in the Business carried on at Willington Mill, near Wallsend, Northumberland, under the firm of

UNTHANK & PROCTER,

To the surviving partner JOSEPH PROCTER, who will answer all Claims against the late Firm, and to whom all Outstanding Debts due thereto are requested to be paid as early as convenient.

JOSEPH PROCTER desires gratefully to acknowledge the favours bestowed on the firm of UNTHANK AND PROCTER, for so many years, by their numerous Friends, and trusts his experience in the Business will enable him to conduct it so as to ensure their continued support.

Willington Mill, 10th Mo. 27th, 1842.

The disposal of George Unthank's estate, as publicly announced in the Port of Tyne Pilot, *28 October 1842.*

Altogether, there were four Josephs attached to the mill, and three of them carried the surname Procter; it is easy to see how researchers often became confused. The most common mistake has been to confuse Joseph Procter Sr with his son, the second Joseph Procter who lived on the premises.

In 1842, Joseph Unthank passed away. This left only two partners, the young Joseph Procter, who had succeeded his father's position, and George Unthank. What happened after this would, in the history of psychical research, prove to be truly fascinating.

Notes

1. *Monthly Chronicle*, June 1887
2. Poole, Keith B., *Britain's Haunted Heritage* (Guild Publishing, 1988), p. 92
3. *Ibid.*
4. Anon, *The World's Greatest Unsolved Mysteries* (Chancellor Press, 2001), pp 502-3
5. Davidson, Robert, *The True Story of the Willington Mill Ghost* (Robert Davidson, c. 1886)
6. Poole, Keith B., *Britain's Haunted Heritage* (Guild Publishing, 1988), p. 92.
7. Boyce, Anne Ogden, *Records of a Quaker Family: The Richardsons of Cleveland* (Thomas Harris & Co., 1889)

Four

1835

In the year 1831, the Unthank family terminated their residence at the mill and moved to Battle Hill Farm in the Battle Hill area of Wallsend, several miles away, and Joseph Procter Jr moved into the mill house. Joseph's diary, in which he kept a record of the bizarre phenomena which occurred in his home, begins in the year 1835. It has been presumed from this that during the first four years of his occupancy nothing of a supernatural nature occurred. Indeed, William Howitt[1] states, 'We learned that the house had been reputed, at least one room in it, to have been haunted forty years ago, and had afterwards been undisturbed for a long period, during some years of which quietude the present occupant [Joseph Procter] lived in it unmolested'.

However, most researchers who have delved into the Willington Mill case have concluded that, almost from the day the Procter family moved in, they were confronted by paranormal phenomena for which they had no explanation. Poole[2], for example, states that strange things began to happen, 'from the very beginning of the Procters moving in', whilst Puttick[3] adds, 'The family had scarcely settled in before the alarming disturbances ... began'.

The first hint that the paranormal activity at the mill house began before 1835 can be found in Edmund Procter's commentary on his father's diary: 'On my father's death in 1875, a diary that he had kept *almost from the outset* of the disturbances, and during many years of their occurrence, was found among his papers' (italics ours).

Edmund Procter's use of the word 'almost' indicates that, even if only briefly, there had been some supernatural occurrences at the house before his father began to keep a diary of them. However, as the authors will show presently, we have reason to believe that the paranormal phenomena had been manifesting themselves long before that.

Joseph Procter Jr was a dynamic businessman. Two years after entering into a formal partnership with George Unthank, he married Elizabeth

Carr of Kendal. Elizabeth was the brother of George Carr, who ran a highly successful biscuit factory. Indeed, the Carr's brandname is still in use today and owned by United Biscuits (UK) Ltd[4].

Despite his large workload and strong business connections, Joseph Procter eventually put pen to paper and started to detail the bizarre things that were happening within his home. It is customary for researchers who have delved into the case to refer to Procter's account as a 'diary', and the authors have fallen in with that convention. However, strictly speaking, the term is inaccurate. Gauld and Cornell[5] have correctly said that, 'it is not strictly a diary, but rather a series of memoranda, some dated and contemporary with the events they describe, some not …' Procter's diary is not an orderly, sequential history of events. At times it is confusing, inconsistent and muddled. In fact, the more one reads Procter's account the more difficult it becomes to follow it. Events are mostly listed in chronological order, but many are completely out of sequence. Unfortunately, too many researchers, unlike Gauld and Cornell, have been willing to trust that Procter laid down his recollections with fastidiousness and meticulousness when, patently, he did not. Once the authors came to see Procter's diary for what it truly was, they also came to see the Willington Mill haunting in a far different light.

Joseph Procter opens his diary as follows:

> *Particulars relating to some unaccountable noises heard in the house of J. and E. Procter, Willington Mill, which began about three months prior to the time, viz., 1 mo. 28th, 1835, still continuing, and for which no adequate natural cause has hitherto been discovered.*

The first thing to note is that Procter does not say that he is about to write a complete history of the paranormal events within his home, but merely that it is an account beginning with 'unaccountable noises' which manifested themselves in January 1835. This allows for the possibility that other phenomena occurred before 1835, although they were not auditory in nature. Poole[6] seems to pick up on this fact and actually dates the beginning of the events within Procter's diary to within a mere six weeks of his family moving into the mill house. In fact, as we shall see, there are some events detailed in Procter's writings which must have occurred before he even moved into the mill house at all. The authors believe that this is a fact of pivotal importance which radically impacts upon the generally accepted view of the entire affair.

At this juncture, we will relate Joseph Procter's diary entry about the first incident he records, and then discuss the profound implications generated by exactly when it took place:

About six weeks ago the nursemaid first told her mistress of the state of dread and alarm she was kept in, in consequence of noises she had heard for about two months, occurring more particularly nearly every evening when left alone to watch the child [Edmund's older brother then about two years old] to sleep in the nursery, a room on the second floor; she declared she distinctly heard a dull, heavy tread on the boarded floor of the unoccupied room above, commonly pacing backwards and forwards, and, on coming over the window, giving the floor such a shake as to cause the window of the nursery to rattle violently in its frame. This disturbance generally lasted ten minutes at a time, and though she did not heed it at first, yet she was now persuaded it was supernatural, and 'it quite overset her'. The latter was indeed evident from the agitation she manifested.

There are several important facts that can be either drawn or deduced from the above diary entry other than the description of the phenomena themselves.

Firstly, Procter states that, 'About six weeks ago the nursemaid first told *her* mistress of the state of dread and alarm she was kept in' (italics ours). It is curious that Procter doesn't say 'told my wife Elizabeth', as if the nursemaid's mistress at the time of the incident was someone other than a member of his immediate family. This makes perfect sense, of course, if the incident took place when the Unthanks lived at the mill and before the Procters arrived. The nursemaid's mistress would then have been Mrs Unthank, and not Joseph Proctor's wife. It is almost certain that after the Unthanks moved out and the Procters moved in the nursemaid was allowed to continue her employment at the home under its new residents. If the incident involving the nursemaid took place before the Procters moved into the mill house, but Joseph describes it as having occurred 'about six weeks ago', then it is clear that he must have written up his account long before 1835. In fact, what Procter wrote in his diary about the occurrence must have been transcribed from notes he made much closer to the time, before his own family moved into the mansion. We can also deduce from this that Procter was aware of supernatural occurrences taking place in the mill house whilst the Unthanks were still living there.

The second crucial piece of information concerns the nursemaid's description of where the phenomena seemed to be occurring. Procter's diary states that 'she distinctly heard a dull, heavy tread on the boarded floor of the *unoccupied room above*' (italics ours). This enables us to determine that the upper floor of the house – or at least one room of it – was, during the time of the Unthanks' residence, already not in use.

These two facts contradict the almost universal assumption amongst researchers that during the tenancy of the Unthank family there had been little or no supernatural activity taking place.

This new version of events is also supported by another of Joseph Procter's diary entries. When discussing the first flurry of incidents which took place shortly after his own family's arrival, he speaks specifically of the haunted room on the top floor and states, 'The room is devoid of furniture, and for some time the door was nailed up'.

If, as is generally accepted, there had not been a hint of supernatural activity in the mill house before the Procters moved in, why would the room be devoid of furniture? Another intriguing thing about Procter's statement is that, whilst he describes the absence of furniture in the present tense – 'the room *is* devoid of furniture' – he then changes to the past tense and adds, 'and for some time the door *was* nailed up'. At the very least, there is a strong hint here that the door to the room had been nailed up in the past but was not nailed up any longer. We know this to be true, for in his diary he talks of servants entering the room on a number of occasions to investigate strange noises.

The number of possible explanations for this circumstance is extremely limited. The first – although highly unlikely – is that as soon as the Procters moved into the mill house Joseph immediately hammered the nails into the door and then, within a few days, changed his mind and removed them. The second possibility – and almost certainly the correct one – is that the door was nailed up before the Procters moved in and hence must have been secured by someone in the Unthank household.

It is not just the nailed-up door which is puzzling; there is also the matter of a plastered-up window. Procter adds in his diary, 'It seems impossible that there can be any trick in the case; there is a garret above, and the roof is inaccessible from without; the house stands alone, and during most of the time *the window was built up with lath and plaster*, whilst the other only [*sic*] communication with the outside, by the chimney, was closed by a fireboard *which was so covered over with soot as to prove that not a pebble or a mouse had passed*' (italics ours).

Again, Procter's change of tense is fascinating. He states in the present tense that 'it *seems* impossible … there *is* a garret above … the roof *is* inaccessible … the house *stands* alone …' but then he switches to the past tense to relate that, 'during most of the time the window *was* built up with lath and plaster, whilst the other only communication with the outside, by the chimney, *was* closed by a fireboard which *was* so covered over with soot as to prove that not a pebble or a mouse *had* passed' (italics ours).

The inference is perfectly clear. Whereas the door had been sealed at one time, it was not now. The window which had once been boarded up was now clear. The fireboard which had sealed off the chimney had now been removed. To suggest that Procter could have done and undone all of this work within days of moving into the house – or even wanted to – is patently absurd. The room had, for some reason, been perfectly sealed off so that no light could enter, no one could see in and nothing could get in or out. Procter specifically mentions an accumulation of soot which had built up, further proving that when his family had moved in the room had already been disused for some time. There can be no doubt, then, that it was someone in the Unthank household who had sealed off the room and not one of the Procter family. The big question, though, is why?

As we shall see, the vast majority of the bizarre phenomena – particularly the auditory ones – took place within the room that had been sealed off and it was sometimes referred to as 'the haunted room' or 'the disturbed room'. The obvious explanation is that someone, patently aware of the fact that something very odd indeed was occurring within its walls, had made an attempt to seal off the room from the rest of the house and, perhaps, 'contain' the problem.

The circumstantial evidence is overwhelming, then, that the Unthanks, far from being blissfully unaware of the problem as they later claimed (Procter recalls that, 'On First day, 2 mo., 15th [1835], my wife and I were informed by our cousin, the Unthanks [*sic*], that they understood that the house, and that room in particular in which the noises now occurred, was said to be haunted before they entered it in 1806, but that nothing that they knew of had been heard during there [*sic*] occupancy of 25 years'), knew that their house was haunted before they moved out.

Before we move on to examine other aspects of the haunting, we must first look at what seems to be an insurmountable impediment to the idea that the 'nursemaid' incident took place before the Procters moved into the house. There is a singular statement in Joseph Procter's diary that would seem to rule this out completely:

About six weeks ago the nursemaid first told her mistress of the state of dread and alarm she was kept in, in consequence of noises she had heard for about two months, occurring more particularly nearly every evening when left alone to watch the child [Edmund's older brother, then about two years old] to sleep in the nursery, a room on the second floor ...

Edmund was Joseph Procter's son. If Edmund and his older brother were being watched in the mill by the nursemaid when the occurrences happened, this would indicate that the Procters were already living in the mill at the time. However, as we have seen, there are numerous other facts which mitigate against this. There are a number of possible solutions to this dilemma.

The first possibility is that Joseph Procter was simply mistaken; mistaken about the fact that it was his own children who were being looked after by the nursemaid when in reality it had been the children of his cousin, and/or mistaken about when the incident had actually occurred. However, Procter was seemingly writing his 'diary' mere weeks after the event, and, if so, it is highly improbable that he would have made such an obvious error.

A second possibility is that the two Procter children were staying overnight at the mill house as guests of their uncle and aunt, the Unthanks. There is nothing implausible about this scenario, except for the fact that it seems odd that Joseph Procter neither mentions it in his diary nor, indeed, attempts to explain it.

A third possibility is that the remark in parenthesis was actually Edmund's own insertion into the text, and this may indeed be the answer.

But there is a fourth solution to the enigma. It is possible that Joseph Procter was actually lying. If so, what on earth could his motive have been?

Both the Unthanks and the Procters were devout members of the Society of Friends, or Quakers. They were renowned for their integrity and honesty, and so the thought of them lying about anything at all is ostensibly hard to swallow. However, a perusal of the evidence demonstrates clearly that, at least insofar as the haunting of the mill was concerned, a culture of deceit or at best a dilution of the truth had already ingrained itself in both families.

We know, for instance, that the Unthanks were being dishonest when they said that they had never experienced a single paranormal incident in the twenty-five years they lived there, as can be demonstrated by the sealed room and the nursemaid incident. Procter, of course, knew that they were lying for he was already well aware of the incident involving the nursemaid.

But the Procters weren't above concealing the truth when it suited them, either. After the nursemaid mentioned in the earlier incident

The surviving factory building of the original Willington Mill as it is today. (Darren W. Ritson)

had left the employ of the Procters, another was hired. Joseph Procter commented in the diary, 'It may be remarked that the nursemaid first mentioned had left, and another engaged, from whom the affair was carefully concealed'.

Of course, concealing from the new maid what had happened to her predecessor is not tantamount to lying, but neither is it being completely honest. One can understand the reluctance of the Procters to tell the new maid that they allegedly had a ghost in the house, as such knowledge might have frightened the girl away before she'd even started, or even encouraged her mind to imagine things if she was of a nervous disposition. And yet, no matter how appreciative we might be of Joseph Procter's motives, the simple fact is that he was prepared to welcome into his house a person whom he knew would inevitably be confronted by bizarre and unsettling supernatural phenomena before very long. Procter had admitted in his diary that, 'Before many days had elapsed, however, every member of the family had witnessed precisely what the girl described, and from that time to the present, nearly every day, and sometimes several times in the day, the same has been heard by one or more of the inmates'.

We can see, then, that although the Unthanks and the Procters were thoroughly decent folk, they were not beyond concealing the truth if they really felt it was necessary. It is against this backdrop that we must consider what motivation might have been behind the telling of each lie, and how the process ended up with Joseph Procter attempting to conceal the fact that paranormal phenomena had not just occurred during his own tenancy of the mill house, but also during that of his cousin.

The first link in the chain of deception concerns the Unthanks' attempt to hide from the Procters the fact that they had personally witnessed some very strange things going on in the mill house. There are at least two powerful reasons why the Unthanks might have felt they had no other option but to do this.

The Unthanks, like the Procters, were deeply religious. As the Quakers were not so doctrinally fastidious as other denominations, and even by the time of the Willington Mill affair had broken into a number of sects and divisions, we cannot say with absolute certainty exactly how the Unthanks and the Procters perceived what was happening in the mill house. However, we can gain a tantalising glimpse into the way that Joseph Procter may have been reading the situation from the following entry in his diary:

> *Those who deem all intrusion from the world of spirits impossible in the present constitution of things will feel assured that a natural solution of the difficulty will soon be obtained on further investigation; whilst those who believe with the poet 'that millions of spiritual creatures walk the earth unseen' and that, even in modern times, amidst a thousand creations of fancy, fear, fraud or superstition, there still remain some well-attested instances in which good or evil spirits have manifested their presence by invisible tokens, will deem it possible that this may be referred to the latter class – especially when they learn that several circumstances tending to corroborate such a view are withheld from this narrative.*

The first question that arises is just what Procter was referring to when he talked about 'the latter class' in his diary. Initially he discusses two positions that observers might hold; the first a denial of supernatural activity, and the second an acceptance of it. Were the two 'classes' that he mentions, then, the polarised positions of scepticism and belief? However, it is also possible that the two 'classes' he mentions were those of 'good or evil spirits'. If so, then 'the latter class' he makes reference to would in essence have been demons. Even if the first explanation is the correct one, it is still likely that Procter thought the entities in his home to be evil spirits. As we shall see presently, his own narrative makes it clear that he thought they were spirits of some kind, and the type of behaviour they engaged in would hardly be the sort of activity one would expect of angels.

Joseph Procter, then, seemed to be leaning towards the idea that the spirits manifesting themselves in the mill house were demonic in nature. It might seem odd, given Procter's spiritual proclivities, that he did not fill every page of his diary with religious and theological perspectives on the affair, but he did not. In fact, other than the above instance, he hardly touched upon the subject. Another point that might raise comment is the fact that Procter, if he believed the ghosts to be of a demonic nature, certainly didn't seem terrified at the prospect. The strange occurrences in the mill irritated him, to be sure, but the authors can see little or no evidence that they ever frightened him. In all likelihood it was his deeply-held beliefs as a Quaker which enabled him to face the situation so stoically.

If Joseph Procter felt that the ghosts of Willington Mill might have been demons, then it is likely that his cousin George Unthank thought so too. But here we see a remarkable contrast between the two cousins. Unthank seems to have been genuinely frightened by what was going on. His response had not been to keep a diary, but to nail shut a door, plaster up a window and do everything physically possible to create a barrier between him, his family and whatever devilish malignancy he believed lay within the haunted room.

It must have been difficult for George Unthank. On one hand, he had a business to run and his professional vocation dictated that his presence on the site of the mill was needed. However, the presence of the ghosts – or demons – was seriously disturbing him and, likely, the rest of his family. There was also the worry of how his religious compatriots would view the matter too, if they got to hear about it. Would they suspect that the implacable and protracted presence of the entities was in some way due to a lack of faith on his part? And what about the other residents of Willington Quay? They weren't all Quakers, but many were deeply religious and might well have suspected that he was either in league with the Devil or in some other way responsible for the perpetuation of the haunting. How would that, in turn, affect his standing as a businessman? If people discovered that he was sharing the mill house with a bunch of spectres, would they distance themselves from him and refuse to purchase the wares of Messrs Unthank & Procter? He was, quite simply, caught between a rock and a hard place. It is for this reason, the authors suspect, that Unthank instructed his family and household employees not to tell anyone about the phenomena that were manifesting themselves – not even his beloved cousin, Joseph Procter.

Much of the remainder of this book will be taken up with the shocking phenomena that occurred after the Procters moved into the mill house, and it is in relation to this where we find yet another powerful motive for Unthank to keep the haunting of the mill house secret.

We must acknowledge that both the Unthank and Procter families exhibited great determination in the face of the supernatural events which took place in the Willington Quay mill house. We do not know for how long the Unthanks were forced to endure the appearance of ghosts, strange lights and other phenomena which will be detailed presently, and it is just possible that it was only for the latter few months or weeks of their tenancy. However, the likelihood is that it was for far longer than that. The mill had a reputation for being haunted when they moved in, and it was certainly being haunted when they moved out. The probability has to be, then, that they also experienced things during the period in between. It is likely that for the entire twenty-five-year period that the Unthanks lived at the mill they would have been subjected to a regular (although not necessarily frequent) exposure to things that they could not explain.

Eventually, in 1831, things became so bad that Unthank knew his family would simply have to move out. It may well have been around this time that he boarded up the haunted room. If this is the case, then it seems likely that there must have been a sharp increase in the frequency and/or the intensity of the phenomena. The only way that Unthank could move his family out of the mill was if the Procters agreed to move in. Obviously, he would have to tell his cousin something, as Procter would no doubt be baffled that after a quarter of a century Unthank and his family were abruptly vacating their home. Just what excuse he gave his cousin we do not know, but it must have been a plausible one. He must also have convinced Procter that moving his own family into the mill house was an attractive proposition. What Unthank couldn't do, of course, was tell Procter the awful truth; that the mill house legends were true.

We know that the two cousins, Unthank and Procter, were extremely close. In at least three areas of their lives they shared an intimate bond; the fact that they were closely related, ran a business together and belonged to the same religious denomination. Procter, as the authors have already detailed, almost certainly knew that George Unthank wasn't being entirely truthful when he said that for twenty-five years neither he nor his family had experienced anything untoward in the mill house. However, if Unthank had promulgated this lie to his family, whom else had he told it to? There must surely have been other residents of Willington Quay who had been told by Unthank that he'd never seen a ghost or anything else supernatural in his home. If the truth eventually came out, and it was proved beyond any doubt that the Unthanks had endured a number of strange experiences during their tenancy, then Mr Unthank would be identified as a liar; something that would undoubtedly have damaged his reputation amongst the residents of Willington Quay and – just as importantly – his fellow members of the Society of Friends. Although Procter may have been irritated at his cousin for withholding the truth from him, he would surely not have wanted Unthank or his family to be publicly humiliated. Hence, he would have been forced to perpetuate the myth that nothing supernatural had happened at the mill before his tenancy and whilst his cousin was living there.

Thus, as we have seen, in his diary Procter changes certain facts in the historical timeline to make it look as if supernatural occurrences which occurred during the Unthanks' tenancy actually happened after his own family had moved in. This would explain why he makes a curious emphasis of the fact that when the nursemaid had her first experience she was allegedly looking after Procter's own children and not those of the Unthank household. The facts demonstrate that this patently could not have been the case. It is also likely that Procter would have been forced to omit from his diary any events which would have proved beyond doubt that the Unthanks were also the victims of paranormal activity. To assess whether this was true, the authors meticulously examined Procter's diary to see if it held any clues suggesting that he had employed this technique to disguise the truth. No less than five clues came to light, providing powerful evidence that the theory was correct.

The first is provided by Edmund Procter, Joseph's son, who added his own introduction and commentary to his father's diary when it was first made public:

> On my father's death in 1875, a diary that he had kept almost from the outset of the disturbances, and during many years of their occurrence, was found among his papers. The publication of this diary has been delayed for two reasons: first, my mother's [Elizabeth Procter] objection to their publicity during her lifetime; secondly, because the manuscript breaks off suddenly, and I have long hoped, but in vain, to find the continuation and conclusion. To such readers as were not personally acquainted with the writer of this diary I may briefly state that he was a member of the Society of Friends, belonging to a family of which had been attached members of that body from its very foundation.

The first thing to note about Edmund Procter's statement is the position his mother Elizabeth, Joseph's wife, took concerning the publication of her husband's diaries. She had no objection to them being published as such, but did not want it done whilst she was still alive. Of course, she may simply have been worried that publication of the diaries might have brought about undue (and unpleasant) media attention upon her family. However, it is also possible that she was aware that the contents of the diaries, although substantially true, also contained inaccuracies deliberately introduced into the text by Joseph. If this had come to light during her lifetime, then the adverse publicity might have been even worse.

The second clue can be gleaned from Edmund Procter's testimony that the latter half of his father's diary had mysteriously gone missing and, despite Edmund's best efforts, was never located. It seems astonishing that Joseph Procter would have gone to all the trouble of keeping such a diary and then accidentally 'lost' a substantial part of it. It is probable that it was either deliberately hidden or, more likely, destroyed. We do not know who was responsible for this, but there are two likely candidates. It is possible that Joseph Procter, in his later years, realised that there were portions of the diary that would, if published, give the game away. To prevent this, he may simply have torn out the pages and consigned them to the fire. The other possibility is that the latter part of Joseph's diary was hidden or destroyed by his wife Elizabeth; probably after her husband's death and for the same reasons. We know that she already felt distinctly uneasy about them being published before her own demise, quite possibly because she knew that, ultimately, the truth would then come out. Parts of the diary that blatantly gave the game away may well have been destroyed by her to both maintain the pretence and also protect the reputations of both her husband and his cousin.

The third clue can be gathered from a rather curious postscript that Edmund Procter added to his explanation of why the publication of his father's diaries had been delayed for so long: 'To such readers as were not personally acquainted with the writer of this diary I may briefly state *that he was a member of the Society of Friends, belonging to a family of which had been attached members of that body from its very foundation*' (italics ours). Why does Edmund Procter suddenly begin to discuss his father's religious affiliations and responsibilities? It seems that, for some reason, after discussing the missing portion of his father's diary, Edmund immediately tries to establish his father's religious, moral and ethical qualifications. The only point to such an exercise that the authors can see is that the postscript is in some way relevant to the missing text. Is Edmund Procter sending a warning shot across the bows of any potential critics not to ascribe any dubious motives to his father regarding the mysterious disappearance of the latter half of the diary? No other explanation seems credible, but it also indicates that, at least potentially, such dubious motives could have been waiting in the wings and ready to make their entrance upon the stage – at least in the mind of Edmund Procter.

But there is a fourth clue that Procter deliberately omitted information from the diary. Speaking of those who disbelieve in the existence of discarnate spirits, Joseph Procter seemed to think that they would eventually have to admit to it, 'especially when they learn that several circumstances tending to corroborate such a view *are withheld from this narrative*' (italics ours).

By Procter's own admission, then, a number of 'circumstances' – powerful enough to convince even the most ardent sceptics – had been deliberately left out of his diary. This seems bizarre, considering that one of his prime motives for compiling the diary in the first place must have been to provide circumstantial proof to others that the events that allegedly took place were real. Surely it would seem sensible to include in the diary every single incident – particularly those that provided the most powerful testimony. Yet, for some reason, Joseph Procter omits from his diary the very examples that logic dictates should have been included.

It is also odd that Procter makes no effort to explain his decision. The reader is left wondering why he should fail to include material which only serves to tantalise us by its absence. The only obvious explanation the authors can think of is that the incidents concerned were set in such a context that their inclusion would have proved the very thing that Procter studiously wanted to avoid admitting; that the paranormal activity at the mill house had been going on throughout the Unthanks' residence.

However, there is a far darker, less obvious reason that may have prompted Procter to keep some things secret which the authors will detail later in this book. At this juncture, though, it is sufficient to quote the words of William T. Stead, who commented, 'In spite of the unwillingness of Mr Procter that these mysterious circumstances should become quite public, and averse as he is to make known himself these strange visitations, they were of such a nature that they soon became rumoured over the whole neighbourhood'[7].

Finally, and perhaps most astonishing of all, is another entry in the diary which was only partially completed. The authors have already discussed this briefly in Chapter One, but must now revisit it from a radically different perspective.

Edmund Procter recalls:

> *... in my father's handwriting is the following memorandum below the above recital; there is a line drawn through them, however, whether by himself I am unable to say, and the sentence is apparently unfinished:*

> *'An infirm old woman, the mother-in-law of R. Oxon, the builder of the premises, lived and died in the house, and after her death the haunting was attributed-----'*

Joseph Procter had started to make an entry in his diary and then, before finishing it, seems to have changed his mind. Someone, almost certainly Joseph himself, then scored out the text. Just what was it that the miller intended to write, and what motivated him to change his mind?

For reasons that will become clear presently, Joseph Procter was deeply disturbed by the story of the witch who, allegedly, had lived in a cottage on the site centuries previously. When William Howitt mentions, in an article he penned for *Spiritual Magazine*[8], the fact that Joseph had seen this story 'in an old book'[9], Procter was deeply unhappy and fired off the following letter to the editor:

> *To the Editor of the Spiritual Magazine.*

> *Tynemouth, 7 mo. 20th, 1863.*

> *The following statement of your able and esteemed correspondent, William Howitt, in the number for July, I believe to be founded in misapprehension, and will thank you to insert this correction in the next month's number:—* *'There are said to be evidences of the spirits haunting Willington Mill, having done so to an older house on the same spot for two hundred years'. I believe no such evidences exist, the premises having been erected in 1800, on ground never before built on. Persons acquainted with the neighbourhood, and knowing the statement I have quoted to be an error, might thus be led to discredit the whole narrative, as truly and circumstantially related in the number for January. There is an older house about two hundred yards from Willington Mill, in which there was a mysterious ringing of bells about forty years ago; and about twenty years since, the person who then occupied it told me that occasionally at night very strange noises were heard, adding, 'It must be rats, you know'. That is, however, more than I know, and may be left as a doubtful question.*

As Howitt gleaned his information directly from Procter, then Procter is, in couched terms, effectively declaring Howitt to be a liar. Procter, we know, had already mentioned the old book and its contents in his own diary. Further, it is almost certain that the words the miller penned and then scratched out were a direct quotation from the book concerned. Yet, Procter attempts to rewrite the past and pretend that there is no truth in Howitt's account. Of course, some critics will argue that it is not Procter's reading of the book that the miller takes issue with, or indeed its contents, but simply the fact that Howitt presents the account about the woman in the cottage as factual. However, Howitt doesn't do any such thing. In his article for *Spiritual Magazine* he simply says, 'There are *said* to be evidences of the spirits haunting Willington Mill, having done so to an older house on the same spot for two hundred years' (italics ours). Howitt, then, reduces the story to little more than hearsay, so why would Procter be so troubled by it?

'R. Oxon', we know, was the builder who constructed the cottage which previously stood upon the site of the mill. Oxon seems to have then given the premises to his mother-in-law or rented them to her. Perhaps he let her live there rent-free, who knows?

Even before Oxon's mother-in-law – aka 'the notorious witch' – died, people were saying that the place was haunted and/or cursed. Catherine Crowe[10] also states that Joseph Procter ascertained this information from 'an old book' that had somehow come into his possession. Crowe was informed about this by William Howitt, who had actually investigated the Willington Mill case himself. In *The Night Side of Nature* Crowe states, 'We have lately heard that Mr Procter has discovered an old book,

The original cover of Catherine Crowe's The Night Side of Nature, *published in 1848 by T.C. Newby.*

which makes it appear that the very same 'hauntings' took place in an old house, on the very same spot, at least two hundred years ago.'

How reliable are the testimonies of Howitt and Crowe on this matter? An earlier article on the Willington Mill haunting had also appeared in an issue of *Spiritual Magazine*, and detailed both Howitt and Crowe's research. Joseph Procter read the article and was thereafter prompted to write to the editor with his own comments[11]:

> *The publicity given to the occurrences at Willington a few years ago, through Crowe's Night Side of Nature, has given occasion to many inquiries similar to thy own, and I have never shrunk from the avowal of undoubting assurance of these appearances, noises, &c., being made by the spirit of some person or persons deceased, notwithstanding that the who and the wherefore have not hitherto been ascertained. In reply to thy inquiry about the accuracy of the narrative in the work referred to.*
>
> *I may state that the portion of it [the article] from p. 125 to p. 137 taken from Richardson's Table Book, a local antiquarian publication, was written by the late Dr Clanny, of Sunderland, and revised by myself before being printed, and is perfectly true and correct.*
>
> *In that other portion, derived from William Howitt's personal inquiries, there are trifling inaccuracies, yet not such as materially affect the nature of the facts referred to.*

Procter's letter was written on 2 September 1853, over a decade before he took issue with Howitt over the 'haunted cottage' story. In the earlier letter he mentions, almost as an afterthought, the fact that there were 'trifling inaccuracies' in Howitt's account but adds the caveat that, 'yet not such as materially affect the nature of the facts referred to'.

Dr William Clanny, who wrote up an approved account of the Procter hauntings in Richardson's Table Book.

As Howitt's assertion that Procter gleaned the information about the 'haunted cottage' from 'an old book' was essentially verified by Procter himself, there can be little doubt about its veracity.

We can deduce little from Procter's half-finished statement, other than that R. Oxon's mother-in-law, who was ill, lived in a cottage Oxon had built. We can also deduce that after her death the alleged haunting of the premises had been 'attributed' to something, although Procter, irritatingly, stops writing just before stating what the attribution was.

What makes Procter's statement so fascinating, though, is the fact that he didn't complete it and actually scribbled it out. But why?

In all probability, he was again acting to protect his cousin. To reduce the risk of exposing his cousin to accusations of lying, Procter needed to minimise if not expunge completely from his diary any ideas that the place had an institutionalised reputation for being haunted. As detailing the story of the haunted cottage would have been counterproductive in that regard, Procter started to write about it and then thought better of it.

Edmund Procter may, deep down, have realised his father's motives and tried to support them. Although he retained the half-finished comment in his transcript of Joseph's diary, he weakens its evidential value by adding, 'I have heard my father speak of this circumstance, but the evidence appeared to be of a slight and hearsay character'.

Edmund Procter obviously loved his father dearly, and says, 'a man with a more delicate sense of what it means to speak the truth I have yet to meet'. The authors believe that in almost all aspects of his life this was true, and also true of his cousin. These two men were not pathological liars; they were two devout Quakers who valued honesty and truthfulness very highly. However, both were faced with a set of extraordinary circumstances that forced them to compromise their principles to a small but significant degree. The final question we must address is how their consciences may have allowed them to do this.

To answer this, the authors decided to contact a Quaker body which provides an on-line service whereby visitors can address questions concerning the movement's doctrinal teachings. The questions we submitted were as follows:

'Could you inform us what the Quaker position is on the telling of lies?'
'Are there any circumstances in which a Quaker could find lying morally permissible?'
'Is it permissible to tell what one might perceive as 'white lies' to perhaps save the feelings of others?'

The answers we received were interesting. Quakers, we were informed, have what was described as 'a testimony to telling the truth', and that telling the truth is actually part of what it means to be a Quaker. However, the response to our question also said that there might be times when it was right to deceive a person. The specific example given was a circumstance in which 'a Gestapo officer was searching for Jews'. The implication was clearly that it would be permissible to lie if the intent was to protect the lives of those who may be harmed or even killed if their location was divulged. However, the writer clarified her position by stating that such an act would 'require [a] strong justification'.

Insofar as 'white lies' or 'saving the feelings of others' was concerned, the writer indicated that this was not really acceptable and that other means should be found to avoid causing offence without resorting to lying.

Unthank and Procter, then, probably both felt able to justify their actions to a degree, but not completely. Their residual guilt would explain perfectly why, not only during their lives but also afterwards, efforts were clearly made to keep their actions hidden from the world at large.

When all is said and done, the fact of the matter is that, in January 1831, the Unthanks moved out of the mill and the Procters moved in. After a while, the supernatural entities in the dwelling began to make their presence known to the new tenants in the most terrifying way.

Notes

1. Howitt, William, *Visits to Remarkable Places; Old Walls, Battle Fields, and Scenes Illustrative of Striking Passages in English History and Poetry* (Longman, Orme, Brown, Green & Longman, 1840)
2. Poole, Keith B., *Britain's Haunted Heritage* (Guild Publishing, 1988)
3. Puttick, Betty, *Supernatural England* (Countryside Books, 2002)
4. http://en.wikipedia.org/wiki/United_Biscuits
5. Gauld, Alan & Cornell, Tony, *Poltergeists* (Routledge & Kegan Paul, 1979)
6. Poole, Keith B., *Britain's Haunted Heritage* (Guild Publishing, 1988)
7. Stead, William T., *Real Ghost Stories* (Grant Richards, 1897)
8. *Spiritual Magazine*, August 1863
9. Undated copy of the *Umanian Magazine*
10. Crowe, Catherine, *The Night Side of Nature, or, Ghosts and Ghost Seers, Vol. II* (T.C. Newby, 1848).
11. *Spiritual Magazine*, August 1863

Five

THE PROCTER
DIARY (PART I)

Joseph Procter passed away in 1875, forty years or so after he began to record the occurrences which would prove then – and now – to be so baffling. Even though the latter half of the diary is missing, we have no reason to assume that he did not continue writing it till he vacated the premises with the rest of his family in 1847. Considering the startling nature of the events contained in the first half of the diary, which we will relate here, one is left wondering what other amazing incidents were written up in the missing portion.

One question is why, after writing his diary, Procter kept it hidden from the world and did not publish it or, at least, make it available for scrutiny. This puzzle is compounded by the fact that the man did not

---

WILLINGTON MILL.

TO BE SOLD BY PRIVATE CONTRACT, the Premises known as WILLINGTON MILL, near Newcastle-on-Tyne, consisting of a large Building having Seven Floors, 90 feet by 30 feet, with Steam Engine and Boilers attached; a commodious Dwelling House, containing Thirteen Rooms; also Cottages and Stables, with space for additional Buildings. These Premises having Water Carriage, and being so conveniently situated between the Four populous Towns on the banks of the Tyne, are well adapted for Manufacturing Purposes, as for Oil, Bone, or Saw Mills, and also for Paper Mills, having a good supply of Fresh Water.—Apply to JOSEPH PROCTER & SON, Willington Mill.

The sale of Willington Mill, as advertised in the Shields Daily News *on 17 April 1866.*

refrain from telling others what occurred on a number of occasions. It is possible that, after writing the diary, Procter belatedly realised that it may contain clues regarding things which occurred when the mill house was owned by the Unthanks. This may have encouraged him to keep the diary secret, whilst at the same time sharing what facts he felt happy to reveal when asked for them.

After Joseph Procter's death, and the later demise of his mother, Edmund Procter (or another member of the Procter family) discovered the diary amongst Joseph's papers and Edmund decided to publish them. Edmund was only seven years old when the family moved out of the mill, which means that he could not have been an eyewitness to any occurrences from 1831–40 as he wasn't alive then, and, one presumes, would be unlikely to recall anything that he did see during the first two or three years of his life. However, in his introduction to his father's diary he candidly admits to having 'vivid recollections of many singular occurrences'. Sadly, Edmund Procter rarely details these events in his own writings, stating that, 'As my parents … ceased to reside there when I was but a child of seven any evidence of my own can be but of trifling value'.

Edmund prefaces his father's diary by relating to the reader just how much attention the haunting of Willington Mill received:

> *The 'Haunted House at Willington' has been a familiar theme on Tyneside for half a century, and the general public have been made acquainted with it in William Howitt's Visits to Remarkable Places[1], Catherine Crowe's Night Side of Nature[2], The Local Historian's Table Book[3], Stead's Ghost Stories[4,5] and other publications.*

Incident 1: Footsteps

We have already discussed the incident in which a nursemaid at the house heard some strange noises, but our examination of the occurrence was almost exclusively restricted to the discrepancies in Joseph Procter's account regarding exactly when it transpired. Regardless, it is the first incident mentioned in his diary and therefore we need to revisit it, but this time to focus upon the nature of the phenomena themselves.

It seems that during the residency of the Unthanks (or the Procters, if you believe the more popular version of the tale) the nursemaid was in the habit of looking after the children each evening and putting them to bed. The room in which the children slept was on the second floor, and commonly referred to as 'the nursery'.

One evening, whilst watching one of the youngsters, the maid heard some strange noises coming from the floor above. They were, she said, 'dull and heavy, pacing backwards and forwards'. So clear were the sounds that the maid could follow them across the floor of the room above and was seemingly able to determine roughly where the person – and we use the term loosely – making them was standing. According to Edmund Procter, the maid told him that, 'on coming over [to] the window, [it gave] the floor such a shake as to cause the window of the nursery to rattle violently in its frame'.

Later in the book the authors will attempt to determine exactly what type of phenomenon may have been responsible for the bizarre noises and rattling windows, but it seems reasonable to suggest that, at least some of the time, they fit comfortably within the symptomology of a poltergeist infestation.

According to Edmund Procter's recital of the nursemaid's testimony, the 'disturbance generally lasted ten minutes at a time' and repeated itself night after night. If the Procters were living in the house at the time, it is impossible to think that such loud noises and violent rattling of windows would only have been heard by the nursemaid. Surely the Procters themselves would have heard them on at least a number of occasions – unless, of course, the incident occurred during the tenancy of the Unthanks, which the authors firmly believe.

On first hearing the disembodied footsteps, the nursemaid 'did not heed' them, but after repeated episodes she 'became persuaded it was supernatural' and – quite understandably – became distressed.

Several days passed, during which the nursemaid heard the footsteps and saw the windows of the nursery rattle violently on a number of occasions. During one bout of activity the maid shouted down to the ground floor for the 'kitchen girl'. This employee ascended the stairs and found the nursemaid 'trembling much and very pale'.

It seems that the 'kitchen girl' exercised a degree of authority over the nursemaid, but whether this was because she was officially higher in the household pecking order, or simply had a more robust personality we do not know. However, it seems that the kitchen girl interrogated the maid or, as Procter put it, 'examined her further in reference to this improbable tale'. Procter adds that the maid stuck to her story and would not deviate from it, thus prompting the already cynical kitchen girl to go to the upper floor of the house and investigate. Procter then adds an intriguing detail; 'on searching the rooms above and finding nothing to cause such results … little credit was attached to the story'.

At the risk of sounding repetitious, the authors must once again point out that this is not consistent with what we already know. We have shown from the historical record that the haunted room on the second floor was already boarded up before the Unthanks left the premises. We also know that Joseph Procter removed the nails, laths, plaster and other bits and pieces and made the room accessible at some point after he moved in. As the kitchen girl searched the rooms of the upper floor, we know that the incident must have taken place either before Mr Unthank boarded the room up or after Mr Procter opened it up for use. It is unlikely to be the latter, for, by Procter's own testimony, the incident involving the nursemaid supposedly occurred almost immediately after they moved in, in addition to which we know for other reasons that it definitely occurred during the tenancy of the Unthanks.

As Procter bravely endeavours to alter the historical facts and essentially airbrush the Unthank family out of the paranormal picture, the inconsistencies simply continue to pile up. For instance, regarding the 'nursemaid incident', he adds, '*Before many days had elapsed*, however, *every member of the family* had witnessed precisely what the girl described, and from that time to the present, nearly every day, and sometimes several times in the day, the same has been heard by one or more of the inmates, varying unimportantly in the nature of the sound' (italics ours).

This statement is telling indeed, for, according to Procter's own words, within a few days of the incident occurring every member of the family had become an eyewitness to the very same phenomena. The phrase 'every member of the family' must, of course, include Joseph himself. And yet, earlier in his diary, he claims to have been blissfully unaware of what had transpired until no less than three and one-half months had passed!

The truth, of course, is easy to see. At some point, probably just a week or two before the Unthanks moved out, the nursemaid had the first experience in a series which involved the hearing of disembodied footsteps and the angry rattling of the windows. These incidents repeated themselves almost every night, and it may have been both the frequency and intensity of them that proved, for the Unthanks, to be the straw that broke the camel's back and finally drove them out. After the Procters moved in, the strange phenomena continued unabated. Within a few days after their arrival, then – and not the first event involving the nursemaid – every member of the Procter household had witnessed something similar. This is the only interpretation of the facts that, to the authors, fits comfortably on the historical timeline.

Incident 2: Spectral Footfalls

Procter begins his narration of this incident by spelling out precisely when it occurred, and already we find ourselves in trouble when we try to marry the date he gives with the known facts. According to Joseph Procter, the event occurred, 'On sixth day, 1st month 23rd, 1835'.

Procter's method of writing down dates is cumbersome, unnecessarily complicated and lacks consistency. Nevertheless, it seems obvious that he is referring to 23 January 1835. Unfortunately he prefixes the date with 'On sixth day', the very presence of which screams out for justification. To be sure we understand exactly what date – and day – that Procter is referring to we need to ask ourselves the obvious question; namely, just what was or is the sixth day of the week? This is not as daft a query as it may look, and neither is it an easy one to answer.

In pre-Christian times, Sunday was generally referred to as the first day of the week. However, with the advent of Christianity – and its subsequent nomination of Sunday as the Sabbath or seventh day of the week, a conflict arose. Was Sunday the first day of the week, then, or the last? The Emperor Constantine gave Monday his official stamp of approval as the first day of the week, thus making Sunday the seventh day and a legally authentic Sabbath. Old habits die hard, though, and in politics, commerce and most other walks of life Sunday still held pole position as the first day of the week, not the last. Since then, from time-to-time, the West has operated a dual system which is internally inconsistent. Sunday is still usually spoken of as the first day of the week, although now we speak of Saturday and Sunday as 'the weekend', which in one fell swoop shunts Monday to the front of the queue. The term 'weekend' – referring to both Saturday and Sunday – did not come into use until after the death of Joseph Procter.

If Procter followed the pattern of identifying Monday as the first day of the week, then the sixth day would have been a Saturday. However, if he accepted Sunday as the first day of the week then Friday would be classed as the sixth day and the veracity of both the date and day given in his diary would be consistent.

A quick check with some members of the Society of Friends allowed the authors to determine that Saturday was usually referred to as 'the seventh day' by Quakers, and that this would almost certainly be a practice adopted by the devout Joseph Procter. Hence, Procter's making of Friday, 23 January 1835 and 'the sixth day' synonymous is understandable, and should not make us doubt the accuracy of his statement.

But there is a second problem. The first incident which Procter describes, involving the nursemaid, allegedly took place on 28 January 1835. The next incident seemingly occurred on 23 January, almost a week prior to that. Why would Procter break his general practise of listing the events in chronological order? Of course, there is a solution to this problem, and it is one which fits in well with the authors' belief that Procter was not being entirely truthful about just when the first incident involving the nursemaid occurred.

It is likely that before Procter commenced writing his diary he compiled a list of incidents that he wished to include. He would, of course, have listed every incident sequentially and in the order they occurred. When Procter began to pen his diary proper, however, he realised that a certain amount of reorganising was necessary to avoid people realising the truth; namely, that the Unthank family, despite their protestations to the contrary, had witnessed paranormal phenomena taking place at their home. To keep up the pretence, he created a fictitious scenario in which the nursemaid incident occurred on 28 January 1835, after Procter and his family had moved in. Unfortunately, he omitted to change the order of the first and second incidents around on his list, and hence the nursemaid incident still appears first, even though, according to Procter's dates, it actually occurred second.

Having dealt with these inconsistencies we can now go on to examine what actually transpired.

According to Procter, 'my wife had in the forenoon requested one of the servants to sweep out the disturbed room in the course of the day …'

The 'disturbed room', of course, was none other than the 'haunted room' on the upper floor, which Procter had now made accessible by removing the nails from the door, taking down the lath-and-plaster inserts from the windows and unblocking the fireplace. Procter then goes on to say that his wife Elizabeth, '… herself in the nursery after dinner, heard a noise in the room like a person stirring about, which she took for granted was the maid cleaning out the chamber, when, to her surprise, she afterwards found that neither of the girls had been upstairs at all'.

The obvious implication, of course, is that Mrs Procter had really been listening to noises made by the 'ghost'.

The intriguing thing is that there were distinct similarities between the incident involving the nursemaid and the second event described above. Both involved sounds with no obvious origin emanating from the 'disturbed' room on the upper floor. In both events the sounds were

– or at least seemed to be – those of an unidentified person moving or walking around. The third commonality is that, on both occasions, the witnesses were in the nursery on the first floor, directly below the haunted room.

Incident 3: Fire Light

From Procter's account we can determine that the next incident – or at least the next that he records – took place on the following day, Saturday 24 January. According to the mill owner, 'one of the maids, being in the nursery, supposed, from the noise she heard, that the other was lighting the fire in the room above, as had been desired, which proved a similar mistake to that preceding day.'

The same principal elements to the story are there; the witness/es are in the nursery on the first floor, while the enigmatic sounds seem to come from the room above on the second floor.

Incident 4: The New Maid

Within a few days before or after Incident 3, it seems that the nursemaid involved in Incident 1 left her employ at the mill house, apparently unable to stand the bizarre occurrences which were taking place. Another servant was immediately engaged, and Procter informed the rest of the staff, and presumably his family, that under no circumstances were they to tell the new employee what had been going on. Procter remarks that, 'A day or two after her arrival the noise was observed by her fellow servant whilst they were together in the nursery, but she apparently did not observe it herself, from her companion talking and using the rocking-chair'.

What Procter seems to be suggesting here is that the second maid – the one using the rocking chair – was rocking back and forth in the chair, presumably making a squeaking noise, and also chatting to the new maid when she heard the sound of footsteps coming from the disused room upstairs. The new maid seemingly didn't hear the sounds due to the chatter of her companion and the noise being made by the chair. The second maid appears to have drawn the attention of her colleague to the sounds, but they seem to have stopped just as she attempted to listen to them.

The new maid appears to have taken an ambivalent attitude to what her fellow worker heard, expressing neither belief nor cynicism.

Incident 5: Encore

On the same day that Incident 4 occurred, the new maid later entered the nursery. We are not told whether she was alone, but the context implies that she was. Procter does not state exactly what she experienced, but relates, 'it began suddenly when she was present, and she, somewhat alarmed, inquired who or what was in the room above'.

The fact that the new maid enquired of someone – we do not know who – 'who or what was in the room above' suggests that the maid tried to determine whether any member of the household could have legitimately been in the room before instantly dismissing the idea. It is also clear that her question regarding 'who or what' might have been in the room displays at least an openness to the idea that the presence might have been something other than human.

Incident 6: A Man with a Strong Shoe or Boot

On Sunday 25 January, the day after Incident 3, Procter relates in his diary that, 'being kept at home by indisposition, my wife was in the nursery about eleven o'clock in the forenoon, and heard on the floor above, about the centre of the room, a step as of a man with a strong shoe or boot going towards the window and returning'.

Incident 7: More Footsteps

On the same day, Procter recalls: 'When we were at dinner, the maid, being with the child in the nursery, heard the same heavy tread for about five minutes; she came into the sitting room to satisfy herself that her master was there, thinking it must have been he who was upstairs'.

Incident 8: Even More Footsteps

The following day 'the dull sound was resumed, and up to this day the boots have not done duty again'. Procter seems to suggest here that the disembodied footsteps, which had been heard on an almost daily basis, had desisted as suddenly as they had begun. By this time the family, obviously both irritated and bemused, had begun to 'examine' the room 'frequently' and 'immediately after the occurrence of the noise'. Nothing was ever discovered, of course; the 'haunted' or 'disturbed' room was invariably found to be empty.

Incident 9: One Exception

In the succeeding months, numerous attempts were made to ascertain the cause of the strange noises. Procter states, 'it has been sat in, in one instance slept in all night, and in every case nothing has been elicited. Several of our friends who have waited to hear the invisible disturber have all, with one exception, been disappointed'.

Incident 10: The John Procter Event

Procter goes on to relate an incident involving his brother John. Superficially this seems to be the 'exception' he mentioned previously, however further examination proves that cannot be the case. In the 'exception' case, Joseph makes it clear that the witness or witnesses successfully attempted to hear the sounds for themselves. The event involving John Richardson Procter, although intriguing, did not involve him hearing the noises for himself.

Like the other incidents, the one involving John Procter must have taken place at some point before the strange footfalls seemingly ceased on 26 January. We do not know the exact date, but it must have been after the Procters moved in and can therefore be fixed between mid-to-late January. Procter's recollection of the event is as follows:

My brother, John Richardson Procter, remained in the room below some time after the usual period of operation, fruitlessly, but within ten minutes of his departure the nurse was so terrified by the loudness of its onset that she ran downstairs with the child half asleep in her arms.

Procter didn't manage to hear the sounds for himself, then, but was an eyewitness to the effects they had upon the nursemaid minutes later. Procter goes on to relate, 'My cousin, Mary Unthank, stayed two nights and was much in the room without being gratified'. Clearly, then, Mary Unthank cannot be the unnamed witness mentioned in Incident 9, as her attempts to hear the noises for herself was also unsuccessful. Procter states:

All the persons who have heard, and six have been so far privileged, are confident that the noise is within the room on the third floor, as the precise part of the floor above on which the impression is made is clearly distinguishable through the ceiling below, and the weight apparently laid on, shaking violently the window in the room below, when no other window in the house is affected, and during a dead calm, is itself a proof of this.

It might prove helpful at this juncture to establish just who the 'six witnesses' mentioned by Procter were. A close scrutiny of his diary highlights the following persons:

Nursemaid 1
Elizabeth Procter
Nursemaid 2
The unnamed witness mentioned in Incident 9
Housemaid 1
Housemaid 2

Some of these witnesses, as we know, had a multiplicity of experiences. The difficulty we have with Procter's testimony is that it does not dovetail with another statement made earlier, in which he said, 'before many days had elapsed [after Incident 1], however, every member of the family had witnessed precisely what the girl [the nursemaid] described.' If we then include 'every member of the family' it is painfully obvious that far more than six persons should have been counted as witnesses. Procter, the authors believe, was specifically referring to the six people who had witnessed supernatural events after his own family moved into the mill house. The evidence has already been presented in abundance to show that Incident 1, involving the nursemaid, took place before the Procters moved in and during the tenancy of the Unthanks. The fact that the 'family' whose 'every member' also witnessed bizarre events is not counted by Joseph is a clear indication that it was not his own family he was referring to, but that of the Unthanks. Here, again, is proof positive that the mill house was being subjected to paranormal phenomena during the Unthank tenancy.

Incident 11: The Mallet

The next portion of Procter's diary is prefaced with the words, 'Additional particulars relating to unaccountable noises, etc. heard at Willington Mill, containing the most remarkable from first month 25th, to the present time, second month 18th 1835.'

So far so good; although there is a slight overlap between the first and second parts of the diary, it is clear that the writer now intends to list the incidents that occurred between 25 January and 18 February 1835. Yet again, though, we hit a snag. Procter specifically dates Incident 11 as having occurred, 'on first day night, the 31st of the month'. We know that, to Quakers, Sunday was acknowledged as the first day of the week. Procter's statement that the following incident took place on the evening of 'first day' suggests that he believes it to have occurred on a Sunday night. The difficulty is that 31 January 1835 was a Saturday. Just why Procter made this mistake – or just possibly a deliberate error – is unknown. Perhaps it was another unsuccessful attempt to cover up the real timeline of events – or possibly just a slip of the pen whilst momentarily distracted.

In any event, Procter relates that, 'soon after retiring to bed, before going to sleep, my wife and I both heard ten or twelve obtuse deadened beats as of a mallet on a block of wood, apparently within two feet of the bed curtain, on one side by the crib in which the child was laid'.

As far as we can tell, this was the first incident during the tenancy of the Procters which deviated from the now well-established 'footfalls' pattern.

Incident 12: The Crib

The next night [likely Sunday 1 February], before undressing, I had hushed the child asleep in his crib, and while leaning over it with one hand laid upon it and listening to some indistinct sounds overhead, which had just ceased, I heard a tap on the cradle leg as with a piece of steel, and distinctly felt the vibration of the wood in my hand from the blow. This might be a sudden crack not infrequent when wood is drying in, but sounded like a knock on the outside ... Since this time the walking in the empty room has not been heard oftener than twice or thrice, of which this afternoon was the last time.

Two things become clear at this juncture. Firstly, Procter's earlier statement that no more spectral footfalls were heard in the haunted room after 26 January simply cannot be true; either that, or the incident involving the crib is not in its proper place on the timeline. It is hard to see how this can be the case, though, for the last of the 'two or three' disembodied footstep incidents happened, according to Procter, on the very afternoon he made his diary entry. As we know that Procter began writing his diary in the latter half of April 1835, then the spectral footfalls must have continued till that very point. The other possibility, of course, is that Procter had already compiled a collection of handwritten notes which he later incorporated into his diary. This allows for the possibility that his notes regarding Incident 12 were actually written on the very day the event occurred and not on the day that the details were added to his diary. In any event, it is hard to justify Procter's earlier statement that no more spectral footfalls were heard after 26 January, for whichever way you interpret his words they simply must have been.

Incident 13: The Cistern

In the early hours of Monday 2 February, Procter was alerted to an incident that had occurred in the yard at the rear of the mill house:

> *On the same evening, I heard that Thomas Mann, the foreman of the mill – a man of strict integrity and veracity, who has been two year in Unthank and Procter's employ – had heard something remarkable, and on questioning him elicited the following statement. It may premised [sic] that U. and P. have a wooden cistern on iron wheels to bring water for their horses, which stands in the mill yard. When in motion, drawn by a horse to be filled, it makes a very peculiar noise which may be heard a considerable distance, especially when the wheels want greasing, and by any person accustomed to it the noise of its going could not be mistaken for that of any other vehicle. The mill was going all night, and T.M.'s place was to attend the engine till 2 a.m. Going out to fill the barrow with coals about one o'clock, he heard this machine, as he thought, going along the yard, which did not at the moment strike him as out of the usual course; but remembering the hour, the apprehension that it was being stolen flashed in his mind; it was creaking excessively, from want of oil as might be supposed, and was then near the yard gates, towards which he pursued after it, when, to his astonishment, he found it had never stirred from its place near where he at first was, and looking round everywhere all was still and not a creature to be found. He afterwards searched round the premises with a lantern, but descried nothing. He was much puzzled, but it was not till the next day that he felt himself compelled to attribute the phenomenon to a supernatural cause.*

Incident 14: Transparent, White Female Figure

The following incident was not actually contained in Joseph Procter's diary, but was found amongst his papers after his death written on a separate sheet of paper. Edmund Procter, in his preface to the event, states: 'I ... believe, although it is not dated, that this is the correct sequence of the manuscript. I have myself heard all the particulars from the lips of all the parties concerned, which completely agreed with this account in my father's handwriting.'

We do not know how Edmund Procter was able to slot this event into the sequence of instances with such confidence, but must presume that he had good reason for doing so. The previous incident, we know, took place on Monday 2 February, and the one immediately after it, although not of paranormal provenance, took place on Friday 13 November. Incident 14, therefore, must have taken place between those two dates.

According to Procter's account, 'a few days previously [previous to what or when we are not told] a respectable neighbour had seen a transparent, white female figure in a window on the second storey of the house'.

There were subsequently a number of 'female spectres' seen in and around the mill house, but as far as the authors can determine this was the first. Procter finishes his account of this incident by stating, 'For about two months previously there had rarely been 24 hours without indications by noises, etc. not in any other way accountable of the presence of the ghostly visitant, to some or all of the inmates'.

The reference to two months of almost daily supernatural noises could have given us an important clue as to when this incident occurred. Had Procter been correct when he stated that the phantom footfalls ended abruptly on 26 January 1835, then the appearance of the female ghost in the second-storey window must have occurred just afterwards. However, as the authors have shown that Procter's testimony in this respect is unreliable, we really can't be sure.

Incident 15: The Object That Could Not Be Real

On Friday 13 November – perhaps ominously – Procter recalls that:

> ... *two of the children in the house, one aged about 8, the other under two years, both saw, unknown to each other, an object which could not be real, and which went into the room where the apparition was afterwards seen and disappeared there.*

There are several puzzling factors within this short account, so perhaps we should dispense with the more mundane ones first.

It is odd indeed that Procter refers to his children as being, 'one aged about 8, the other under two years'. If Procter was writing his diary in 'real time', as he claimed he was from the latter half of April 1835, it is baffling that he doesn't seem to be able to recall the current ages of his children. It is hard not to suspect that some of Procter's diary at least may not have been written up at the time the incidents occurred, but actually much later.

The most cryptic statement made by Procter concerns the nature of the phenomenon; it was, he said, 'an object which could not be real'.

What the good miller meant by this is anybody's guess. We can't even be sure that in nineteenth-century Geordie brogue the word 'object' had the same specific meaning that it does today. Richardson[6] recalls a multiple-witness sighting of a male spectre which appears in one of the windows and the same incident is detailed in the *Monthly Chronicle*[7]. In both accounts, the clearly anthropomorphic ghost is described as an 'object'. This could mean that the 'object' the children saw entering the room was actually a spectral person. However, Procter seems to differentiate between the 'object' seen by the children and the ghost, for he describes the 'object' as entering the room, 'where the apparition was *afterwards* seen and disappeared there' (italics ours).

Whilst the haunting of Willington Mill was at its height, some five years later an anonymous hack wrote an extremely sarcastic piece in a local paper[8] making fun of the entire affair. Derogatory though the article is, it does contain material that the authors haven't seen elsewhere. Presumably the journalist carried out his own research and perhaps spoke to witnesses independently. Towards the end of his diatribe the writer mentions, 'that the tongs, poker and fire-irons have been heard (or seen) dancing with themselves, and that various other mysterious actions have been at different times performed in the house, apparently by an invisible agency'.

The authors thus tend towards the idea that the 'object' in this case was not anthropomorphic but household, and was clearly moving or behaving in a manner that objects of its kind weren't supposed to do. The 'object' then seems to have moved into the bedroom where the apparition had been seen before promptly disappearing. Likely it was this latter act – the disappearance of the object – which prompted Procter to say that, 'it could not be real'.

Another question thrown up by Procter's account is his statement that the two young witnesses saw the 'object' enter the room 'unknown to each other'. Whether the children were together when they saw the apparition but simply didn't mention it to each other at the time we do not know. They may not have been together and witnessed it from different vantage points, or indeed they may both have witnessed the same phenomena at different times of the day independently.

The room which the 'object' was seen to enter was, according to Procter, the same one in which a 'transparent, white female figure' had been seen 'in a window on the second storey of the house'. It is important at this point to detail exactly what Procter meant by the phrase, 'second storey'. In the USA, the ground floor of a building is usually referred to as 'the first floor', the next level as 'the second floor', the level above it as 'the third floor', and so on. However, this is not the case in the UK. In the UK – and this applied in Procter's day – the bottom floor of a building was usually described as the 'ground floor', the next floor up as the 'first floor', the level above it as the 'second floor' and so forth. The phrase 'second storey' would have applied to what we now call the first floor, or second level, of the building. This means that the apparition appeared not in a window on the upper level of the house, where the haunted or 'disturbed' room was, but on the one below it. This enables us to determine that the paranormal activity in the house was, by November 1835, occurring not just on one level of the house but two.

This begs the question as to which room specifically the mysterious object entered before it disappeared. It is highly likely that the two witnesses, if they were both together, were in the nursery at the time the incident occurred. This means that it must have been one of the adjacent rooms, and not the nursery itself, that the object was seen to enter. Unfortunately, a lack of further detail prevents us from being more precise.

According to Edmund Procter, his father places the 'unreal object' incident immediately after the 'transparent, white female' incident. However, he then says that the 'unreal object' incident took place before a sighting of the apparition in the same room. This means that there must have been a second sighting of the 'transparent, white female' after the 'unreal object' incident. Sadly, that account is not written up by Procter for our edification.

Incident 16: Backwards and Forwards

Procter does not give a date for this incident, so the authors have left it in the same place on the historical timeline as the miller himself.

It seems that Joseph Procter's sister-in-law, Jane Carr, came to visit. Procter says that 'for obvious reasons' she did not stay at the mill house but lodged for the evening with the mill foreman, Thomas Mann, and his wife Elizabeth (Bessy). There were numerous houses and cottages on the mill site, and we know that the Manns inhabited one of them; specifically, the cottage directly opposite the back of the mill house. However, there is some slight circumstantial evidence that Mann maintained a small apartment within the mill itself where he could be on hand in case of an emergency. Further circumstantial evidence suggests that the Mann family was initially in the mill apartment on the night of the incident in question. The 'obvious reasons' for the woman not

Above: *The mill as it appeared from Willington Gut in the mid-nineteenth century. (Courtesy, Bridon Ropes)*

Right: *The mill as it appears today, from Willington Gut. (Darren W. Ritson)*

staying at the mill house itself seem to have been the presence of the ghosts that had troubled so many others.

At some point, the Manns left their apartment at the mill and returned to their cottage. Then, at around 9.15 p.m., Jane Carr left the mill house and made her way to the Manns' home, where she promptly went to her bedroom.

At around 9.30 p.m., Mrs Mann left her house to get some coal for the fire. There was a large coal bunker attached to the side of the mill house, and it seems that the Manns had permission to avail themselves of its contents. This would explain why Mrs Mann actually passed the mill house on her way to fetch the coal. On leaving the front door of her cottage she would have turned right, passed a small kitchen garden and walked along the road in between her own home and the rear of the mill house, which was then, as now, called Gut Road. As she did so, she happened to glance up at a first-floor rear window where the apparition of the 'white, transparent female' had previously been seen and, to her amazement, saw for herself a spectral figure.

Mrs Mann immediately shouted for her husband, who promptly left their cottage and joined her at the back of the mill. He too saw the same figure, which the couple later said had been, 'passing backwards and forwards and then standing still in the window'. According to Procter, the apparition had been, 'very luminous and likewise transparent, and had the appearance of a priest in a white surplice'.

Thomas Mann then went back to his cottage and roused both Mr Procter's sister-in-law and his own daughter. The three then joined Mrs Mann, who was still standing outside staring at the spectre in the mill house window.

'When they came,' said Procter, 'the head was nearly gone and the brightness somewhat abated, but it was fully ten minutes before it disappeared by fading gradually downwards. Both when standing and moving it was about 3 feet from the floor of the room'.

At this point, Thomas Mann crept across the road until he was directly beneath the window in question, perhaps to see if he could get a better look. Then, perhaps not satisfied, he decided to wake up Joseph Procter. This would have involved walking around to the front of the mill house where the main entrance was. On arrival at the front door, Mann found the place in darkness. He made several knocks upon the door, but it seems that the Procters had all gone to sleep and did not hear him. He then retraced his steps around the mill house and rejoined the others.

It was, according to Procter, 'a dark night, without a moon, and there was not a ray of light, nor any person anywhere near the house. The window blind was closed, and the figure seemed to come both through it and the glass, as had the brightness been all inside of the glass the framing of the window would have intervened, which was not visible. In walking, the figure seemed to enter the wall on each side. The occupier of the house slept in that room, and must have gone in shortly after the disappearance of the apparition'.

As with most of the other entries in Joseph's diary, there are seeming inconsistencies. The first problem is that the room in which the apparition could be seen was on the first floor, or 'second storey', and it is puzzling how the witnesses could have seen the apparition walking through walls, etc., from their vantage point on the ground. However, Robert Davidson, in his book *The True Story of the Willington Ghost*, which he published privately in 1886, recalls how a long window ran vertically from the top of the house to the first floor, illuminating the entire stairwell and landings. This, says Davidson, was done in preference to installing several smaller windows, which would have increased the 'window tax' levied upon the owners. It is likely, then, that this huge window would have given witnesses on the outside a much better view of what was going on in the interior.

The second difficulty arises from the fact that when Thomas Mann went to the front of the house in an attempt to wake the Procters he found the building in darkness and said that the family had all gone to bed. However, he later stated that Procter must have entered the room just after the apparition had finally disappeared. The problem is that the apparition was still visible after he rejoined the others at the back of the mill house, which means that Joseph Procter could not have been in bed when Mann tried to rouse him. The only conclusion that the authors can reach is that Procter must have been fully awake when Mann was knocking at the door but, for some reason, refused to answer. Just why he would have done this remains a mystery.

Incident 17: The Winding of the Clock

Edmund Procter introduces the next entry in his father's diary with the words: 'The following account in my father's diary has no year stated, but it appears to be about this time. J.C. is Edmund's aunt, Jane Carr, of Carlisle'. As Joseph Procter gives a specific date – 16 December – we must trust Edmund Procter's assertion that it occurred in 1835:

> *In the 16th of 12th mo., a little before twelve o'clock at night, J.C. and her bedfellow were disturbed by a noise similar to the winding up of a clock, apparently on the stairs where the clock stands, which continued for the space of ten minutes. When that ceased footsteps were heard in the room above, which is unoccupied, for perhaps a quarter of an hour; whilst this was going on the bed was felt to shake, and J.C. distinctly heard the sound of a sack falling on the floor.*

It is clear that all three of the bedrooms on the first floor, plus the nursery, had by this time been subjected to paranormal phenomena or at least held witnesses to phenomena taking place in the 'disturbed room' above.

Incident 18: Five Knocks

> *On the 31st of 1st month [31 January 1836], about twelve o'clock at night, J.C. being quite awake was disturbed by a noise similar to a person knocking quickly and strongly five times on a piece of board in the room; when that ceased she distinctly heard the sound of a footstep close by the side of her bed.*

It is interesting to note that the two times Jane Carr stayed at the mill house she was able to hear anomalous sounds without any obvious natural origin.

Incident 19: Bullet

The following event is also undated, but as it follows on from an Incident 18, which took place on 31 January 1836, and occurred 'about the beginning of the year', we are probably safe in assuming that it took place in early February of the same year.

> *About the beginning of the year J.P. was awoke by the sound like a bullet lodged in the floor above or in the wall of his bedroom, and looked at his watch to ascertain the time; he found next morning that his wife in the next room was awoke by the same sound.*

Incident 20: Raise Me Up

Procter prefaces this event by saying it occurred, 'About the 21st inst.', which likely means 21 February 1836. For the first time we are given the name of the household's nursemaid, which is Pollard. 'E.P.' is obviously Elizabeth Procter, Joseph's wife: 'About the 21st inst. E.P. and nurse Pollard both felt themselves raised up and let down three times'.

Edmund Procter adds a footnote to this entry, in which he recalls:

> *My mother has described this experience to me; she said the bed was lifted up as if a man were underneath pushing it up with his back. She did not speak to nurse Pollard, nor the nurse to her, each thinking the other was asleep; this not being disclosed until breakfast time.*

Incident 21: Begging For Light

The next entry in the Procter diary is simply dated, 'On the 15th, about 8 p.m.'. It is tempting to suggest that this must be referring to 15 March, less than a month after the occurrence of Incident 20, but it is unlikely. The difficulty is that Incident 22, detailed below, actually occurred on 11 January 1837. This means that almost a year had gone by in which, supposedly, Joseph Procter had made Incident 21 his only entry. Either there had been an uncharacteristic lull in the supernatural activity or, as is more likely, many incidents went unrecorded. The authors have already shown how Procter himself admitted this to be the case.

In any event, some time between February 1836 and 11 January 1837, the following event occurred:

> *J.P.[Joseph Proctor] jun., who had been in bed about half an hour, called of someone to come to him and begged for light; he said that something under the crib raised him up very quickly many times, and wished to know what it could be.*

There is some evidence that the supernatural phenomena operating within the precincts of the mill house tended to 'cluster' specific types of action together. For a while it would do little else other than make phantom footfalls in the 'disturbed room' and rattle the windows, then it would focus upon 'lifting' the beds. Later, the reader will be able to pick out other 'event clusters'. As the incident on this occasion involved the repeated raising and lowering of Joseph Junior's bed, there may be some suggestion that it occurred in close proximity to Incident 20, which was nigh-identical in nature. We simply can't be sure, however.

Incident 22: Closet Ghost

On 11 January 1837, or, 'on the 11th of 1st mo,' as Procter puts it …

> *… whilst the servants were at dinner, E.P. [Elizabeth Procter] was lying on the sofa in her lodging-room when she felt the floor vibrate as from a heavy foot in an adjoining room; in the writing room underneath J.C. [Jane Carr] at the same heard the sound of a person walking backwards and forwards in the room above. Soon after this E.P. heard the sound of a closet door in the room above shutting three times, after which footsteps came into the middle of the room and then all was silent. E.P. feels assured there was nobody upstairs at the time.*

Procter's rendition of this incident is a little confusing, and it will help clarify matters if some fuller detail is presented to the reader regarding the layout of the house. On the ground floor of the building were five main rooms; a lounge, a parlour, a dining room, the kitchen (or scullery, as it was then called) and a study or 'writing room'. On the floor above were a nursery and three bedrooms. One of these seems to have been the sole province of Mr Procter and another that of Elizabeth. Procter, we know, was often called upon by his business to work during the night or see to emergencies at the mill. It made sense, therefore, for him to have a separate room so that he did not continually disturb Elizabeth's sleep.

The third floor of the house contained four rooms, all of which were probably designed for sleeping purposes. Under normal circumstances the rooms on the upper floor would be used by live-in staff such as maids, cooks, etc., but as one reads through Procter's diary and the vast array of other material available on the Willington haunting, one thing becomes starkly noticeable by its absence; apart from the 'disturbed room', almost nothing is said of the other rooms on the same floor. Rarely if ever is mention made of anyone entering or leaving them. This has led some researchers[9] to suggest that it was not only the disturbed room which was sealed off, but that, during the periods when the paranormal activity was at its worst, the entire floor was effectively abandoned. If this was indeed the case, it must have been difficult for the Procters to manage the sleeping arrangements of their staff. Although we can't be sure, they may have been billeted in one of the numerous houses or cottages on the site, or possibly lived close enough to the mill so that they were excused from living on the premises at all.

On the day in question, Elizabeth Procter seems to have been resting in her first-floor bedroom, quaintly called her 'lodging-room' by her husband. On the ground floor, in the study, was Jane Carr. The study was directly underneath the nursery. Elizabeth's bedroom was adjacent to the nursery.

Elizabeth's attention was drawn to noises coming from the nursery. She seemingly, 'felt the floor vibrate as from a heavy foot'. Until that juncture the phantom footfalls had almost exclusively been restricted to the 'disturbed room', but now they were coming from within the nursery itself. One can only imagine the thoughts that were running through Elizabeth Procter's head. Her main concern would, the authors think, have been the possibility that the 'ghost', which had hitherto inhabited the 'disturbed' or 'haunted' room, was now starting to invade other places in her house.

Meanwhile, on the ground floor in the study, Jane Carr could also hear noises coming from the nursery directly above her head. They were, she testified, like 'the sound of a person walking backwards and forwards'.

As soon as the noises in the nursery stopped, Elizabeth heard them again almost immediately, but this time they were upstairs in the 'disturbed room'. According to Mrs Procter, she 'heard the sound of a closet door in the room above shutting three times, after which footsteps came into the middle of the room and then all was silent'.

During much of the remainder of Joseph Procter's diary, he refrains from his previous habit of giving the day, date, month and year of each recorded incident. However, a careful scrutiny of the text allows us to state with a reasonable degree of confidence that Incidents 23–36 all occurred during the month of January 1837. The events which follow are not strictly in the order they appear within Joseph Procter's diary, as the writer was in the habit of detailing an incident and then relating another which had happened previously. The authors have slightly re-sequenced the incidents so that they are, as far as they can tell, in the correct order.

Incident 23: Jingling

On the 17th, at 7 p.m., the two elder children and two nursemaids were in the nursery when a loud clattering or jingling was heard in the room; it sounded from the closet; the girls were very much terrified as also was Jane P., who is four years and a half old. Little Joseph, perceiving his sister affrighted, endeavoured to calm her by saying, 'Never mind, Jane, God will take care of thee.'

Incident 24: Fast Walkers

… little Joseph said in the morning to his aunt, Jane Carr, who was sleeping with him, that he was a long time in getting to sleep the night before from some people walking very fast in the room above; he wondered who it could be. This was an unoccupied room.

By this time, the 'disturbed room' had long been left empty. Superficially, it seems as if this was the room that Joseph jnr was referring to, as he heard the footsteps in 'the room above'. If he was sleeping in the nursery then this would fit perfectly. However, it is odd that Procter specifically states that 'This was an unoccupied room', as if he is pointing out to the reader something that they were previously unaware of. The authors feel it is possible that the footsteps may not have emanated from the 'disturbed room' but one adjacent to it, hence prompting Procter to clarify the matter. If this conjecture is correct – and it may not be – what led Procter to determine this is unknown.

Incident 25: Close to the Bed

One night, whilst sleeping in a crib in his parents' room, he [Joseph Junior] awoke to say that someone had stepped close to his bed.

Incident 26: Beating of Wood

One night about this time J.P. heard early in the morning a noise as of wood moving from the middle of one side of the boarded floor of the empty room above; after which he heard a loud beating in the mill yard.

Incident 27: Whistling or Whizzing

Another night he [Joseph Procter] heard two very peculiar sounds as of whistling or whizzing … I have sometimes heard my father imitate this peculiar and horrid sound.

Incident 28: Thumps or Blows

About 11 o'clock on the night of the 23rd, J.C. [Jane Carr] and her little bedfellow heard a succession of thumps or blows in the empty room above which continued for the space of ten minutes.

Incident 29: A Single Beat

A little after one o'clock the same night [as Incident 28] J.P. was awakened by a single beat or blow in the room above, after which one of the chairs in his own room seemed shifted.

Incident 30: Footsteps in the Attic

On the night of 26th J.P. heard the sound of footsteps in the attic, and afterwards as of setting things down in the room above, from about 11.30p.m to 2a.m.

This event is intriguing, for it is the first time that a phenomenon is reported as occurring in 'the attic', which is essentially the fourth level of the house.

Incident 31: Peculiar Whistles

A little after eleven he [Joseph Procter] had heard several prolonged and peculiar whistles, which were also heard by the nurse in another room; they seemed to come from the landing; she had described it without knowing that J.P. had heard it.

Incident 32: Shaken Crib

Joseph [Junior] was shaken in his crib early the same night.

Incident 33: Clashing

On the 27th no one slept in the third storey; about eleven o'clock Jane C. and the nursemaid heard in the room above the sound of some person with strong shoes sometimes walking, sometimes running backwards and forwards, moving chairs and clashing down box lids, and sometimes thumping as with a fist. These sounds also moved onto the stair-head.

Two statements are of interest in this short account. Firstly, Procter says that on the evening in question 'no one slept in the third storey'. This might indicate that, by the time the incident occurred, at least some of the rooms on the upper floor – excepting the 'disturbed room', obviously – were now being occupied, probably by household staff.

It is also interesting to note that on this occasion, 'These sounds also moved onto the stair-head'. It seems that by the time of this event the phenomena had moved beyond the 'disturbed room' and were now beginning to manifest themselves in the nursery, several of the bedrooms and, as we shall see, virtually everywhere else in the house.

Incident 34: Two Lifts

About midnight J.C. felt the bed raised up on one side as if to turn it over, giving two lifts.

Incident 35: Lord Have Mercy Upon Me!

Nurse Pollard in another room on the same floor heard a noise which roused her as she was going to sleep; something then pressed against the high part of the curtain and came down on to her arm, which was weighed down with the same force; in great terror she called out, 'Lord have mercy upon me!' Nothing further occurred to her that night, nor was the maid who slept with her aroused.

Incident 36: A Loud Shriek

This incident seems to have taken place on 3 February 1837, or as Procter puts it, '2nd month 3rd':

On nearly every day or night since the last entry more or less has been heard that could be referred to no other than the same cause; amongst them the following may be noted: Joseph and Henry [Joseph Procter's sons] have been several times disturbed in their cribs during the evening; once they heard a loud shriek which seemed to come from the foot of the bed. On going up Joseph was found trembling and perspiring from the fright. Another time Joseph said his bed moved backwards and forwards; also a voice by the foot of the bed said, 'Chuck' twice; he is very inquisitive as to the origin of these noises, and says he never heard or felt anything like it whilst we lived at Shields.

Incident 37: Up and Down

This event seems to have occurred on 30 March 1837.

It may be proper to mention that neither he [Joseph Junior] nor any of the children have any idea of anything supernatural. Jane sleeps in another room; she told her mother that she felt the bed go up and down, and other things of that kind, not having heard of her brother Joseph, or any of us, having felt anything of the same kind.

Incident 38: Footsteps in the Night

About the 30th J. and E.P. heard loud thumps in the room above, also footsteps in the night, when they knew no one was upstairs, as the cook was at that time sleeping for company with the nurses on the second floor.

Incident 39: Heavy Pieces of Wood

A day or two later, about six in the evening, whilst the servants were at tea in the kitchen, E.P. and J.C., whilst in the nursery on the second floor, heard what seemed to be heavy pieces of wood jarring on the floor above.

The following incidents probably occurred in February of 1838. However, if the authors are correct in this assertion then it leaves us with the puzzling fact that virtually no events are recorded in Procter's diary for the year 1839. If some of the incidents listed below did take place in 1839, then it seems that the phenomena were not presenting themselves anywhere near as frequently as before. As previously noted, however, by Procter's own admission he deliberately omitted a good number of incidents from his diary. It is possible, therefore, that almost all of the events which did occur in 1839 were consciously left out of the text.

Incident 40: Moving Chairs

2nd mo., 1st [1 February 1838]. About 11 p.m., some little time after all had gone to bed, the sound of chairs etc., being moved about on the kitchen floor was heard.

Incident 41: The Phantom Cook

2nd mo., 4th [4 February 1838]. Jane C. had been poorly, and was awake about 4.30 a.m., as well as her companion, when they heard footsteps descending from the upper storey which passed their door and went down into the kitchen; they thought it was the cook and wondered at her being so early. They then heard the sound of the kitchen door opening and then of the kitchen window being thrown up and the shutters opened with more than usual noise. At about seven o'clock they were surprised by the cook calling at their room for a light; having been up early to do the washing the previous morning she had this time over-slept herself. She had clearly not been downstairs.

Incident 42: Mallet Beats

In the afternoon of that same day [4 February 1838] Jon. D. Carr [Elizabeth Procter's brother, from Carlisle] came to the house and stayed all night, sleeping alone on the second storey. Soon after going to bed he heard noises in the room above, as of a piece of wood or a balance rapidly striking each end of the floor; afterwards many beats as with a mallet, some very loud; also like a person stamping in a passion. He also heard a peculiar whistle, which he imitated so as exactly to resemble what J.P. heard some time before. He further heard a noise on the stairs and landing, and for some time felt his bed to vibrate very much; he put his hand down to the stock and felt it shaking. This suddenly ceased. He was quite awake and collected; indeed he did not sleep till two o'clock though unusually disposed to it. He said in the morning he would not live in the house for any money. The account he gave to Jonathan Carr [Jon. D. Carr's father and Elizabeth Procter's father] induced ... [him]... to come over from Carlisle next morning to see if he could assist with his advice under such disagreeable and dangerous disturbances.

Edmund Procter adds, 'I can find no other allusion to my grandfather's visit among my father's papers'.

Incident 43: A Night of Horror

On 2nd mo., 5th, between 11 and 12 at night, Jane C. heard a thump on the landing near the bedroom door, upon which she awoke her companion, Mary Young'.

At this point in the diary, Edmund Procter inserts, 'This was the cook whom my aunt had to sleep with her, not daring to sleep alone in such a house; she was a most respectable and intelligent woman whom I well remember; she was eight years in my mother's service when she married the principal tradesman in the village'.

Joseph Procter's diary then continues:

Mary Young heard the slot in the door apparently slide back, the handle to turn and the door to open. A rush light was burning on the dressing-table, but the bed was an old four-poster, and the curtains being drawn nothing could be seen. A step then went to the rush light and appeared by the sound to snuff it and then lay down the snuffers. In the act of snuffing the light was transiently obscured, as when that act is customarily performed. Jane C. then felt it raise up the clothes over her twice; then they both heard something rustle the curtains as it went round the bed; on getting to Mary Young's side she distinctly saw a dark shadow on the curtain. On getting to the bed-board where Jane C. lay a loud thump as with a fist was heard on it; something was then felt to press on the counterpane on M. Young's side of the bed, the bed curtain being pushed in but nothing more seen. Whatever the visitor might be was then heard to go out, seeming to leave the door open. In the morning they found the door still bolted as it was left when they went to bed. In this occurrence Jane C. heard and felt everything described, but having her head under the bedclothes could not see the shadow as her companion did.

Edmund Procter adds a second footnote:

I have on three or four occasions heard a graphic account of this night of horror both from my aunt Jane Carr in later life, and from Mary Young some years after her marriage. The description they both give exactly agreed with the above narrative from my father's pen except that one or both of them stated that a few minutes after the unknown dreadful visitor left the room they arose, found the door locked as when they came to bed, and searched the room in every way. This is the only discrepancy I notice. One would naturally expect that my aunt would refuse to stay longer in the house after such an experience, but such was not the case; she was as I remember her to be, a woman of strong nerve, of very cheerful temper, and not easily disturbed. She died on board the steamer Prussian Eagle, in Plymouth Sound, in 1859.

Incident 44: Unaccountable Thumpings

The following incident occurred on 6 February 1838:

There had been unaccountable thumpings and bed shakings but nothing of special note.

Incident 45: The Box

On the 7th [7 February 1838] J.C. heard the noise of a box trailed over the floor above the nursery when she was certain no one was upstairs, the servants being at dinner in the kitchen and the rest of the family in the parlour downstairs.

Incident 46: A Queer Looking Head

The following incident is interesting, as it involves the appearance of an anthropomorphic entity. The puzzling factor is that Procter prefaces it with the words, 'From 2nd mo., 6th to the 20th [6-20 February 1838] nothing particular has been heard'. However, Incident 45, we know according to Procter's own writings, took place on 7 February and Incident 47 took place on 17 February – both in the time period when Procter alleged 'nothing particular has been heard'. The authors can only conclude that Procter had another one of his unfortunately familiar errors with dates or that he believed the phenomena which manifested themselves in Incidents 45 and 47 were barely worth a mention. The details of Incident 46 are as follows:

> *…but Jane, about 4 ½ years old, told her parents that when sleeping with her aunt she one night [between 6-20 February] saw by the washstand at the foot of the bed where the curtains were open, a queer looking head, she thought of an old woman; she saw her hands with two fingers of each hand extended and touching each other; she had something down the sides of her face and passed across the lower part of it. She saw it plainly though it was darkish in the room. She was afraid and put her head under the clothes and by-and-bye fell asleep.*

Incident 47: The Head on the Landing

> *On the 17th, [17 February 1838] about dusk, she [the young Jane Procter] described having seen a head on the landing as she was coming downstairs, and appeared to be very much terrified.*

Incident 48: Icy Coldness

> *Some night previous [probably between 18-24 February] E.P. was awoke by feeling a pressure on the face over the eye, of icy coldness; it was suddenly laid on with a good deal of force and as suddenly withdrawn.*

Edmund Procter adds the comment:

> *I have heard my mother describe this on different occasions 20 or 30 years after it occurred; her face always had a pained expression when she related this experience, which I think was more distressing to her than anything she underwent in the house.*

Incident 49: Heavy Pressure

> *About the 25th [25 February 1838], pretty late at night, whilst J.P. was asleep, E.P. felt a heavy pressure which unnerved her very much; it seemed to take her breath away and she felt quite sick after it, but did not tell J.P. of it until the morning.*

From this point onwards, it is possible to date the events as having occurred in the year 1840.

Incident 50: Rattling Rings

3rd mo., 3rd. [3 March 1840]. About 5 a.m. E.P. was awake when several beats were felt on one side of the room, which awoke J.P.; a vibration was felt in the room, the bed shook considerably and the curtain rings rattled. The knocks were repeated on the floor above.

Incident 51: A Heavy Box

On the night of the 5th [5 March 1840] E.P. heard what appeared to be a heavy box turned over twice in the room above, where no one was sleeping, and the entire household being asleep except herself, and everything still.

Incident 52: His Name Being Called

3rd mo., 13th, 1840 [13 March 1840]. Since the last entry Joseph [Junior] has heard the sound of a thick stick being broken in his room; of a stepping backwards and forwards; of his name being called, etc. About the same date J. and E.P. heard unaccountable drummings and vibrations; also the sound of someone stirring in the closet.

Incident 53: The Bells

On the 21st [21 March 1840] J. and E.P. heard a handbell rung upstairs; they were quite satisfied at the time that no one was there.

Incident 54: Thumps in the Night

On the 28th [21 March 1840] heavy thumps in the middle of the night …

Incident 55: The Hand Bell

… and after breakfast the next morning [21 March 1840] E.P heard a handbell upstairs when she was quite certain everyone was downstairs. J. and E.P. are sure it is no actual bell in the house that is rung, the tone being altogether different.

Incident 56: Voices

Joseph [Junior] has been disturbed nearly every night lately; he says when there is nobody upstairs the voices are loud; he is now afraid of going into his room in the daytime. The words he reports as being uttered, such as 'Never mind' and 'Come and get', seem to have no particular application. Tonight [some time between 21-30 March] he has heard footsteps twice, and felt a bat on his pillow. At the time two of the servants were at a temperance meeting, the other in the kitchen.

Edmund Procter adds the footnote:

The inference that my brother was simply dreaming, or else shamming, so as to get someone to come beside him, will no doubt readily occur to some minds. I can only say that a more truthful boy, or one more transparently honest I do not think ever breathed. He was six years of age at this time, and died eleven years afterwards from an accidental blow on the head at a boarding-school.

Incident 57: Someone Talking

On the 30th [30 March 1840] Henry (3 years old) was awakened by his brother Joseph ringing the bell at his bedside, saying his bed was shaking, and that he heard someone talking in the room; Henry being asked if he did not think it was Joseph that spoke, said No, and showed where the sound came from; they both heard it again about ten minutes later on.

Incident 58: Stirring and Rustling

4th mo., 4th. [4 April 1840] This evening E.P. plainly heard someone or something stirring and rustling about in a room she knew no one was in, and there and then found that no one was in it.

Incident 59: Stirring in the Night

4th mo., 6th. [6 April 1840] During the last nine days J. and E.P. have often heard something stirring in the night, and knocks in the servants' room above; these they afterwards found the girls had not heard, being very sound sleepers.

Incident 60: Knocks

6th. [6 April 1840] During last night there seemed to be but little quiet in the house till daylight; noises as of a shoe dragged over the boards just outside the door, and as though the servants had got up and were going about; knocks loud and knocks gentle, indeed all sorts of knocks.

Edmund Procter adds, 'It may be well to mention here that the Newcastle and North Shields Railway, which passes about a quarter of a mile from the house, was opened on June 19th, 1840'.

Edmund Procter's reason for adding this suffix is obvious; he wishes to kill off any speculation before it arises that the sounds heard in the mill house could have been caused by the noise of the trains passing nearby.

Notes

1. Howitt, William, *Visits to Remarkable Places; Old Walls, Battle Fields, and Scenes Illustrative of Striking Passages in English History and Poetry* (Longman, Orme, Brown, Green & Longman, 1840)

   Howitt, like Procter and Unthank, had actually been a Quaker at one time. However, in 1847 he disassociated himself and became an ardent proponent of Spiritualism. How much influence his investigation into the Willington Mill affair might have influenced his decision is hard to say, and is something that even Howitt himself may have had difficulty in assessing

2. Crowe, Catherine, *The Night Side of Nature, or, Ghosts and Ghost Seers, Vol. II* (T.C. Newby, 1848)

3. Richardson, Moses Aaron, *The Local Historian's Table Book Vol. VI* (M.A Richardson, 1847)

4. Stead, William T., *Real Ghost Stories* (Grant Richards, 1897)

5. Stead, William T., *More Ghost Stories* (London, 1922)

   William T. Stead was a former editor of the *Northern Echo*, and relates that, 'I spent most of my boyhood within a mile of the famous haunted house or mill at Willington'. That he should later have developed an interest in the case is thus even more understandable

6. Richardson, Moses Aaron *The Local Historian's Table Book Vol. VI* (M.A. Richardson, 1847)

7. *Monthly Chronicle*, June 1887, p.178

8. *Tyne Pilot*, 11 July 1840

9. Anon; *The Willington Quay Ghost* (Privately published, *c.*1972)

Six

THE VIGIL

Perhaps the most extraordinary incident connected with the entire Willington enigma was an overnight vigil held at the mill house on Friday, 3 July 1840. What transpired that evening caused a sensation in Willington Quay itself, and news of it rippled throughout the entire nation. Despite the fact that more has been written about this event than any other aspect of the case, much of it is grossly inaccurate. To unearth all the available documentation on the event – or at least most of it – was indeed a difficult task for the authors. For that reason they are sympathetic in the most part towards others who have accidentally incorporated factual inaccuracies into their own works. What you are about to read here is, the authors believe, the most complete and accurate account to date on the event in question.

The Procter family was well connected throughout Tyneside, and had forged powerful relationships with local businesses, many of which were run by Quakers, and many professionals. One highly-regarded local doctor was Edward Drury, who worked in a surgery owned by a Dr Embleton at 10 Church Street, Sunderland, just south of the River Tyne and north of the River Wear. As far as the authors can tell, Drury was not known to the Procters – contrary to the assertions of some contemporary investigators – but it seems that they did have a number of mutual acquaintances. Drury was a rather serious-minded medic with little in the way of a sense of humour.

Drury had, for a number of years, been friends with a Willington farmer by the name of Davison. At some point, Davison told Drury about the strange events at Willington Mill, and excited the doctor's curiosity to such a degree that he desired to investigate them himself. Without delay, Drury put pen to paper[1]:

To Mr Procter. 17th June, 1840.

SIR,— Having heard from indisputable authority — viz., that of my excellent friend, Mr Davison, of Low Willington, farmer, that you and your family are disturbed by most unaccountable noises at night, — I beg leave to tell you that I have read attentively Wesley's account of such things, but with, I must confess, no great belief; but an account of this report coming from one of your sect, which I admire for candour and simplicity, my curiosity is excited to a high pitch,— which I would fain satisfy. My desire is to remain alone in the house all night, with no companion but my own watch-dog, in which, as far as courage and fidelity are concerned, I place much more reliance than upon any three young gentlemen I know of. And it is also my hope that, if I have a fair trial, I shall be enabled to unravel this mystery. Mr Davison will give you every satisfaction if you take the trouble to inquire of him concerning me.

I am, Sir, yours most respectfully,

EDW. DRURY.

At C.C. Embleton's, Surgeon, No. 10, Church-street, Sunderland.

Joseph Procter looked kindly upon Drury's request, and on 21 June had the following note sent to him[2]:

EDW. DRURY.

At C.C. Embleton's, Surgeon, No. 10, Church-street, Sunderland.

Joseph Procter's respects to Edw. Drury, whose note he received a few days ago, expressing a wish to pass a night in his house at Willington. As the family is going from home on the 23rd instant, and one of Unthank and Procter's men will sleep in the house, if E.D. incline to come, on or after the 24th, to spend a night in it, he is at liberty so to do, with or without his faithful dog, which, by-the-bye, can be of no possible use, except as company. At the same time, J.P. thinks it best to inform him that particular disturbances are far from frequent at present, being only occasional and quite uncertain, and therefore the satisfaction of E.D.'s curiosity must be considered as problematical. The best chance would be afforded by his sitting up alone in the third storey till it be fairly daylight— say 2 or 3 a.m.

Drury promptly contacted Procter and enquired whether 3 July would be a suitable time to carry out his investigations into 'the ghost', and was told that would be perfectly acceptable. The Procter family had planned to still be away in Carlisle on the date the vigil was carried out, and so Drury fully expected no one to be there except himself and the aforementioned servant. Things didn't quite work out that way.

Another person known to the Procters, but not really associated with them, was a local chemist by the name of Thomas Hudson. Hudson was highly respected by his colleagues, but also had a great sense of social responsibility. He served as a local councillor in South Shields, just across the River Tyne, and was well known for taking a principled stand on just about any affair that caught his attention. Hudson was one of the principal proponents of an Act of Parliament which culminated in the provision of a direct steam ferry between North Shields and South Shields, and, in 1854, was one of a number of influential characters who met with the Italian General Garibaldi when he visited England. On one occasion, Hudson received what he believed to be an 'excessive' payment for the value of some shares. This so troubled his conscience that he deducted what he thought he had reasonably deserved and gave the rest away to charity.

Late in the afternoon of 3 July 1840, Hudson was in the company of another North Shields chemist, his employer, Joseph Ogilvie – whom he teasingly referred to as 'his young governor' – when the younger man posed a question to him:[3]

THE HAUNTED MILL, WILLINGTON-ON-TYNE, 1887.

A sketch of 'The Haunted Mill' by C.X. Sykes, which appeared in the Monthly Chronicle *in June 1887.*

'Tom, the doctor [Drury] is going tonight to make the acquaintance of the ghost at the haunted house at Willington. How would you like to go with him, and see that he doesn't come back with a cock-and-bull story about it?'

Hudson later recalled, 'To give the "powdered aloes" the go-by, even for one afternoon was a prospect too tempting to give up, especially having had for many hours the acute aroma of that dust in my nostrils'.

'Most willingly', he replied. Probably to the amazement of Ogilvie, the chemist left his company 'within minutes' and promptly made his way towards Willington Quay.

Hudson recalled, 'That was before the days of railways, and as the Newcastle omnibuses, which then ran hourly to and beyond Willington, charged two shillings for the journey, we decided to tramp it'. He also remembered that:

> It was a beautiful evening. Golden clouds shone in the sky, the air was rich with the scent of wild flowers, the trees and hedges seemed clothed in gold, and the peaceful hum of the industrious bee in the green fields around us fell like dreamy music on the ear. These were the 'delightful days of old' before 'buzzers' were born; when old Father Tyne kept sand beds right up the river for sleepy steamers to get stranded upon for hours daily at low tide; and when fiddlers were always part of the crew, for the amusement of the company on board. Palmer [Sir Charles Mark Palmer, the shipping magnate] had not then built his palaces of labour nor his plantations of iron ships at Jarrow on the opposite shore … Quietude reigned everywhere. There was nothing ghostly about except the memory of the many tales told of the headless old lady who it was our vaunted ambition to accost on her nocturnal excursion from the other world.

Hudson arrived at Willington Mill at precisely 8 p.m., seemingly at the same time as Edward Drury the doctor. Drury would have been surprised at two things; firstly, the presence of Joseph Procter, whom he had believed was on vacation with his family, and secondly the presence of Thomas Hudson, as he had no idea that the chemist was going to join him on the vigil. Drury may have been more than a little piqued at Hudson's arrival, as we shall see.

We know that Procter and his family, along with a retinue of servants, departed for Carlisle on 23 June to spend time with Elizabeth's family. They had not planned to return to Willington until the week beginning Monday 6 July. However, something prompted Joseph Procter to cut short his holiday. Leaving his family in Carlisle, he took a train on the morning of 3 July and arrived in Newcastle late that afternoon. Procter was home well before either Drury or Hudson arrived. Later, he would simply claim that he had cut short his vacation because he 'had business' to attend to. This is odd, because as the owner of the mill there were any number of people he could delegate work to, including the ultra-trustworthy and experienced foreman, Thomas Mann. Even more suspicious is the fact that Procter suddenly decided to travel home on the very day that Hudson and Drury were going to spend the night in the old mill house.

Something seems to have unsettled Joseph Procter. It is clear that the only 'business' he wanted to engage in was being present when two strangers spent the night in his house. As will become clear later, Procter almost certainly regretted agreeing to allow the men to stay overnight at the mill house.

Throughout this book it will become apparent that Joseph Procter was very cautious about allowing people into his home – particularly those who were intrigued by the ghost or tales of the old 'witch's cottage' which once stood on the site. Mill employees needed to ask special permission to enter the Procter home, and on one occasion two employees who spent the night at the mill house when the family was absent were locked in their bedroom by the foreman and had to remain there until 6 a.m. the following morning when he released them. The truth is that Procter really didn't like people having the free run of his house when he wasn't there.

The reason why Procter probably agreed to the unsupervised visit initially was due to the fact that one of the Procters' servants would be present with Hudson and Drury. However, as the days whiled away at Carlisle, Joseph had time to reflect upon this.

The elderly servant on duty was named Bell and was technically no longer an employee of the Procters as he had retired on health grounds. However, Joseph Procter had persuaded him to spend the night on the premises in case his services were required. As things transpired, this would prove to be a fortuitous move on the mill owner's part. However, there were places in the mill house where Procter certainly didn't want his visitors to go, and it probably struck him that if they were really determined to visit somewhere off-limits, the ageing, fragile Bell may not have been in a position to stop them. By the morning of 3 July the anxiety became too great and Procter sped home.

In his account in the *Monthly Chronicle*[4] Hudson the chemist recalls that they …

... were most kindly entertained to supper by the genial and worthy miller, whose memory will long be revered on Tyneside. Mr Procter told us he had never seen the apparition himself, but he had heard many utterly unaccountable sounds on several remarkable occasions. However, from the accounts given to him by his children (who felt not at all alarmed by the 'old lady's' appearance by night or day) – accounts which, he told us, agreed in every detail – he was quite satisfied that the story of the supernatural appearance in his house was founded on fact. 'Moreover' said he, 'the testimony of most trustworthy witnesses, such as friends, neighbours and people on the premises, seem proof enough for the most sceptical'.

'If', continued our interesting and respected informant, 'if [sic] you feel inclined to stay all night on the chance of seeing it [as the visits, it seemed, were ever erratic], you are welcome to do so, or to return upon any future occasion when curiosity may call you here again'.

Hudson then related that they had enjoyed 'a salubrious but anti-stimulative supper' whilst being regaled further by Procter with his tales of the haunted mill house. Afterwards, both Bell and Procter gave their guests a guided tour of the premises and thus enabled the investigators to satisfy themselves of 'the impossibility of any intrusion or hoax-playing'. This was something that had apparently troubled Drury more than it had Hudson.

Wilson[5] and even Joseph Procter himself both state that Drury had taken with him a brace of pistols, intending to let one of them 'accidentally' fall to the floor to deter any would-be practical joker.

Hudson[6] puts a different gloss on the story, and seems to have detected more than a hint of fear in his companion who had consistently been sceptical about the whole notion that the mill house was haunted. In his recollections he sarcastically scolded, 'So brave was he [Drury], indeed, that at my request he left his pocket pistol downstairs, being now assured that whatever might appear would be skinless, and not susceptible to shot'.

Some researchers, such as Liddell[7], have fostered the idea that both Drury and Hudson were in the possession of pistols at the vigil. Liddell states, 'When they heard the sound of bare feet in a bedroom to Hudson's right they remembered that *they'd left their pistols* downstairs, well out of reach' (italics ours). As Hudson testified, not only did the one pistol he knew about belong to Drury, but he actually convinced the doctor to leave it downstairs.

Drury appears to have concealed his possession of the second pistol from Hudson and the assumption must be that during the vigil he still had the second weapon on him.

Just before 10 p.m., Procter and Bell took the two investigators up to the top landing which housed the 'haunted room'. On the landing itself Bell, at Procter's instruction, had placed two chairs, a small table holding two candles (already lit) and 'two silk night-caps' for the guests. Both Procter and Bell then went to bed – the master in his own room on the floor below, the servant in what is referred to as 'the camp room' on the ground level.

Hudson and Drury then began, with the aid of the candles, to take in their surroundings. Hudson recalls, 'Four bed-room doors stood open around us. All the bed-rooms were furnished, but none of them was occupied on the night in question, Mr Proctor's [*sic*] family being away from home at the time'.

It is obvious from Hudson's account that the 'disturbed room' had already been opened up by this time and furnished at least to some degree. It is also obvious that some of the rooms on the upper floor were indeed being occupied, and were only disused because the family was away. This does not mean that they were being occupied by the family itself, however, as the upper floor would normally be used by staff. It seems that during the family's absence the staff were given a holiday, thus explaining why the servant Bell had to be temporarily brought out of retirement and the rooms were vacant. The testimony of Procter and other witnesses is consistent that the 'haunted' room in question was never used at all.

In his recollection Hudson – who doesn't seem to have liked Drury particularly – adds, 'Dr Drury, being my senior, took the choice of seats, and sat upon one nearest the stairs, without, of course, any intention of beating an ignominious retreat at the advance of the ghost'.

Hudson says that he 'occupied a central position, two rooms being to the right of me and two to the left, while the stairs were at a right angle. Both of us looked so profoundly philosophical as possible in the light of the two stately wax candles, and there was not a sound save the occasional creech of the old-fashioned snuffers'.

According to Drury, 'Two hours crept slowly by in this solemn silence. The clock struck the ghostly hour of twelve without a single incident having occurred worthy of a word of comment'. Not long after, however, all hell broke loose.

According to Hudson, it started when …

> … *Fifteen minutes afterwards, however, a most unearthly hollow sound broke upon our ears. Knowing that coming events often cast their shadows before, we*

The railway line that leads past the site of Willington Mill, as it appears today. (Darren W. Ritson)

awaited breathlessly in the anticipation that these sounds might be the prelude to sights. But we waited in vain.

Later on, sounds came in a sort of rumbling and unequal fashion, such as might have been caused by waggon wheels travelling over the skeleton of the Willington Bridge, then in course of construction'. [Hudson's memory is failing him on this point; the bridge was actually opened for use on 19 June 1840, just two weeks before the vigil was carried out].

Anon my friend was a little excited by a vibrating noise which he said sounded 'like the fluttering of an angel's wing!'

My answer was that it was more likely to be the echo of a steamer's paddle wheels on the adjoining river. Then there came another awfully perplexing sound, as if something was trying to squeeze itself through the floor at our feet. This was simple as a matter of fact, yet it produced in us a great degree of nervous uneasiness. Not, however, to an alarming extent, as we knew that the house was built upon piles, and was, therefore, more sensitive to sounds than other buildings resting on more substantial foundations. This thought calmed our feelings.

It is perhaps significant that both men went into the house sceptical – even cynical – and yet the anomalous sounds were odd enough to make them both feel uneasy.

At 12.45 a.m., Hudson and Drury both noticed something distinctly odd. It was another strange sound, but the chemist later described it as 'the most unaccountable disturbance we had yet heard'.

Both men heard the noise, which they agreed was coming from 'one of the rooms close by'. Hudson describes it as being, 'the room to my right hand'. It was, said Hudson, 'as if someone were really there, walking on his or her bare feet, and approaching us. But nothing met our vision'.

After the noise had ceased, both men simultaneously felt tired. They had both been up since 6 a.m. the previous morning, and the chemist confessed that, 'nature was weighing my eyelids down'.

The doctor made a suggestion: Why didn't both men retire to bed and keep watch from there? Tempted though Hudson was, he dismissed the idea. If an extremely tired person lies down upon a bed, then he will fall asleep. Hudson told Drury that if the experiment was to be a success, then they needed to stay awake at least until daybreak. This seems to have upset Drury. Hudson suggested a compromise, and volunteered to be 'captain of the watch' whise the doctor went to bed for a nap.

According to Hudson, 'he refused somewhat testily, and not only so, but in a bad temper refused all further conversation, nursing his "pet" [his grievance] to keep it warm'. (When Drury first contacted Procter about the possibility of conducting his vigil, he had suggested bringing along his dog. This has caused some writers to speculate that the dog was the 'pet' mentioned by Hudson. However, we know that the doctor did not bring his dog in the final event.)

Hudson, seizing the opportunity, decided to wind Drury up even further:

> *To retaliate, lad-like, I took out a cigar in a strong spirit of independence, and jocosely [sic] remarked that I would take his white hat for a spittoon. This annoyed him, and he reminded me that we were engaged on too serious a matter for levity or laughter. Thus, after sitting there nearly three hours, without a book to read or a friend to chat with – the doctor refusing to speak – I naturally became exceedingly drowsy, yet I was awake enough for any emergency. I saw my friend reading a note which he had taken from his waistcoat pocket, and I closed my eyes for a few seconds only.*

Whether Hudson actually fell asleep or not has been a matter of some debate, and we will return to this subject later. For the moment we will give him the benefit of the doubt, however, and assume that he did not. Whatever the truth, what happened next would remove any possibility of slumber.

According to Drury, after finishing reading his note he took out his pocket watch to check the time. Then …

> … *In taking my eyes from the watch they became rivetted [sic] upon a closet door, which I distinctly saw open, and saw also the figure of a female attired in greyish garments, with the head inclining downwards, and one hand pressed upon the chest, as if in pain, and the other, viz., the right hand, extended towards the floor, with the index finger pointing downwards. It advanced with an apparently cautious step across the floor towards me; immediately as it approached my friend, who was slumbering, its right hand was extended towards him ; I then rushed at it, giving at the time, as Mr Procter states, a most awful yell; but instead of grasping it, I fell upon my friend, and I recollected nothing distinctly for nearly three hours afterwards. I have since learnt that I was carried downstairs in an agony of fear and terror[8].*

Hudson's recollection, as we might imagine, is slightly different[9]: After informing the reader that he closed his eyes 'for a few seconds only', he then goes on to say:

> *I was quickly startled, however, by a hideous yell from Drury, who sprang up with his hair standing on end, the picture of horror. He fainted and fell into my arms, like a lifeless piece of humanity. His horrible shouts made me shout in sympathy, and I instantly laid him down and went into the last room from whence the noise was heard. But nothing was there, and the window had not been opened.*

Drury's screams, and Hudson's own efforts to mimic them, did not go unheard. Procter would later discover that two or three of his neighbours had been woken by them, as were the miller and his trusty servant Bell.

According to Hudson, 'Mr Procter and the housekeeper came quickly to our assistance, and found the young doctor trembling in acute mental agony. Indeed, he was so much excited that he wanted to jump out of the window'.

This point – that Drury may have even been on the verge of committing suicide – has been almost universally overlooked by other writers.

For some reason, Hudson then glosses over what happened next with breathtaking brevity, which is all the more curious for there is nothing in the reports we have that paint him in anything other than a favourable

light. According to the chemist, 'Coffee was kindly given to us, and we
shortly afterwards left for North Shields'[10].

Hudson's rendition hardly does the incident justice. Drury, writing much
closer to the time of the actual incident, recalls with commendable candour;
'I recollected nothing distinctly for nearly three hours afterwards. I have
since learnt that I was carried downstairs in an agony of fear and terror'[11].

In a letter to his wife written the very next morning, Joseph Procter
recalls:

> *I called up Bell to make on the fires, get coffee, etc. but he [Drury] continued in
> a shocking state of tremour [sic] for some hours, though not irrational. He had a
> ghastly look and started at the smallest sound – could not bear to see anything
> white; he had not been in the least sleepy, and was not at all frightened till
> the moment when the ghost met his gaze. They had both previously heard
> several noises, but all had been quiet for about quarter of an hour, and E.D was
> thinking of getting his companion to go to bed, not expecting anything more
> that night … E.D. has got a shock he will not soon cast off.*[12]

Procter's recollection of events is in some respects closer to Hudson's and
in others to the good doctor. In the letter to his wife[13] he relates:

> *About one o'clock I heard a most horrid shriek from E.D., slipped on my
> trousers and went up. He had then swooned, but came to himself again in a
> state of extreme nervous excitement, and accompanied with much coldness and
> faintness. Had seen the G[host]., had been struck speechless as it advanced
> from the closet in the room over the drawing room to the landing, and then
> leapt up with an awful shriek and fainted. The other young man had his head
> laid against the easy-chair and was dozing, and as the G[host] made no noise
> in coming up he did not wake till the yell of his friend called him to his help.*

There are a number of discrepancies in the above accounts which need
to be addressed. The first concerns the time when the ghost was said to
have appeared.

According to Drury[14]:

> *At a quarter to one, I told my friend that, feeling a little cold, I would like to go
> to bed, as we might hear the noises equally well there. He replied that he would
> not go to bed till daylight. I took up a note which I had accidentally dropped,
> and began to read it, after which I took out my watch to ascertain the time, and
> found that it wanted ten minutes to one.*

It was immediately after looking at his watch that Drury saw the apparition which caused him to scream. If his watch was keeping good time, and in the dim candlelight he read it correctly, then we can identify that the incident occurred at 12.50 a.m. This is supported by Procter, who in his letter to Elizabeth[15] stated that, 'About one o'clock I heard a most horrid shriek from E.D.' However, according to the testimony of Thomas Hudson[16]:

> *To retaliate, lad-like, I took out a cigar in a strong spirit of independence, and jocosely [sic] remarked that I would take his white hat for a spittoon. This annoyed him, and he reminded me that we were engaged on too serious a matter for levity or laughter. Thus, after sitting there nearly three hours, without a book to read or a friend to chat with – the doctor refusing to speak – I naturally became exceedingly drowsy.*

According to Hudson, it was only at 12.45 a.m. when he began to tease the doctor, causing Drury to refuse to speak further, after which he had to sit for 'nearly three hours, without a book to read or a friend to chat with' before he eventually closed his eyes. If this reading of Hudson's account is correct, then the chemist identifies the time of the ghost's appearance as 3.45am.

Of course, if we allow the 'three hours' to begin at 10 p.m., at the beginning of the vigil, then the appearance of the apparition would have been at 1 a.m. the following morning. It would also pretty much bring Hudson's timeline into agreement with those of Drury and Procter. The difficulty with this is that it would necessitate accepting that, from the outset of the vigil, virtually no conversation at all took place between the two investigators. This is something that Hudson's testimony does not suggest. Perhaps the safest course would be to accept the testimonies of the doctor and the miller, as both were writing almost immediately after the event. Hudson's recollections were not given to, and printed in, the *Monthly Chronicle* till 1887, by which time his memory may have dimmed considerably.

Another minor difficulty arises when Drury, in his letter of 13 July 1840, describes Hudson as 'my friend'. The evidence suggests that the two barely knew each other, so we can only presume that in the days immediately following the vigil the two overcame their mutual disdain for each other and became friends.

Another problem relates to the time the vigil began. Hudson is emphatic that it started at 10 p.m. – a time accepted by almost all researchers. However, Drury states that it started at 'eleven o'clock p.m.' The authors have been unable to resolve this discrepancy, but cannot see that it impacts upon the veracity of the tale in any meaningful way.

Drury, writing much closer to the time, recalls, 'About ten minutes to twelve we both heard a noise, as if a number of people was pattering with their bare feet upon the floor'. Hudson's statement was that it was only the sound of one person's feet they heard, but this is a minor matter and should not trouble us too much.

Drury also recalls other noises that the passage of time seems to have caused the chemist to forget:

A few minutes afterwards, we heard a noise, as if someone was knocking with his knuckles among our feet; this was immediately followed by a hollow cough from the very room from which the apparition proceeded. The only noise after this was as if a person was rustling against the wall in coming upstairs.

Regarding the apparition, Drury states:

I ... saw also the figure of a female attired in greyish garments, with the head inclining downwards, and one hand pressed upon the chest, as if in pain, and the other, viz., the right hand, extended towards the floor, with the index finger pointing downwards. It advanced with an apparently cautious step across the floor towards me; immediately as it approached my friend, who was slumbering, its right hand was extended towards him.

Hudson recalls:

He said he had seen the grey, old lady in a grey gown proceed from the room at my right hand side, and slowly approach me from behind. She was, he said, just about to place her hand on my slumbering head, whilst he was strongly endeavouring to touch my foot with his, but though our feet were only a few inches apart, he had not the power to do so.

These two accounts are perfectly compatible, save for one small part. According to Hudson, he was sitting in a chair on the landing and could see into four bedrooms opposite. If the ghost appeared from one of those rooms and drifted towards Hudson, it is hard to see how it could have approached him from behind. The authors believe there is probably a simple explanation for this, could we but interview the now deceased participants.

After the participants in the vigil departed, Joseph Procter appears to have been deeply troubled by the effect the investigation had on Edward Drury. For three hours the man had been in a state of semi-consciousness and, on waking, had no recollection of them. On 5 July, just two days after the vigil, Procter decided to journey to Sunderland to call upon Drury and see how he was faring. Unfortunately the doctor wasn't in and did not return home till the following day. Presumably Procter must have left a note or message for Drury to let him know he had called. Touched by his kindness, the doctor wrote a letter of thanks[17]:

To Mr Procter. Monday morning, July 6th, 1840.

DEAR SIR, — I am sorry I was not at home to receive you when you kindly called yesterday to inquire for me. I am happy to state that I am really surprised that I have been so little affected as I am, after that horrid and most awful affair, the only bad effect that I feel is a heavy dulness in one of my ears—the right one; I call it heavy dulness, because I not only do not hear distinctly, but feel in it a constant noise; this I was never affected with heretofore; but I doubt not it will go off.

I am persuaded that no one went to your house at any time more disbelieving in respect to seeing anything peculiar; now no one can be more satisfied than myself. I will, in the course of a few days, send you a full detail of all I saw and heard. Mr Spence and two other gentlemen came down to my house in the afternoon to hear my detail; but, sir, could I account for these noises from natural causes, yet, so firmly am I persuaded of the horrid apparition, that I would affirm that what I saw with my eyes was a punishment to me for my scoffing and unbelief, that I am assured that, as far as the horror is concerned, they are happy that believe and have not seen. . .
EDWARD DRURY.

Procter replied[18]:

Willington, 7th mo. 9, 1840. Respected Friend, E. Drury,
Having been at Sunderland, I did not receive thine of the 6th till yesterday morning. I am glad to hear thou art getting well over the effects of thy unlooked-for visitation. I hold in respect thy bold and manly assertion of the truth in the face of that ridicule and ignorant conceit with which that which is called the supernatural, in the present day, is usually assailed.

I shall be glad to receive thy detail, in which it will be needful to be very particular in showing that thou couldst not be asleep, or attacked by nightmare,

or mistake a reflection of the candle, as some sagaciously suppose.
I remain, respectfully,

Thy friend,

JOSH. PROCTER.

P.S. I have about thirty witnesses to various things which cannot be
satisfactorily accounted for on any other principle than that of spiritual agency.

It is clear from the correspondence that Edward Drury had gone
through a conversion of sorts, and he was no longer cynical regarding
supernatural phenomena. Thomas Hudson, however, remained far more
cautious. In the *Monthly Chronicle*[19] he said:

Drury declared his unbounded belief in the ghost. He said he had seen the grey
old lady … My opinion, however, is that Drury saw the appearance of the
mysterious lady, as others had seen her, in much the same way as Macbeth [sic]
saw the ghost of Banquo and the dagger; but whether it was or was not a spirit in
form will remain a mystery to some, a fact to a few, and simply a mental delusion
to many. The latter will be the more prevalent opinion in this age of materialism,
when the question is asked, How can there be a shadow without substance, or
mind without matter, except in our dreaming eyes and foolish fancies?

Hudson's version of events concerning the vigil was eventually published
in the *Newcastle Weekly Chronicle*[20] and later the *Monthly Chronicle*[21] and
the writer of the latter feature felt obliged to explain why it had taken
the chemist nearly half a century to tell his side of the story:

Mr Drury's version of the adventures in the haunted house had been before
the public for more than forty years ere Mr Hudson consented to give his …
How it happened that Mr Hudson so long remained silent on the subject was
thus explained: When the permission of Mr Procter was given to the last visit
in 1840, he requested the visitors not to make known their experiences, because
of the difficulty he found in retaining domestic servants, who were naturally
terrified of the idea of residing in a house that was reputed to be haunted. Mr
Hudson scrupulously observed Mr Procter's injunctions. But the reasons for
silence had disappeared in 1884. Mr Procter is dead, his family had removed
from Willington, and the premises had been converted to other uses. There was,
therefore, no longer any reason for reticence.

All of this is understandable, of course, although it demonstrates yet again the consistent desire on the part of Procter to keep the haunting of the mill under wraps, whilst, enigmatically, vouching forth the truth of it whenever asked.

The vigil at the mill is a fascinating vignette for the affair that makes intriguing reading, but as evidence it is at best circumstantial. The reader must make of it what they will. One of the most accurate accounts of the haunting, including the vigil, that the authors have came across, although extremely brief, is contained in *500 British Ghosts and Hauntings* by Sarah Hapgood[22].

Notes

1. Letter from Dr Edward Drury to Joseph Procter, 17 June 1840
2. Letter from Joseph Procter to Dr Edward Drury, 21 June 1840
3. *Monthly Chronicle*, June 1887, p. 179
4. *Ibid.*
5. Wilson, Colin, *The Supernatural – Unlock the Earth's Hidden Mysteries* (Parragon, 1995), p. 119
6. *Monthly Chronicle*, June 1887, p. 180
7. Liddell, Tony, *Otherworld North East: Ghosts and Hauntings Explored* (Tyne Bridge Publishing, 2004)
8. Private letter from Dr Edmund Drury to Joseph Procter, dated 13 July 1840
9. *Monthly Chronicle*, June 1887, p. 180
10. *Ibid.*
11. Private letter from Dr Edmund Drury to Joseph Procter, dated 13 July 1840
12. Private letter from Joseph Procter to Elizabeth Procter, dated 4 July 1840
13. *Ibid.*
14. Private letter from Dr Edmund Drury to Joseph Procter, dated 13 July 1840
15. Private letter from Joseph Procter to Elizabeth Procter, dated 4 July 1840 INS. REF
16. *Monthly Chronicle*, June 1887, p. 180
17. Private letter from Edward Drury to Joseph Procter, 6 July 1840
18. Private letter from Joseph Procter to Edward Drury, 9 July 1840
19. *Monthly Chronicle*, June 1887, pp. 180-1
20. *Newcastle Weekly Chronicle*, 20 December 1884
21. *Monthly Chronicle*, June 1887, pp. 180-1
22. Hapgood, Sarah, *500 British Ghosts & Hauntings* (Foulsham, 1993)

Seven

LOOK INTO MY EYES

Thomas Hudson was, as we know, an influential character who was well-respected for his professional abilities as a chemist. He was also a slight eccentric who, despite his impeccable honesty, was never afraid to court controversy in his social or political life.

It was 1846 before Hudson first gained a mention in any of the trade directories published on North and South Tyneside, by which time he had left his former employment with the chemist Joseph Ogilvie and opened up his own dispensary at 23 Long Row, South Shields while his brother, George, operated a second dispensary at 76 West Holborn. Although running his business in South Shields, Thomas Hudson maintained a comfortable residence at South Preston Cottage, North Shields. By 1871, Hudson had also qualified as a 'surgeon-dentist' and opened up a practice at 3 Thrift Street, South Shields, with his brother. Several years later, Hudson purchased the adjacent property at 4 Thrift Street and converted it into yet another dispensary.

Hudson was not only a chemist and a surgeon-dentist, but also – and this is not well known – revered for his abilities as a hypnotist. Even the vast majority of Tynesiders who are aware of Hudson and his life are oblivious to his skills in mesmerism. However, at the peak of his career he became embroiled in a case which was to make international headlines.

Harriet Martineau was born in Norwich on 12 June 1802. Her family members were devout Unitarians, and Harriet was raised in a strict but devoutly spiritual household. From an early age she suffered from ill health, including, nervous debility, poor eyesight and sensitivity to light, diminished hearing, poor appetite and, apparently, a reduced capacity for taste and smell.

At the age of eighteen, perhaps because she was unable to enjoy the more robust pursuits of other teenagers, Harriet started to write. Her first literary attempts were a number of articles for *The Monthly Repository* – a liberal Unitarian journal founded by Robert Aspland.

A year later she published her first book, *Devotional Exercises and Addresses, Prayers and Hymns.*

After the death of her father in 1826, the family fortunes took a radical downturn. To compensate for this, Harriet returned to her writing with renewed vigour. Within five years she had become a celebrated success and she found herself feted by celebrities such as Florence Nightingale, Charles Darwin and Emily Brontë, who were all admirers of her work. Perhaps through their influence, and an inherent sense of justice, Harriet became something of a social reformer.

By 1838 Harriet's health was deteriorating. Her pre-existing conditions were being exacerbated by the presence of a cyst on one of her ovaries, for which she was recommended to the care of Thomas M. Greenhow, her own brother-in-law and one of Newcastle-upon-Tyne's most respected surgeons. Greenhow had attended a lecture on mesmerism at Newcastle City Hall, and had seemingly been impressed by it. He made contact with the speaker, Spenser Hall, and asked him if he would accompany him to see Miss Martineau. In June 1844 the consultation took place. Initially, Hall's hypnotherapy precipitated some unpleasant symptoms, but overall Martineau said that she felt somewhat better. Hall and Greenhow were encouraged enough to arrange a second visit the following day. This session too produced an overall improvement. Unfortunately, when the two arrived at Martineau's Tynemouth home on the third day, her condition had deteriorated and they were not able to attend her. Not to be outdone, Greenhow taught Jane Arrowsmith, a maid in the employ of Harriet's landlady, how to conduct the 'mesmeric hand-passes' favoured by Hall. The maid did as instructed, and witnessed a sudden and astonishing improvement in her mistress's condition. The symptoms which had plagued Martineau all her life were greatly reduced, and she lived quite happily until she eventually succumbed to heart disease years later.

It seems that Hall and Greenhow had intended to visit Martineau further, but their visits were curtailed. Martineau eventually left Tynemouth and relocated to Ambleside in 1845. Although this did not have a deleterious affect upon Martineau, it proved disastrous for the maid, Jane Arrowsmith, who had also been subjected to several sessions of mesmerism under their supervision. Much has been written about how Arrowsmith, whilst hypnotised, demonstrated some remarkable clairvoyant abilities. However, what is not so well documented is the fact that she was also being mesmerised to treat some debilitating medical conditions. Arrowsmith, amongst other things, had been suffering from a degenerative ocular condition which had rendered her partially blind, and a digestive disorder which had left her almost unable to eat.

A friend of Harriet Martineau's took pity upon the girl and introduced her to none other than the celebrated chemist, dentist and hypnotist, Thomas Hudson. Martineau herself had been introduced to Hudson, whom she described as, 'a benevolent druggist, accustomed to mesmerise'.[1] Hudson arranged to meet Arrowsmith at the home of an aunt who, it seems, was none too disposed towards hypnotism, despite the desperate straits her niece found herself in. When Hudson arrived, the aunt refused to grant him entry. Hudson somehow managed to communicate his presence to some friends of Jane Arrowsmith before making his way surreptitiously to the bottom of the aunt's garden. There, Jane's colleagues gently helped her into a seat and, without further ado, the chemist got to work. Almost immediately Jane displayed an astonishing improvement in her condition. Her eyesight improved instantaneously and she exclaimed that, unlike before, she could now see an object placed in her lap. She also expressed a desire to eat – something that she had not done for weeks.

Jane's aunt, on seeing the positive results of Hudson's handiwork, suddenly changed her tune and bade the chemist to stay for tea. Her hypocrisy was self-evident, however, and it seems that Arrowsmith never really forgave her for attempting to deny her an opportunity to improve her health for no good reason. Word soon reached Harriet Martineau of the incident, and she immediately made arrangements for Jane to come

The author Harriet Martineau, whose maid was 'mesmerised' by Dr Thomas Hudson. The Monthly Chronicle, November 1887.

and stay with her. There she lived for seven years until she relocated to Australia and married. Some years later her eye condition returned and she eventually died.

What we are able to determine from this vignette in Tyneside's history is that Thomas Hudson possessed some considerable skill as a hypnotist. This fact, which is historically undeniable, has forced the authors to confront a very important question: If Hudson could mesmerise Jane Arrowsmith so powerfully, could he have done the same to Dr Edward Drury during their vigil at the mill house? It is certainly possible.

Hudson, we know, was something of a sceptic concerning the paranormal, and he may well have decided to play an outrageous prank on Drury in this way. We have already seen how, by his own admission, he teased his ghost-hunting companion to the point where the latter stopped speaking to him for a period of three hours. However, there are aspects of Hudson's personality, already ably demonstrated, which do not fit comfortably with this scenario. He was a man of almost fanatical honesty, and it is hard to believe that he would have sunk so low as to perpetrate such a trick upon Drury even if he were irritated by the man's pomposity.

But there is another factor to consider. Hudson had an impeccable reputation in his field, but if it were later discovered that he had mesmerised someone without their consent the result could have been incredibly damaging. Hudson was already playing with fire simply for dabbling with hypnotism for medical reasons with willing patients, as the entire art of mesmerism was at that time provoking furious debate in the medical profession. To hypnotise someone unwillingly, and for no more reason than to humiliate them, would have been a risk too far.

Even if Hudson had carried out such an outrageous parlour trick, his honesty and integrity would, the authors think, have forced him to admit to it almost immediately. He did not, and towards the end of his life doubted that what Drury had witnessed was a ghost at all.

Hudson, although given to teasing Drury from time-to-time in later years, never took to being malicious or making capital from the doctor's dramatic reaction to seeing the ghost.

It is unlikely in the extreme that Hudson mesmerised poor Dr Drury and convinced him that he'd had a supernatural experience, but at least the facts have now been presented here and readers can make up their own minds.

Note
1. *Monthly Chronicle*, November 1887, p. 418

Eight

THE PROCTER DIARY (PART 2)

The following events recorded in Joseph Procter's diary all took place after the notorious 'vigil' of 3 July 1840.

> *5th mo., 1841 [May 1841]. Since the latter end of 12 mo [December], 1840, we have been entirely free from those very singular disturbances which had been occurring with intermissions for about 14 months before; and as we now appear to be threatened with a renewal of them, I here make some memoranda of the circumstances.*

It is interesting that Procter here indicates specifically that there was a lull in paranormal activity between the end of December 1840 and May 1841. However, his previous diary entry is dated 6 April 1840, which means that the events which cover the period 7 April 1840 till the end of December 1841 are not discussed. It is indeed sad that Procter consciously omitted so much material that could have proved invaluable to researchers. Regardless, Procter goes on to say:

Incident 61: Rustling and Running

> *Our servants for some time have shown no symptoms of timidity, and seemed to have no apprehension of any recurrence of former visitations. E.P. has not been well lately, and has thought she observed something in the demeanour of the servants indicative of fear within a day or two past; on questioning them this afternoon they said the ghost had come back, but they wished to keep it from her if possible, as she was poorly.*
>
> *On the 29th [probably 29 April], about 9 p.m., J.P., hearing Joseph call, and going upstairs, heard a rustling, like a female running out of the room, but saw no one and was satisfied no one was there. Joseph said his name had been called several times from near the foot of the bed in a voice like his own.*

Incident 62: Drumming and Tapping

That night [probably 29 April] J. and E.P. heard a drumming and tapping in different parts of their room; at one moment it seemed to be something heavy falling on the floor of the room above, then on the floor of the room adjoining where it awoke the youngest child, and then to pounce down in the room below on the ground floor.

Edmund Procter adds, 'I have frequently heard my father describe this peculiar case'.

Incident 63: Bare Feet

6 mo., 1st. [1 June 1841] The two maids, Davis and E. Mann, report they were unable to sleep before 2 a.m. from constant noises, particularly the apparent treading of bare feet backwards and forwards at the foot of their bed, the noise several times awaking the youngest child; some times the tread seemed to pass out on the landing and run up and down stairs. The nursery door was of course bolted.

Incident 64: Roll Out the Barrel

7 mo., 14th, 1841 [14 July 1841]. – J. and E.P. heard the spirit in their own room, and in the room overhead, making a noise as of something heavy being hoisted or rolled, or like a barrel set down on its end; also noises in the camp-room of various and most unaccountable character. Edmund, who is about a year and a half old, roused up with every symptom of being dreadfully frightened; he screamed violently, was very long time in sleeping again, and frequently awoke in a fright; he became feverish and continued so all the following day, seeming frightened at the sight of his crib, and alarmed at any noise he did not understand.

Incident 64: The White Face

On the 26th of 10th mo., 1841, [26 October 1841] about 9 a.m., Joseph and Henry were playing at the foot of the stairs; they both saw a white face looking down upon them over the stair rails leading to the garret. Joseph called for his aunt, Christina Carr, to come and see it, but just as she was coming he saw it hop away. Henry heard it give a great jump, but Joseph, being very dull of hearing, did not. They both agreed in the description of what they saw.

Incident 65: The Funny Cat

This incident appears to have occurred in either late October or early November 1841:

Edmund, who is under two years old, was frightened a short time before by what he called a 'funny cat', and showed a good deal of timidity the rest of the evening, looking under chairs, etc., lest it should be lurking there, and it is to be noted that he has no fear of a cat.

Incident 66: The Sound of an Animal

On or about the 1st of 11th mo. [1 November 1841] E.P. awoke at night, heard the sound of an animal leaping down off the easy-chair which stood near the bed; there was no noise of its getting up and running off, but a dead silence.

Incident 67: The Monkey

7th day, 11 mo., 13th, 1841 [Saturday, 13 November 1841]. About 4.30 p.m. Joseph, now eight years old, was in the nursery with his brothers and sisters; he had seated himself on the top of a chest of drawers and was making a pretended speech to them, when he suddenly jumped down, and the nursery door being ajar, J.P., who was in his own bedroom adjoining, heard him exclaim there was a monkey, and that it had pulled his leg by his shoe-strap. J.P. did not himself see the monkey, but coming out of his room saw the children peering under the curtains of the bed in the Blue-room where, they alleged, the animal had disappeared. Joseph afterwards stated that the monkey had given a sharp pull at his shoe-strap, and had tickled his foot; he did not suppose any other but it was a real monkey.

Edmund Procter comments:

Now it so happens that this monkey is the first incident in the lugubrious hauntings, or whatever they may be termed, of which I have any recollection. I suppose it was, or might easily be, the first monkey I had ever seen, which may explain my memory being so impressed that I have not forgotten it. A monkey, and upstairs in the nursery, that is the business.

My parents have told me that no monkey was known to be owned in the neighbourhood, and after diligent inquiry no organ-man or hurdy-gurdy boy, either with or without monkey, had been seen anywhere about the place or neighbourhood, either on that day or for a length of time.

Although I freely admit the evidence of an infant barely two years old is of very small import, yet I may say I have an absolutely distinct recollection of that monkey, and of running to see where it went to, as it hopped out of the room and into the adjoining Blue-room. We saw it go under the bed in that room, but it could not be found or traced anywhere afterwards. We hunted and ferretted [sic] about that room, and every corner of the house, but no monkey, or any trace of one, was more to be found.

I don't know what to make of such a visitation, and have no explanation to offer; but that it was a monkey, that it disappeared under the bed in the Blue-room that Saturday afternoon, and was never seen or heard of again – of this not merely from my own childish recollection, but from the repeated confirmation of my brothers and sisters in after life, I am perfectly certain. I am merely recording the facts as simply as I can; readers may smile or mock as seemeth good unto them – I cannot alter what has taken place to suit either them or anyone else.

Incident 68: Labouring Breathing

About the middle of the 11th mo., 1841 [November 1841], Christina Carr went with Eliz. Mann into a bedroom about 10 p.m. They heard a heavy labouring breathing, first at the far side of the room and then very near them, the floor at the same time shaking with a constant vibration. They hastily retired.

Incident 69: Threw up the Sash

On the 24th of 11th mo., Joseph, who had gone to bed about 8 o'clock, presently called of his father in some alarm; he said a man had just been in who went to the window, threw up the sash, put it down again and then walked out; he had light or grey hair and no hat on. He was astonished J.P. had not met him. Within a few minutes he called out again; he had heard a step from the door to the closet at the far side of the room where he heard something like a cloak fall. He durst not look up to see who it was.

Edmund Procter commented:

If any readers exclaim that these are but the dreams and nightmares of children, I will only remind them that I am simply transcribing from my father's diary, written on the dates given by his own hand, and that they must form their own conclusions. The diary goes on to say that my mother had her own mother staying with her and sleeping with her at this time for about a fortnight.

Incident 70: Cinders

One night, when E.P. was asleep, Jane Carr heard a sound like a continued pelting of small substances which at first she took for cinders from the fire; afterwards she sat up in bed, with a light burning, and seeing nothing, she heard the sound of somebody going gently about the floor, the dress rustling as it passed from one part of the room to another.

Incident 71: A Miscellany of Sounds

*On first day evening, 19th of 12th, 1841 [Sunday, 19 December 1841] about
8 o'clock, E.P. and her sister, Christina Carr, were in the nursery with the
infant, and heard a heavy step coming up the stairs. They at first thought it
might be J.P., but recollected that he had put on his slippers, and the step was
with heavy shoes; it seemed to pass into the adjoining room in which were
some of the children asleep. They soon heard the sounds in that room as of
something falling, and by-and-bye Henry, about five years old, began to cry
as if afraid. The only maid then at home came up to him, when he could not
speak for a length of time for sobbing; at last he said something spoke to him,
and had also made noises with the chairs.*

Incident 72: Two Stamps

*8 mo., 3rd [3 August 1842] – Since the last date there have been few nights
during which some branch of the family has not heard our visitor. One night
J.P. was awoke and heard something hastily walk, with a step like that of a
child of 8 or 10 years, from the foot of the bed towards the side of the room, and
come back seemingly towards the door, in a run; then it gave two stamps with
one foot; there was a loud rustling as of a frock or night dress. I need scarcely
say the door was locked, and I am quite certain there was no other human
being in the room but E.P., who was asleep. The two stamps aroused E.P. out
of her sleep. About this time Joseph, on two or three occasions, said he had heard
voices from underneath his bed and from other parts of the room, and described
seeing on one occasion a boy in a drab hat much like his own, the boy much
like himself too, walking backwards and forwards between the window and the
wardrobe. He was afraid but did not speak.*

*Noises as of a band-box falling close at hand, as of someone running
upstairs when no one was there, and like the raking of a coal rake, were heard
about this time by different members of the family.*

Incident 73: Clothes Horse

*'8 mo., 6th. On the night of the 3rd [3 August 1842], just after the previous
memorandum was written, about 10.30 p.m., the servants having all retired
to bed, J. and E.P. heard the noise like a clothes-horse being thrown down
in the kitchen. Soon the noises became louder and appeared as though some
persons had burst into the house on the ground floor and were clashing the
doors and throwing things down. Eventually J.P. got one of the servants
to go downstairs with him, when all was found right, no one there, and
apparently nothing moved. The noises now began on the third storey, and*

the servants were so much alarmed that it was difficult to get them to go bed at all that night.

Incident 73: Steppings and Loud Rumblings

8 mo., 6th to 12th [6-12 August 1842], my brother-in-law, George Carr, was with us. He heard steppings and loud rumblings in the middle of the night, and other noises.

Edmund Procter then comments:

At this point the diary comes to an end. I know, however, that disturbances of a varied character continued more or less, perhaps less rather than more, for years. One episode during the period has been frequently told to me by my father, and I think no account of it has been published.

All his family were in Cumberland and he was sleeping alone, only one servant being in the house. He had retired about 10.30. Owing to the disturbances he and my mother, as well as the domestics, usually burnt a rush light during the night, a description of candle at that time in common use; but on this occasion he had no light whatsoever. He had not been two minutes in bed when suddenly, seemingly close to the bedside, there was an awful crash as of a wooden box being wrenched open with a crowbar with terrific force; he started up and cried out with a loud voice, 'Begone! Thou wicked spirit!' As if in defiance of this adjuration the fearful crash was almost immediately repeated, and if possible, louder than before. Cool-headed as my father was, and inured to unwelcome surprises from the unknown, he was painfully agitated by this ostentatious outburst of ill-will or wanton devilry; he arose, struck a light, searched the room, opened his bedroom door, listened on the stairs, looked into the other rooms, and explored the house generally, but found everything perfectly quiet. There was no wind, and indeed there seemed no explanation, but one only, of this horrid visitation.

Nine

PROBLEMS WITH THE PROCTER DIARY

We must be thankful indeed that Joseph Procter decided to keep a diary of the bizarre occurrences which took place at the mill house at Willington. Had he not done so, it is almost certain that the case would have quickly faded into obscurity. However, as the authors picked through Procter's account it became obvious that there were certain difficulties with it which, to their knowledge, had never been previously addressed by other researchers.

The first problem concerns the sporadic nature of the entries. There are times when Procter details two and sometimes three incidents within one day, but there are others when over a year seems to go by without a single entry being made. There are, as far as the authors can tell, three possible explanations for this.

The first solution is that, quite simply, nothing happened during the time periods concerned. Later in this volume the authors will detail their thoughts regarding the nature of the phenomena which occurred at Willington, and one of those under consideration will be that of a poltergeist infestation. A poltergeist phenomena normally has a very short shelf-life, and rarely lasts for more than a few weeks. However, in more protracted cases it is not unusual for there to be long breaks in between bouts of supernatural activity – sometimes for months or, rarely, even years. If a poltergeist infestation of unusually long duration was part of the problem at the mill house, then this might explain some of the large gaps in the diary. Joseph Procter had commented on the sporadic nature of the manifestations himself. In a letter to Dr Edmund Drury he stated that the 'disturbances are far from frequent at present, being only occasional and quite uncertain'[1].

There can be no doubt that this explanation might well account for some of the gaps, but it is far from a perfect solution to the problem. After protracted lulls in activity, one would expect Procter to comment upon them when resuming his diary entries. Only once does he even obliquely seem to do this, and on all other occasions he simply takes up where he had left off as if the last incident happened the day before, and not weeks or months earlier.

A second possibility is that during the time periods covered by the blank spots in the diary there were indeed strange things going on at the mill house, but, for whatever reason, Procter deliberately didn't commit them to paper. As we know, Procter admitted on at least one occasion that he had indeed refrained from detailing a number of occurrences. However, there are simply too many gaps in the diary to allow for this explanation to be applied on every occasion.

A third possibility – and one which needs to be given serious consideration – is that there were diary entries made during the time periods in question but that they were subsequently removed. If pages were removed, who could have done so and what might their motivation have been? Is it possible that the missing pages, if indeed there are any, could still be in existence? These are questions which the authors will address later in this chapter.

Who Wrote the Diary?

This may seem like a strange question, however it is worth considering. The appearance of a person's writing is unique, as are the idiosyncrasies in their writing style. Like everyone else, Joseph Procter had a number of idiosyncrasies that manifested themselves when he wrote. It isn't necessary to detail them all here, but there is one which gives the authors rise for concern: Procter continually swaps between the first and the third person pronouns. This might simply have been an idiosyncratic characteristic of Joseph Procter's writing. Unfortunately, a much more disturbing possibility also has to be considered; that the portions of the diary written in the third person had not been penned by Joseph Procter at all.

For examples of first-person pronouns in the diary we may consider the following:

My brother, John Richardson Procter …

My wife and I …

On the same evening I heard …

On dozens of occasions, however, Procter seems to use the third-person pronoun when speaking of himself:

About the beginning of the year J.P. [Joseph Procter] was awoke by the sound …

… he found next morning that his wife in the next room …

One night about this time J.P. heard early in the morning …

Sometimes Procter flips between the first-person plural and the third-person singular within the space of a single entry:

Our servants for some time have shown no symptoms of timidity, and seemed to have no apprehension of any recurrence of former visitations … On the 29th about 9 p.m., J.P. hearing Joseph call …

Speaking about oneself in the third person like this is unusual, but certainly not without precedent. Throughout this book the authors speak of themselves as 'the authors' in keeping with literary etiquette. The difficulty with Procter's diary is not so much that he employs the third-person pronoun or indeed the first-person pronoun, but rather that he continually seems to flip between the two, which may well point to a second hand being involved in the writing.

The fact that the diary was not published until 1892, seventeen years after Procter's death, suggests the possibility that additional information may have been added in the intervening years by a second hand. Edmund Procter does give reasons for the delay: 'my mother's [Elizabeth Procter] objection to their publicity during her lifetime; secondly, because the manuscript breaks off suddenly, and I have long hoped, but in vain, to find the continuation and conclusion'. However, his mother died only a few years after her husband and it is hard to believe that the hunt for the missing portion could have taken up the intervening years. Joseph Procter died in 1875 and we must presume that, within days of his death at most, Edmund, and perhaps other family members, would have begun to go through their father's personal papers in order to finalise any outstanding business. It is reasonable to assume, then, that soon after Joseph's death Edmund would have become aware of the diary's existence if he did not know of it already.

How long it took Edmund to discover that a portion of the diary was missing we do not know. He may have spotted it immediately, or it may have been within a month or two. We can safely say that it mustn't have been too long, though, for Edmund states that he had, 'long hoped, but in vain, to find the continuation and conclusion'. This indicates that he had been searching for the missing portion for many years. The diary was first published in the journal of the Society for Psychical Research in December 1892, seventeen years after Joseph Procter's death. This leads us to conclude that for most or all of that time Joseph's son was engaged in looking for the missing portion. Joseph's complete diary – in one or two parts – would almost certainly have been kept in the study of his new home. There is also a faint possibility that the missing portion was in the possession of a family member. In beginning his search, then, Edmund would have initially looked through his father's study. Having failed to find it, he would no doubt have contacted family members who might have had the latter portion of the diary. After exhausting these possibilities, it is difficult to see where Edmund could have planned to look next. The entire process of searching for the missing portion could have been completed within days. This makes it difficult to understand just why Edmund waited for well over a decade before eventually allowing the existing portion to be published.

When one looks at the numerous incidents in the diary in which Procter apparently slips into using the third-person pronoun, it is hard to escape the conclusion that someone else collaborated with him in writing it. If Procter did have help in compiling his notes we need to try and work out who did it and why, for the presence of an unseen and unnamed 'second hand' could potentially have a great impact upon the reliability of the text.

The first clue lies in the fact that some of the text does not seem to have been compiled until long after the incidents concerned. The writer – whomsoever they may have been – regularly states the ages of the children in the household when reciting incidents that they may have witnessed. Here are some examples:

He was six years of age at this time, and died eleven years afterwards from an accidental blow on the head at a boarding-school …

On the 30th Henry (3 years old) was awakened by his brother Joseph ringing the bell at his bedside …

7th day, 11 mo., 13th, 1841. About 4.30 p.m. Joseph, now eight years old, was in the nursery with his brothers and sisters …

Edmund, who is under two years old, was frightened a short time before …

However, on other occasions the diarist seems to struggle to recall the ages of the children, even when relating events that supposedly happened only a short time before:

> *About six weeks ago the nursemaid first told her mistress of the state of dread and alarm she was kept in, in consequence of noises she had heard for about two months, occurring more particularly nearly every evening when left alone to watch the child (Edmund's older brother then about two years old) …*

> *On the 13th of last month, early in the evening, two of the children in the house, one aged about 8, the other under two years, both saw, unknown to each other, an object which could not be real, and which went into the room where the apparition was afterwards seen and disappeared there …*

> *From 2nd mo., 6th to the 20th, nothing particular has been heard; but Jane, about 4½ …*

There is a possible solution to this problem, and it lies in a statement made by Edmund Procter in his commentary to the diary:

> *If any readers exclaim that these [the paranormal phenomena reported at the mill house] are but the dreams and nightmares of children, I will only remind them that I am simply transcribing from my father's diary, written on the dates given by his own hand.*

Edmund admits to 'transcribing' his father's notes; that is, copying them from the original. It may well be, then, that the guesses at the ages of the children – some of which appear in parentheses – were added by Edmund long after the events described and that it was he, not his father, who could not clearly remember the ages of his siblings at the time.

However, some of the guesses appear to be the diarist's own as they appeared in the original text. This leaves open a number of possibilities.

1. That Procter did not pen his diary as the events were happening, but actually years later.
2. That the hypothetical 'second hand' involved in the writing of the diary was unaware of the exact ages of the children.
3. That Joseph Procter never wrote the diary. It is a forgery.
4. That the original diary of Joseph Procter was not merely 'transcribed' by his son Edmund but essentially re-written.

In the diary we find the following entry: '8 mo., 3rd – Since the last date there have been few nights during which some branch of the family has not heard our visitor. One night J.P. was awoke and heard something hastily walk …'

The first thing to note is that the writer talks about Joseph Procter in the third person. However, in the same sentence they also employ the first-person plural and talk about 'our visitor' or ghost. Taken together, this identifies the writer as not Joseph Procter, but, crucially, someone who can describe the spectre as 'our visitor'. The writer, therefore, is almost certainly a member of the Procter family and someone who lived in the mill house.

Currently, in business, it is common for a personal secretary or assistant to type a letter in his or her employer's name and then get them to sign it later. Alternatively, if the boss isn't around, the secretary may simply 'pp' it. The prefix 'pp' is an abbreviation of the Latin *per procurationem*, which simply indicates that the signatory is signing the letter on behalf of someone else. However, in the case of Joseph Procter this method of writing and/or signing letters does not seem to have been consistently employed. However, there is some evidence of this. When Dr Edward Drury wrote to Procter and asked if he could spend a night in the mill house looking for the ghost, he received a reply. The reply does not seem to have actually been written by Procter himself, however:

EDW. DRURY.

At C.C. Embleton's, Surgeon, No. 10, Church-street, Sunderland.

Joseph Procter's respects to Edw. Drury, whose note he received a few days ago, expressing a wish to pass a night in his house at Willington. As the family is going from home on the 23rd instant, and one of Unthank and Procter's men will sleep in the house, if E.D. incline to come, on or after the 24th, to spend a night in it, he is at liberty so to do, with or without his faithful dog, which, by-the-bye, can be of no possible use, except as company. At the same time, J.P. thinks it best to inform him that particular disturbances are far from frequent at present, being only occasional and quite uncertain, and therefore the satisfaction of E.D.'s curiosity must be considered as problematical. The best chance would be afforded by his sitting up alone in the third storey till it be fairly daylight— say 2 or 3 a.m.

This clearly seems to be someone writing on behalf of Joseph Procter, and not Procter himself.

To recap, then, we know that Joseph Procter normally answered his own personal mail, but also that someone close to him was occasionally allowed to answer correspondence on his behalf whenever necessary. We also know that when that person answered correspondence on Procter's behalf they did not write the letters *per procurationem* but in the first person, referring to Procter in the third person. In addition, we know that there was almost certainly a second hand in the diary who also spoke of Joseph Procter in the third person and who must have been intimately acquainted with him; someone who, in fact, Procter trusted so much he was happy to collaborate with them in the creation of the diary itself.

Even a cursory view of the evidence leads us to point the metaphorical finger at one person; Elizabeth Procter, Joseph's wife. The other persons living there were essentially domestic staff who would not have been given such authority. This now leaves us with the knotty problem of trying to come up with a hypothetical scenario that not only allows for the numerous facts we have uncovered but also answers all of the conundrums thrown up by them.

Another potential issue is that Procter was in the habit of freely utilising archaic terms such as thee, thine, thy, thou and art in his correspondence:

> *Having been at Sunderland, I did not receive thine of the 6th till yesterday morning. I am glad to hear thou art getting well over the effects of thy unlooked-for visitation.*
>
> > *(Letter from Joseph Procter to Dr Edward Drury, 9 July 1840)*

> *The publicity given to the occurrences at Willington a few years ago, through Crowe's Night Side of Nature, has given occasion to many inquiries similar to thy own.*
>
> > *(Letter from Joseph Procter to the editor of* Spiritual Magazine*, 2 September 1853)*

> *I remember very well having corresponded with thee on the subject of the mysterious occurrences in my house at Willington, about three years ago.*
>
> > *(Letter from Joseph Procter to the editor of* Spiritual Magazine*, 7 January 1858)*

This was common in Quaker circles at that time, so we should not be surprised at it. However, in some correspondence allegedly written by Procter such terminology is entirely missing, for instance in the letter sent by Procter to the editor of *Spiritual Magazine* on 20 July 1863, which read in part:

> *The following statement of your able and esteemed correspondent, William Howitt, in the number for July, I believe to be founded in misapprehension, and will thank you to insert this correction in the next month's number.*

All the letters were seemingly written by the same person and yet the presence of archaic words in one and the absence of it in the above example could lead one to think that two different people had written them. Is it possible that the miller could have employed two different writing styles, depending on whom he was corresponding with, or is only one style representative of the real Joseph Procter?

The one epistle written by Joseph that we know his wife could not have had a hand in was that written by Joseph to Elizabeth the morning after the Drury-Hudson vigil. In that piece of correspondence, Joseph not once employs any of the archaic English terms used in other letters. If we are forced to choose between the two styles, then the one employed when writing to his wife must be the authentic one. However, it is possible, as previously stated, that Joseph used two different styles depending on whom he was addressing. Maybe in more formal letters to 'professional' people he used the archaic style, whilst in more informal, personal correspondence he used the modern vernacular. Or, just maybe, it was the other way around. Quakers were, in fact, known to employ archaic English in certain contexts, such as when engaging in debate about religion. The term thou was also often used by members of the movement to demonstrate an intimate spiritual bond with their fellow believers. In writing, Quakers were known to slip between the modern and the archaic within the same sentence, employing both thou and you interchangeably. Yet this would not explain Procter's style as in one letter to the editor of *Spiritual Magazine* he consistently uses the archaic terms, whilst in another he restricts himself to purely modern ones.

To get to the bottom of this mystery the authors contacted Professor Katie Wales, Special Professor in English at the University of Nottingham, who is an expert in the use of English for the period concerned. On 23 July, the authors wrote to Professor Wales with the following questions.

Can you shed any light on the seemingly inconsistent use of archaic English in the man's [Procter's] writing? Is there a consistency there that the authors might be missing?

Could you state whether, during the time period in question, it was common to speak of oneself in the third person in ordinary correspondence?

On 27 July Professor Wales kindly responded:

It would be much easier to answer your queries if I had some concrete examples, but here goes:

By your use of the term 'modern vernacular' for the diary I am assuming that the language is relatively unmarked. And one wouldn't expect terms of address or vocatives (hence 2nd person forms) since the diary is for oneself. Now in his correspondence, this is where it gets interesting. In section 5.3. of my book on Northern English (Cambridge, 2006, pp. 181-5) it is clear that many dialects until the mid-20c used the thou-thee forms as a matter of course, but especially in the North, where the distinction survives in places to this day. And so one would expect in the 'far' North Tyneside area!

  Contrary to popular opinion, where 'thou' is used only in religious registers, thou was not at all formal, as you suggest, or 'professional' but very informal! It would be used amongst family members and to close friends and neighbours; and to indicate affection, etc. It came into English in the Middle Ages from French, and is comparable to French uses of 'tu'. But died out in Standard English from 18c onwards. However, in English, there has been quite a lot of apparent inconsistency and switching (it is noted in Shakespeare's plays, for example).

  You say you have switching in your correspondence, but imply that it was consistent in one letter, and then changed for another, even to exactly the same person. This is unusual, I admit. But you would be wise to check the emotions in each case. is he being affectionate, or angry, or rebuking? Talking of personal things? That could be Thou. Then more professional or business-like and neutral would be 'you'.

  The other thing to bear in mind is that you say that your business man was a Quaker. Now Quakers used thou a lot until the present-day, and may still do. This goes back to the 17c, and the rise of Quakers and other non-conformist sects, who wished to follow Biblical/ King James Bible style (where Thou addressed to God), and Old English style (where thou was simply singular in all uses, you was plural only).

  (a) I have been fascinated by the so-called third person for first-person address for many years. I noted it first in Dickens. Usually it suggested someone either very pompous, or very old, or a bit sinister!!! Since you say that it occurs in

the diary, that might simply be the answer: that he is reporting events quite dispassionately; or that someone else is writing the entries for him …

(b) This might explain when you say that sometimes 'it seems to be someone else talking about him' Possibly, he is reporting actual conversations, or assumed conversations by others, about himself?

NB at the end of Q2 you refer to 'the third person in ordinary correspondence': NOT the diary – which you refer to above – is that what you mean?

If it is found in correspondence then this might mean that he has used a scribe or secretary for his letters sometimes (cf. 'Miss Otis regrets …') Otherwise, it sounds overly formal and pompous.

Hope this helps a bit,
Katie

It seems that questions such as 'Who was he writing to?' and 'What was his purpose in writing?' are rather too simplistic. Instead, as Professor Wales had pointed out, of crucial importance was his temperament and state of mind. To determine whether Procter's mood could have influenced his writing style, and possibly made him utilise two different vocabularies under broadly similar circumstances, the authors decided to examine afresh three pieces of correspondence; specifically, the letters sent by Joseph Procter to *Spiritual Magazine*. If it could be established that Procter had 'written' three broadly similar letters to the same person under similar circumstances, whilst in the same mood or temperament, and yet in at least one instance had utilised radically different vocabulary, then it could well point to the fact that Procter had not been solely responsible for writing all the epistles at all.

Letter from Joseph Procter to the editor of *Spiritual Magazine*, 2 September 1853:

Camp Villa, North Shields, 9 mo. 2nd, 1853.

The publicity given to the occurrences at Willington a few years ago, through Crowe's Night Side of Nature, has given occasion to many inquiries similar to thy own, and I have never shrunk from the avowal of undoubting assurance of these appearances, noises, &c., being made by the spirit of some person or persons deceased, notwithstanding that the who and the wherefor have not hitherto been ascertained. In reply to thy inquiry about the accuracy of the narrative in the work referred to, I may state that the portion of it from p. 125 to p. 137 taken from Richardson's Table Book, a local antiquarian publication, was written by the late Dr Clanny, of Sunderland, and revised by myself before being printed, and is perfectly true and correct. In that other portion, derived from William Howitt's personal inquiries, there are trifling inaccuracies, yet not such as materially affect the nature of the facts referred to. The disturbances had become much less frequent before I left the house in 1847, and, with a very few exceptions, have not since occurred; nor has anything of that nature ever followed us to our present dwelling.

Extract from a letter sent by Joseph Procter to the editor of *Spiritual Magazine*, 7 January 1858:

Tynemouth, 1 mo. 7th, 1858.

I remember very well having corresponded with thee on the subject of the mysterious occurrences in my house at Willington, about three years ago; and it is a satisfaction to me to have the opportunity given me to assure thee that the statement referred to in thy favour of yesterday, as given by a gentleman who has lived at Newcastle, that I had found the disturbances described in Mrs Crowe's Night Side of Nature to have been a trick practised upon me from interested motives, is entirely void of truth.

Extract from a letter sent by Joseph Procter to the editor of *Spiritual Magazine*, 20 July 1863:

To the Editor of the Spiritual Magazine.

Tynemouth, 7 mo. 20th, 1863.

The following statement of your able and esteemed correspondent, William Howitt, in the number for July, I believe to be founded in misapprehension, and will thank you to insert this correction in the next month's number:— 'There are said to be evidences of the spirits haunting Willington Mill, having done so to an older house on the same spot for two hundred years.' I believe no such evidences exist, the premises having been erected in 1800, on ground never before built on. Persons acquainted with the neighbourhood, and knowing the statement I have quoted to be an error, might thus be led to discredit the whole narrative, as truly and circumstantially related in the number for January. There is an older house about two hundred yards from Willington Mill, in which there was a mysterious ringing of bells about forty years ago; and about twenty years since, the person who then occupied it told me that occasionally at night

very strange noises were heard, adding, 'It must be rats, you know.' That is,
however, more than I know, and may be left as a doubtful question.

In the third letter, Procter is taking William Howitt to task for suggesting
that the Willington Witch once lived on the same site as the mill house.
Could the fact that Procter was in a somewhat critical mood have been
responsible for his avoidance of archaic English in the third letter? It is
certainly possible according to Professor Wales.

However, in the second letter he also criticises an anonymous writer
who suggested that Procter had admitted to being tricked regarding
some of the incidents listed in Catherine Crowe's book *The Night Side
of Nature*. As in both instances Procter seems to have been disturbed by
alleged inaccuracies published about the Willington Ghost, one would
have thought that in both cases his mind-set and emotional state would
have been pretty much the same; and yet, in one letter he uses the
archaic terminology and in another he avoids it. This led the authors
to conclude that a second hand must have been involved in writing
Procter's correspondence to *Spiritual Magazine*.

On 30 July, Professor Wales again contacted the authors after having
had the opportunity to review both the Procter diary and the miller's
correspondence to *Spiritual Magazine*:

> *I think the third person forms are best accounted for by the fact that either it
> was dictated, or written by someone else (e.g. the wife). 'Our' pronouns are
> common if the speaker or writer does not live alone in a house.*
>
> *I've already commented on the 'thou' actually not being formal but informal,
> etc. In the letters to the editor of the spiritualist publication, it is interesting
> that in the 1863 letter he appears to be rather annoyed – which could plausibly
> explain the shift from thou to you. Otherwise, the thou certainly fits with the
> Quakerism and close friends or regular correspondents.*
>
> *… Thou was usual Quaker usage, even in correspondence. Clearly Drury
> quickly progressed from being a polite new acquaintance (hence JP's 'respects',
> June 1840 and even the 3rd person OK in this context: either formal or dictated
> perhaps) to someone about whom he is very concerned. It's interesting to note
> from the son's account that little Joseph uses 'thou' to his sister: Again, perhaps
> Quaker usage, but also for affection and to calm her. On p.17 the utterance,
> 'Be gone! Thou wicked spirit!'- very dramatic, almost theatrical – thou used
> to address ghosts since the 16c plays of Shakespeare and his contemporaries
> … Back in the transcript of the diary, p.14/15, there is the clause 'as seemeth
> good'. This archaic third person singular ending of the verb is common of*

course in Biblical usage of the King James Bible, and again suggests Quaker
influence, or a religious 'echo'.

The authors are now in no doubt that a second hand helped Procter
pen some of his correspondence, and also influenced to a considerable
degree the contents of the diary.

The word 'diary' suggests a book filled in day by day containing the
thoughts, experiences and emotions of the owner. The diary of Joseph
Procter was just not like this.

Edmund Procter testified that, 'On my father's death in 1875, a diary
that he had kept almost from the outset of the disturbances, and during
many years of their occurrence, was found among his papers.' From this
statement we can deduce that the diary was not a collection of loose
papers but a book. It is also likely that the diary was in Joseph Procter's
own hand throughout, as Edmund makes no mention of anything odd
or inconsistent in this regard. In short, when Edmund Procter first saw
the diary it appeared to be just that; a diary, in a book, written in his
father's hand. But appearances can be deceptive. What Edmund Procter
had in his hand was not the original article, but rather the end product of
a sequence of complex events.

It seems that from the time when Joseph Procter began to make a
record of the extraordinary events in the mill house, he did not make his
entries in a book but on separate sheets of paper which he perhaps kept
in a file. This would explain why, amongst other things, his method of
recording dates is inconsistent. Over the first few months – or perhaps
even years – he would have accumulated a whole sheaf of such notes.

At some point the thought seems to have struck him that the notes
should be incorporated in a proper diary. However, transcribing such a
large accumulation of notes would have been a cumbersome and arduous
process, particularly for a busy mill owner. To facilitate the project the
authors believe that he asked his wife Elizabeth to help him. It is also
likely that, at the same time, he encouraged Elizabeth to include her own
recollections. This would explain why, throughout the diary, the writer
repeatedly seems to swap between the first- and third-person pronouns.
The passages written in the first person would have been Joseph's own
thoughts, whilst those in the third person could have been Elizabeth's
recollections of what Joseph said or did.

If Procter's original notes were kept on separate sheets of paper, this
would also explain why, in the diary, some of the entries are out of sequence
on the timeline. Some of the sheets may well have been accidentally mixed

up, so that when Elizabeth transcribed them she did so not in their proper order, but simply in the order in which they were found.

It seems that some years after the diary was completely transcribed by Elizabeth, Joseph then re-wrote it again in his own hand, adding even more thoughts, recollections and observations. This would explain why, so long after the events, he had trouble recollecting details such as the ages of his children.

As the authors have already discussed, the enigma of the missing portion of the diary is problematic. In Edmund Procter's commentary on it he finishes off the text by saying, 'At this point the diary abruptly comes to an end. I know, however, that disturbances of a varied character continued more or less, perhaps less rather than more, for years'. There does not seem to have been any final comment from Joseph Procter stating that he no longer intended to make entries in the diary, which begs the question how Edmund Procter knew that there was a missing portion of the diary at all. For all he knew, his father might simply have tired of writing the journal and left it where it 'abruptly came to an end'. There are three possible answers:

1. Edmund Procter saw the full diary before either his father or mother died. After his mother's passing he noticed that portions of it that were there before were now missing.
2. Before Edmund's mother passed away she informed him that the diary detailed events which took place after 1842. When Joseph later examined the diary he discovered that the latter portion was no longer there.
3. Edmund Procter noticed, on examining the diary after his father's death, that the pages of the missing portion had been torn out.

Edmund states, 'On my father's death in 1875, a diary that he had kept almost from the outset of the disturbances, and during many years of their occurrence, was found among his papers.' Crucially, however, Edmund Procter does not state that he was the person who found it, merely that, 'a diary ... was found amongst his papers'. This seems to suggest that it was someone other that Edmund who discovered it, which leaves the possibility that the discoverer may have been the one who removed the missing portion. Whatever the truth, we know that Edmund Procter knew of the diary's existence shortly after his father died but before his mother had passed away. If, as we know, Elizabeth Procter instructed Edmund not to publish the diary until after her death, then mother and son had obviously discussed the matter. It seems curious, then, that at that juncture the issue of the missing portion did not come into the conversation. Did Elizabeth Procter know that the latter part was missing and simply not tell Edmund? If not, then why not? Or was it that the missing portion was not removed from the diary until after Elizabeth also passed away? If the latter is correct, then who removed it and for what purpose?

Edmund Procter makes no reference to his mother having collaborated with his father in any way on the construction of the diary The likelihood is that he either didn't know, or did know and was told by Elizabeth not to disclose the fact. Perhaps Elizabeth saw the diary, even in its amended form, as 'her husband's baby' and did not feel it was appropriate to share the credit for compiling it.

What happened to the missing portion of the diary may never be known. The authors have already suggested that it might have been removed and/ or destroyed by Elizabeth – or even Joseph himself – due to the fact that it contained material which would demonstrate that both George Unthank and Joseph Procter had not been entirely candid about certain matters in the early stages of the affair. There may, of course, have been other reasons why certain parties wanted the latter portion of the diary hidden or destroyed, although what they might have been we can only speculate on. This is a matter the authors will return to later in this book.

It is of course possible that it wasn't actually removed at all, but simply mislaid and subsequently lost. This is an idea which has been in currency for some time, and first stated almost as an accepted fact by W.T. Stead[2], who asserted, 'Such is the story of the haunted house at Willington. Mr Proctor has lost the diary which he kept of the strange occurrences in that undesirable residence'.

When Joseph Procter died, his diary would almost certainly have been in his study. It is just possible that the latter part of the diary was, like the earlier part initially, on loose sheets of paper. Joseph may have had the intention of re-writing and elaborating on their contents before adding them to the book-version of the account and simply never got around to it. After his death his family would have gone through his papers and may have thrown out the loose-leaf, latter portion of the diary without realising its significance. This is highly unlikely, the authors feel, but not impossible. If this was indeed the case, then Elizabeth herself may have been mystified as to where the later accounts had gone.

Given the small number of people who would have had access to Procter's private papers, however, it is far more likely that the missing

Left: *W.T. Stead, the celebrated Victorian researcher who investigated the Willington Mill haunting and detailed the affair in his book* Real Ghost Stories.

Right: *The original cover (paperback edition) of W.T. Stead's* Real Ghost Stories *(Grant Richards, 1897). (Grant Richards)*

portion of the diary was not accidentally lost but rather deliberately removed. If the removal of the missing portion took place after Joseph's death, then suspicion must fall upon Elizabeth. Knowing how much finding the missing portion meant to Edmund, who had developed a passion not just for finding it but also having it published, she may not have been able to bring herself to admit that she had actually been responsible for its removal and likely destruction.

Earlier the authors acknowledged that there may have been 'another party' who had a motive for seeing the latter part of the diary removed, particularly if it cast doubt upon the truthfulness of George Unthank and Joseph Procter. That 'other party' would have been none other than George Unthank himself.

It is possible that Unthank knew that Joseph Procter had been keeping a diary of the events at the mill house and realised that if the diary was made public everyone would know that Unthank's claim never to have seen or heard the ghost simply wasn't true. George Unthank had a powerful motive, therefore, to find and destroy the diary – or at least that part of it which could have given the game away. We cannot preclude the possibility, then, that shortly after Joseph died George Unthank may have made an excuse to enter his late cousin's study and engage in a frantic search for the diary. Of course, removing the entire book would have raised too many suspicions. Hence, if Unthank were responsible, he would likely have removed only those pages that gave the lie to his strident assertions made all those years previously. By merely removing a number of pages from the book instead of the entire volume itself, the theft may have gone undetected for some time, if not forever. It is perhaps more than coincidental that the remaining portion of the diary is the one which contains Unthank's denial of the supernatural phenomena at his former home, and nothing overtly critical of it in the immediate context. It is only when one studies the diary in depth that the gaping holes in Unthank's story begin to appear.

After finally accepting that the missing portion of the diary wasn't going to show up, Edmund Procter decided that the time had come to release his father's notes to the world. He then transcribed the diary, added his own thoughts and memories, and posted the finished result to the Society for Psychical Research in London. It was duly published in the December 1892 issue of the society's journal.

If Unthank did remove the missing portion of the diary, then he almost certainly destroyed it. However, we can't be sure and it is just possible that he secreted it away somewhere. There is a chance, of course, that it still survives although this is highly unlikely.

Despite the intrigue surrounding the diary and the myriad problems attached to it, we have no reason to think that the events described in it are anything but truthful. Joseph Procter, Elizabeth Procter and George Unthank may have bent the truth a little, but they did so under great pressure. Their few misdemeanours aside, they were decent, hard-working people, devoutly religious and highly respected in their community. Joseph Procter's diary, though highly edited and incomplete, is still enough for us to determine that the old house next to the mill was well and truly haunted.

Notes
1. Private letter from Joseph Procter to Edward Drury, 21 June 1840
2. Stead, William T., *Real Ghost Stories* (Grant Richards, 1897)

Ten

FURTHER INCIDENTS

There were numerous other incidents which occurred at Willington Mill other than those detailed in Joseph Procter's diary. These help us to gain a more complete picture of the nature of the phenomena there.

On one occasion, a Mrs Hargrave, one of Elizabeth Procter's sisters, saw an apparition uncommonly similar to that seen by Dr Edward Drury during the infamous 'vigil'. She described the ghost as, 'the figure of a woman in a grey mantle, which came through the wall' of her room from the adjacent one.

In the room at the time was her 'sister', whom we must presume was Elizabeth Procter, asleep. According to Mrs Hargrave the apparition drifted towards her bed before fading away. Curiously, she noticed that the feet of the ghost seemed to be about 3ft above the level of the floor.

Mrs Hargrave had several other chilling experiences, often shared by others. On a number of occasions she heard sounds as if someone wearing clogs was coming downstairs and rapping every rail beneath the banister with a stick. She also heard a rhythmic 'ratcheting' sound identical to that of a clock being wound up.

Incredibly, this woman slept in the 'disturbed room' for a period of three months. She repeatedly heard bizarre noises, just as everyone else had done, but stoically chose to say nothing about them. Then, one day, she struck up a conversation with her youngest sister, identified only as 'Mrs Wright'. Wright had seemingly heard a loud noise emanating from the room and told her older sibling about it. Hargrave then told her sister about her own experiences.

Mrs Hargrave also 'often felt her bed shaken as if some one was standing at the bottom of it and striking blows against a board placed to keep a child from falling out'. The 'shaking bed' phenomenon was, as we know, also experienced by others in the household.

Perhaps one of the most intriguing incidents regarding Mrs Hargrave concerned a room on the upper floor which was occasionally used as a classroom by the Procter children (Joseph Procter was passionate in his belief that all children should be well educated, and was responsible for setting up a school in Willington to that end). Sometimes, Hargrave would hear 'dancing and noises' in the room, which was almost always empty. She also heard 'the shaking of the window frame' in the room below – the nursery – when the children were playing in the rooms upstairs. Sometimes, when Mrs Hargrave and Mrs Wright, were playing with the children, they would have doors banged in their faces. This would happen when the windows were shut and there were no identifiable draughts to cause such a thing.

Later, Mrs Hargrave was interviewed by Professor Henry Sidgwick (1838–1900) who was one of the founders of the Society for Psychical Research. Sidgwick, also an ardent educationalist, later wrote up his findings[1], which included Hargrave's recollections of when the eminent clairvoyant 'Jane', from Newcastle-upon-Tyne, visited the mill personally.

W.T. Stead[2] details a number of incidents which are hard to locate in other sources. Some of them provide a fascinating insight into the nature of the Willington Mill phenomena:

> *On one occasion Mr Robert Davidson's father spent a night in the house. He saw nothing, but at midnight a noise began which continued about fifteen minutes, and gradually became louder and louder, until it became so deafening that it was as if rivetters [sic] were at work on a boiler in the room. His companion was asleep, Davidson nudged him, said 'Jack,' [and] instantly the noise ceased. When Jack went to sleep again the noise began worse than ever in half an hour; the building seemed to shake to its very foundations. The bed curtains shook, the rings rattled; this continued for a long time; again he said 'Jack,' and the noises ceased.*

Henry Sidgwick, a founding member of the Society for Psychical Research, who interviewed Mrs Hargrave about her experiences.

Another:

> *There was one feature of the Willington ghost … which was peculiar. Most ghosts pass through unbolted, and even when they seem to open them, the doors are found locked as before. The Willington ghost, however, not merely passed through doors, but left them open.*
>
> *On one occasion, when family prayers were being conducted by Mr Proctor [sic], a noise began in the room above, a heavy footstep descended the stairs, passed the room door, and then proceeded to the front door, then the bar was removed, the lock turned, two bolts drawn back, the latch lifted, the door flung open, and the footsteps pass into the front garden. Mr Proctor [sic] ceased reading, went out into the passage, and, behold, the door was wide open. Mrs Proctor [sic] was almost fainting, and Mr Proctor [sic] filled himself with gloomy reflections as to the opportunities which such ghostly habit would afford to burglars.*

Stead also details an incident in which Robert Davidson's aunt felt a heavy blow on the back of her chair as she was sitting in the nursery with the children; then a table was moved from one side of the room to the other, without anyone apparently touching it. The disturbances were so continuous that one of the millers was sent for, and he sat up all night. Stead notes that, 'Mr Carr had a terrible night of it, and left next morning, saying that he could never come back again'.

Whether 'Mr Carr' and 'the miller' are synonymous is difficult to work out from the text, as the Procters had relatives in Carlisle called Carr. In either event, it is possible that the person was related to the Carrs of Carlisle, Elizabeth Procter's family.

On the evening after the incident above, according to Stead, Mr Davidson's aunt and Bessy Mann saw a whitish figure glide downstairs, cross the nursery floor, and enter a closet, from which an hour before they had heard a prolonged groan.

Sometimes the ghosts seemed quite well disposed towards the children, and even engaged in games with them. Stead[3] recalls one occasion when, 'a boy of two years old was charmed with the ghost; he laughed and kicked, crying out, "Ah, I dares somebody, peepee, peepee!"'.

Notes
1. Proceedings 8 P.E., Vol. VII. pp. 64, 82–84, 86, 87
2. Stead, William T., *Real Ghost Stories* (Grant Richards, 1897)
3. *Ibid.*

Eleven

'OLD JEFFREY'

According to some, the first spectre to manifest itself at the location of Willington Mill was that of a man who was allegedly dubbed 'Old Jeffrey'[1]. Just who Jeffrey was we may never know. Ghosts are often given epithets that bear no relationship to either the buildings they haunt or their personal nomenclature. Witnesses sometimes pluck names out of the air, perhaps thinking that by personalising the ghost it will in some way become less frightening. Over time, these names can become accepted as the 'real' ones that the ghosts were supposedly known by during their lifetime. There are some doubts that the name Old Jeffrey really refers to one of the Willington spectres at all, and these need to be addressed.

In his excellent work, *The Supernatural – Unlock the Earth's Hidden Mysteries*[2], Colin Wilson draws parallels between the Willington haunting and the notorious case which became known as the Epworth Poltergeist. The Epworth case centred around some extraordinary events which occurred in the home of Samuel Wesley, grandfather of John Wesley, who founded the Methodist movement. Wilson mentions that the entity in the Epworth dwelling was known as 'Old Jeffrey'. To the authors' knowledge, Wilson is the only modern researcher to actually mention both the Willington and Epworth cases quite literally on the same page and in the same chapter. The book *The World's Greatest Unsolved Mysteries*[3] does actually mention the Willington Mill and Epworth cases on the same page, but in different chapters. In any case, the text on that page makes no mention of 'Old Jeffrey', who only makes his début on the following page. As far as the authors are aware, the most recent written reference to the Willington entity as 'Old Jeffrey' appears in the small but well-written book *Ghosts and Legends of Northumbria*[4], which was published by Sandhill Press in 1992 and then released again in 1996.

The authors had to consider the possibility that the anonymous author of *Ghosts and Legends of Northumbria* may have read Wilson's book and erroneously drawn the conclusion that 'Old Jeffrey' referred to the

Willington ghost and not the Epworth poltergeist. Initially this didn't seem possible, as Wilson's book was actually released four years after the publication of *Ghosts and Legends of Northumbria*. The authors then discovered that Wilson's book had previously been published as a co-edited work with Damon Wilson as *The Mammoth Book of the Supernatural* in 1991[5]. As this was released before the first print of *Ghosts and Legends of Northumbria* it still left open the possibility that the anonymous author of that work may well have drawn his information from Wilson's book.

Further research by the authors precipitated an answer. In 1848, Catherine Crowe wrote her excellent book *The Night Side of Nature, or, Ghosts and Ghost Seers*[6]. Crowe relates the Willington Mill case in great detail, had personal correspondence with some of the experients, and carried out her research shortly after the events had drawn to a close. In her book, Crowe talks about the appearance of a man whom she specifically refers to as 'Old Jeffrey'. As Crowe's book was written well over 100 years before *Ghosts and Legends of Northumbria*, we can now state confidently that the anonymous author of the latter work drew his material from authentic historical sources and any suggestion that he may have misunderstood something in Colin Wilson's book and subsequently introduced the 'error' into his own work can now be thoroughly discounted. Since then, the authors have discovered several other old, authentic sources which call the ghost 'Old Jeffrey'.

Why, then, was the Willington Quay ghost referred to as 'Old Jeffrey'? The Epworth poltergeist case occurred long before the haunting of Willington Mill and the 'Old Jeffrey' of Epworth gained considerable notoriety, the witnesses at Willington may have heard the name of the Epworth entity and decided to apply it to their own spectre.

Despite the fact that Old Jeffrey was and is of uncertain provenance, we do know a little about his appearance. Old Jeffrey was seen on several occasions at the mill house, almost always after the hours of darkness. Crowe relates that the apparition, 'is sometimes that of a man … which is often very luminous, and passes through the walls as though they were nothing'.

On one occasion, Old Jeffrey was said to have appeared at a window; the same window, in fact, that another apparition had been seen in previously. This has caused some writers to assume they were one and the same. It's just possible that this may be correct, but the subtle differences between the two apparitions have encouraged the authors to believe that they are different. Old Jeffrey, then, is essentially a luminous figure whom witnesses do not seem to be able to describe in any detail other than the fact that he is male. Unlike some of the other apparitions at Willington Mill, he seemed to appear at a number of different locations both inside and outside the dwelling.

Another interesting fact about Old Jeffrey is that he may have already been putting in appearances at the mill before the principal experients listed in this book even moved into the premises. As Crowe says, he was 'well known', as he had already established himself with locals.

Notes

1. Wilson, Colin, *The Supernatural – Unlock the Earth's Hidden Mysteries* (Parragon, 1995), p. 119
2. *ibid*
3. Anon, *The World's Greatest Unsolved Mysteries* (Chancellor Press, 2001), pp 502-3
4. Anon, *Ghosts and Legends of Northumbria* (Sandhill Press, 1996), p. 45
5. Wilson, Colin & Wilson, Damon, *The Mammoth Book of the Supernatural* (Robinson Publishing, 1991)
6. Crowe, Catherine, *The Night Side of Nature, or, Ghosts and Ghost Seers, Vol. II* (T.C. Newby, 1848)

Twelve

THE GHOST PRIEST

The other apparition which appeared regularly at Willington Mill was described as wearing a 'priestly surplice'. It seems that not long after the mill was built, but possibly before the principal experients moved in to the mill house, the figure of a man wearing 'a priest's garb' was spotted in the garden behind the mill[1]. The 'arrival' of the Ghost Priest, seems to have occurred around the same time or shortly after the first sightings of Old Jeffrey.

The author of *Ghosts and Legends of Northumbria*[2] certainly seems to indicate an early date for the sighting of this apparition as he mentions witnesses seeing a 'bare-headed man' appearing in 'an upper window' in the same paragraph as he discusses the alleged murder which took place whilst the mill was being constructed. The writer's narrative clearly seems to place both events in the same time frame. The authors have reason to believe that the 'bare-headed man' was the same as the priestly spectre that inhabited the land immediately adjacent to the mill. However, there is also a possibility that the event mentioned in *Ghosts and Legends of Northumbria* is the same one detailed in Chapter Five where the ghost was seen by the Mann family and one of Joseph Procter's relatives.

To the authors' knowledge, the first people to describe their encounter with the Ghost Priest in detail were the members of the Mann family. The distinguishing feature of the priest was that, apart from dressing in a 'priestly surplice' he was again described as 'bare-headed'. This characteristic is intriguing as there are two possible interpretations of the phrase 'bare-headed'. Just which interpretation we choose will impact upon our understanding of both the identities and the number of apparitions which were associated with Willington Mill.

The first interpretation is that it meant bald. If this is the case, then the first thing we are able to determine is that witnesses must have been able to see the physical features of the apparition in reasonable detail. This contrasts sharply with the descriptions given of Old Jeffrey, who is simply described as being 'male' and 'glowing'.

The second interpretation of the phrase 'bare-headed' – and probably the correct one – is that the term was not used to indicate baldness but actually the lack of a head-covering or hat.

Whatever spin one puts upon the phrase 'bare-headed', it is clear that, to the witnesses, the absence of either hair or a head-covering was important enough to mention. Neither baldness nor the lack of a head-covering would normally be seen as of crucial importance, but there is one hypothetical scenario in which that would not apply. If two people of broadly the same appearance were standing side by side, and the only obvious difference between the two is that one is bald and the other is not, or one has his head covered whilst the other does not, then the lack of hair/a head-covering becomes the perfectly obvious way to distinguish between the two. The authors believe that this was the case with the 'bare-headed' man who appeared in the window. The reason why witnesses referred to him as 'bare-headed' was probably to distinguish him from another apparition at the mill who normally had his head covered. There is some slight circumstantial evidence[3] that another priestly figure may have been seen at the mill apart from the 'bare-headed' devotee described by the Manns, but to date the authors have not been able to substantiate the story.

It should be noted here, however, that one author[4] did specifically describe the entity as 'bald-headed', although as he was not an eyewitness it is likely that he had read the term 'bare-headed' in other accounts and simply presumed it was referring to baldness.

As we shall see, the 'bare-headed' Ghost Priest will come to play an important role in the authors' attempts to solve the Willington Quay mystery.

Notes

1. Anon, *The Willington Quay Ghost* (Privately published, *c*.1972)
2. Anon, *Ghosts and Legends of Northumbria* (Sandhill Press, 1996), p. 45
3. Anon, *The Willington Quay Ghost* (Privately published, *c*. 1972)
4. Davidson, Robert, *The True Story of the Willington Ghost* (Robert Davidson, *c*. 1886)

Thirteen

AFTER THE PROCTERS

After the last event detailed in the extant portion of Joseph Procter's diary, paranormal phenomena of different kinds continued to manifest themselves at the mill house and, we now know, the mill itself. During the 'diary years' the Procters had faced each incident with dignity and courage. However, as the years passed by the family became weary. Each event chipped away at their fortitude until they reached the point where they could take it no more and the Procters decided to leave the mill house.

Edmund Procter, in his commentary on Joseph's diary, recounts, 'Finding life in the house to be no longer tolerable, fearing also an unhappy effect, if not a permanent injury on the minds of their children should they remain longer in such a plague-ridden dwelling, they finally [left] it in 1847, and went to reside at Camp Villa, North Shields'.

Enigmatically, Edmund also then adds that 'social and other reasons also influenced them to take this step'. What could he have meant by this? It is interesting to note that after the Procters moved into the mill house – and specifically after George Unthank had tried desperately to convince Joseph that he was unaware of any supernatural phenomena taking place in the dwelling – the Unthanks are rarely mentioned. The authors believe that although the cousins remained on friendly terms their former close bond had been irreparably weakened. Procter had terminated his business relationship with Unthank, and it is likely that the former simply wanted to distance himself from a place that now held so many unhappy memories and, just possibly, go into semi-retirement.

Edmund Procter relates:

My parents have both repeatedly told me that during the last night they slept in the old house, the rest of the family having preceded them to the new one, there were continuous noises during the night, boxes being apparently dragged with heavy thuds down the now carpetless stairs, non-human footsteps stumped on the floors, doors were, or seemed to be, clashed, and impossible furniture corded at random or dragged hither and hither by inscrutable agency; in short, a pantomimic or spiritualistic repetition of all the noises incident to a household flitting.

A miserable night my father and mother had of it, as I have often heard from their own lips; not so much from terror at the unearthly noises, for to these they were habituated, as dread lest this fanfaronade might portend the contemporary flight of the unwelcome visitors to the new abode.

According to Edmund Procter, then, it wasn't simply the phenomena that disturbed the couple on their last night at the mill house but also the worry that the entities may follow them to their new home. This is an intriguing thought, and one which the authors will examine in more detail presently. Edmund continued:

Fortunately for the family, this dread was not realised. So far as I know, and in this I am confirmed by my elder brother and sisters, the eight years' residence in the new home was absolutely free from all forms of annoyances and uncomfortable knockings, the stealthy steps and the uncouth mutterings that for ten or eleven years had disturbed the even tenor of a quiet Quaker family in the old house at Willington mill.

Unfortunately, as we shall see, there are strong reasons to believe that Edmund Procter was being decidedly less than candid when he made this statement.

There are numerous suggestions in the literature devoted to Willington Mill regarding just where the Procters vacated to. Richardson[1] states that the family relocated to Benton and then to Gosforth. Edmund Procter, however, who was in a far better position to know, states that in 1847, 'they finally … went to reside at Camp Villa, North Shields'. We do know that the Procters did eventually move again – to Gosforth – after living at Camp Villa.

Richardson[2] flatly contradicts Edmund Procter's statement that the family had no more trouble in their new home. In fact, he details an event concerning one of the maids in the Procters' employ. The young woman had seemingly been working for the Procters at Willington, and, shortly after the family moved to North Shields, relocated there herself to continue working for them. The maid had sent ahead of her a box 'securely corded and locked' which contained her belongings. On her arrival, the woman went to her room and found the box on the floor, still secured in exactly the same way it had been when it left the mill house. However, to her horror she saw that its contents had been liberally scattered around the room. Someone – or something – had apparently removed her belongings from the box without opening it. Distressed, the maid told the elderly cook – a long-time employee of the Procters – what had happened. Instead of being surprised, the cook told the maid that 'it' did this to every new resident and that three serving girls had already vacated the premises in a 'terrified' state.

Edmund Procter, by denying that anything untoward had occurred at the new residence at all, was simply falling into a by now well-established pattern set by both his father and his uncle of playing down certain aspects of the whole affair. In fact, it was common knowledge regarding the Procters that 'the ghost had followed them'.

Many researchers have suggested, or at least intimated, that immediately after the Procters' departure the mill house was divided into 'tenements' for rent. The mill house was so divided into smaller residences, but not straight away. In the first instance the house was taken over by the sturdy foreman Thomas Mann and his family, who seemingly had no qualms about moving into a haunted building. For the next few months the family was repeatedly disturbed by 'unaccountable noises', but resolutely refused to move out. After a short while the builders arrived to rework the interior and create a number of small flats. Crowe[3] suggests that only two tenements were created – presumably upstairs and downstairs – but later there seems to have been more, including one or two smaller 'bed-sits'.

Despite the continuing presence of 'the ghost', the Manns lived at the mill house for a further twenty years, sharing the building with another family who were unnamed but undoubtedly related to one of the mill's employees. During this time, Thomas Mann 'once or twice' reported seeing 'apparitions'. However, both the Manns and the second family were later reluctant to speak about their experiences. According to Edmund Procter they, 'suffered but little through their occupancy' and, relatively speaking, he was probably correct.

In 1865, Joseph Procter closed the flour mill for good. It stood empty for two years, until a ferocious fire consumed another mill in Newcastle-upon-Tyne and Joseph Procter agreed to rent a portion of his own mill and the adjacent mill house to the company whilst their own premises were rebuilt. Edmund Procter adds, 'I have been informed that those then occupying the house were much troubled, one family declining to stay on any terms'.

Edmund Procter, though no longer living at the mill, still had a fascination with the ghosts that haunted it. On one occasion, whilst the house was unoccupied shortly before its sale, Edmund and four others decided to hold a vigil in the house. We do not know the identities of the others, save that one was a doctor. The five men spent the night on the premises, but nothing of any consequence seems to have happened.

Undaunted, Edmund decided to organise a second vigil (or third, if you include that carried out by Drury and Hudson) and this precipitated something far more interesting. Unfortunately, Procter felt that the things that came to pass were not worth recounting:

> *I was one of another larger party, including two ladies, who spent an evening in another upstairs room, accompanied by a 'medium' of repute at that time well known in Newcastle; no person whatsoever being in the house besides our own party. The séance was not without incidents, well understood by those acquainted with such proceedings, and which it would be useless, at the moment, to describe, to those who are not, but absolutely futile as to establish any communication with the alleged spirit or spirits supposed to haunt or to have formerly haunted the premises.*

The author of *Ghosts and Legends of Northumbria*[4] also mentions a vigil held on the premises by several people, including Thomas Davidson, J.D. Carr, Mr Procter, John Ridley, Revd Mr Caldwell and Revd Mr Robertson. Davidson, as we will see, was also the witness to a 'mystery animal' event at the mill. 'J.D. Carr' was Elizabeth Procter's sister Jane, and 'Mr Procter' is no doubt a referral to Edmund.

Interestingly, the writer W.T. Stead[5] once made reference not to a séance or vigil, but to a somewhat more scientific attempt to 'capture' the ghost:

> *The noises that went on intermittently in the mill were only too frequent and unmistakable. Mr Proctor [sic] did his level best to ascertain what caused the noises, but it was all in vain. The floors of the house were taken up, but nothing was found; then the floors were covered with meal, in order that the foot marks might be detected; but the ghost of Willington Mill trod with too light a step even to leave a trace upon the flour-strewn floor, and the utmost diligence of the inquirers was baffled. Sometimes the noises were very violent.*
>
> *On the Whit-Monday on which Mrs Davidson saw the lady in the lavender silk dress [more of which later], the uproar in the house was the worst that was known during the eight years. Noises were kept up so violently all night that neither the family nor the servants got a wink of sleep.*

In 1871, Joseph Procter relinquished his business entirely and sold it to a man called Sampson Langdale. Langdale was the proprietor of the Langdale Chemical Manure Works, which specialised in selling a substance called guano. Guano, for the uninitiated, was simply a fancy name for bird dung which was then extensively employed as fertiliser.

There is an amusing anecdote attached to the sale of the mill to Sampson Langdale[6], in which, when the sale took place, Procter allegedly said to the buyer, 'Now, Sampson, I will sell thee the mill with the ghost'. Langdale allegedly retorted, 'All right, see that you deliver the ghost'. Langdale – apparently in jest, although we can't be sure – at some point sent his solicitor to see Procter due the ghost's failure to manifest itself.

Langdale, it must be said, was something of an inventor and an entrepreneur. He invested no less than £20,000 – a tidy sum in those days – in a scheme to manufacture soap from partially crushed olives. The problem was that the process involved was incredibly risky and some of the ingredients utilised extremely inflammable; so much so that even having any form of lighting in the building was simply too dangerous. As a solution, Langdale spent another fortune on having specially-designed lights bolted to the outside of the building to reduce the risk of a fire or explosion. It probably seemed like a good idea at the time, but the entire project withered on the vine and was subsequently abandoned.

Langdale employed two machinists – one of them described simply as 'a German' – who worked in the main body of the old mill. Whether the two had endured any anomalous experiences themselves we are not told, but it seems that before long they at least became aware of the stories attached to the mill house. As it was currently uninhabited, the two men had little difficulty in gaining permission from their foreman to spend several nights there in an effort to 'catch the ghost'. Just what occurred there during their vigils we do not know, but something did. Edmund Procter comments, 'information reached us that [they] spent some restless evenings and unhappy nights in the house in fruitlessly trying to discover the origin of fitful and exasperating disturbances. No effort was made, so far as I know, to test the accuracy of these rumours'.

Edmund Procter then momentarily digresses from discussing the history of the mill and relates his father's views about the propriety or otherwise of attempting communication with the spirit world:

My father never made any attempt to open up communication in this way; his experiences were prior to the time when modern developments of spiritualism made the lingo of the séance familiar to the public ear, and although he took an earnest interest in the subject, he never attended a séance and laid stress upon the application of the well-known text about 'seducing spirits and doctrines of demons'.

At the time of writing, the mill was merely being used as a warehouse. The mill house had been divided into even smaller tenements, but as the building was by then in a dilapidated condition the new owners had considerable trouble in finding tenants. Edmund Procter also noted that its reputation for being haunted only exacerbated the problem. To circumvent this difficulty, the company even began offering the apartments free of charge on short-term leases.

By 1873, Joseph Procter had again relocated – this time to a new home in Fairfield, Gosforth. On Saturday, 6 November 1875, he passed away peacefully in his sleep. Whatever secrets he held about Willington Mill – and there were more than a few – he took to the grave with him.

By 1887, the mill was no longer used as a factory and had been turned into a warehouse for the storage of 'oilcake'[7]. In 1889 or thereabouts, Edmund Procter revisited the place and spoke to some of the tenants. None of them – according to Procter – had any stories about seeing ghosts. However, he lamented sadly about the condition of the house and the mill itself:

Although of modest pretensions, it was formerly a comfortable, old fashioned house of ten or twelve rooms, but the untidiness of its present aspect is a painful spectacle to those who remember it at its best; the stables and adjoining out-buildings have been pulled down, the garden wall has disappeared, the jargonelle pear trees that formerly blossomed up to the third storey are represented by the mere ghosts of blackened stumps, the large old thorn tree of red blossom, and the abundance of iris and auricular that were wont to bloom in the garden are as far off as the snows of last winter. The singular record of the house gives it an interest nevertheless, even in its squalid present and its ungracious decay.

Procter then adds his own thoughts on the nature of the phenomena at the mill:

Some may think the whole affair altogether a very paltry story. I admit it is not a very picturesque 'ghost'; but whatever its merit it is at least authentic, and that is rather an important feature in a ghost. The truth has been told without extenuation or reserve, and if the recital points to the conclusion that the spirit or spirits, or whatever you choose to call them, belonged to the residuum of the spirit world, I hope my family may not be held responsible.

I may be permitted finally to briefly indicate some of my own conclusions. If the gibberings, the preposterous incivilities, and the unwholesome uproar committed in that house for ten unforgettable years by these unhallowed genii may be accepted as an argument tending to establish the continued existence of the individual after death, the seductions of futurity are scarcely increased to exhausted travellers that have undergone the scorching heats of life's intemperate zone. Such questionable intimations of immortality are hardly calculated to soothe us when worn with adverse passions, furious strife, and the hard passage of tempestuous life.

Nevertheless, this singular history, taken in connection with others of its class, may to the impartial and philosophic mind hide a lesson of the highest import. M. Renan, in one of the very last of his many charming pages, troubled with doubts as to a future existence, whilst smiling at the superstition of the old-fashioned and orthodox hell, exclaims how glad he would be to be sure even of hell, a hypothesis so preferable to annihilation.

In the same way, may we not justifiably postulate this: that if we can prove the existence of spirits of a low or inferior order, then faith, analogy, and evolution, if not logic and conviction, can claim those of a progressive, a high and superior order? Is it not rational to suppose that the more debased and the most unhappy have the greatest facility in giving tangible proof of their existence, under certain conditions imperfectly understood; whilst the purer and nobler souls find intercourse painful or impossible, but are yet occasionally able to achieve it in those picturesque and beneficent instances where their visitation is recorded, not only in the Old and New Testaments, but scattered all through literature; cases which possibly the many may still deride, but which others cherish as indications of the divine and proofs of immortality. Each must draw his own conclusions; as the prophet of Treguier says, 'Let us all be free to make our own romance of the infinite.'

Other attempts to resolve the mystery of the mill house are detailed by William T. Stead[8], and include a time when, 'The Rev. Mr Caldwell … at the Congregational Church, Howden [sic][9], sat up all night with another minister, but saw nothing, although they heard noises as if bass mats were being drawn over the floor'.

Stead also notes that Mr John Richardson, an old and trusty servant of the Procters, on one occasion sat up with an old Quaker gentleman who had come to discover the cause of the disturbances. The old Quaker asked Mr Richardson to get a Bible, and he would read a chapter. No sooner did he begin to read than the candle began to jump in the candlestick and to oscillate to such an extent that the Quaker could not see to read. The moment he stopped, the candle became quiet. The old Quaker looked at Mr Richardson, and said, 'Strange!'

He began to read again, and again the candle began to sway from side to side. 'Art thou afraid, John?' said the Quaker. 'No', said John, 'but I feel a peculiar sensation which I cannot describe'. 'Let us pray, John', said the Quaker. Immediately a terrific noise arose in the room, all the furniture seemed to be driven from its place, the candlesticks rattled on the table, newspapers seemed to be scattered to and fro in great profusion, the whole building seemed shaken. So terrible was the hubbub that John could not hear a single word of the Quaker's petition. The moment the Quaker arose from his knees everything became quiet. When they looked around the room was perfectly tidy and nothing was out of place.

Another Quaker, who faced the intruder with a bold 'Who art thou? In the name of the Lord, I bid thee depart', was received with a mocking sound described as 'a spasmodic suction of the air through the teeth'.

During the entire affair at Willington Mill strenuous efforts were made on numerous occasions to unravel the mystery. Often, as we have seen, vigils were held to that end and eyewitnesses to the bizarre events attempted to offer up rational explanations for the phenomena. They were never successful, but the fact they even made such efforts demonstrates that they were neither credulous nor instinctively disposed towards 'supernatural answers'. Stead notes pertinently, 'The usual explanation is entirely out of the question, that of rats. Not all the rats that followed the Pied Piper of Hamlin to destruction could make the row which occasionally disturbed the peace of Willington Mill. From time-to-time various explanations were invented to account for the phenomenon of the objective reality of the manifestations of which there can be no doubt unless all the most reliable human evidence is to be regarded as worthless. But no explanation held water'[10].

On 5 October 1891, in response to a request from W.T. Stead for an update on the situation at the mill, Edmund Procter wrote:

> I fear I cannot help you. Tomlinson's 'Guide to Northumberland', or the Appendix to 'Quaker Records – the Richardsons of Cleveland' by Mrs Boyce,

contain the references to all that is published in regard to the Haunted House at Willington.

Of what is unpublished there is little, if anything, except my father's diary, which I am under promise to send to Mr Myers for the ' Journal of Psychical Research,' but which is not ready yet.

The house is not pulled down, but is outwardly a wreck, and inwardly divided into tenements. There have, I believe, been no disturbances of any sort for many years.

When the house was unoccupied, perhaps ten years ago, I visited it twice – once with a well-known 'medium', once with a party of five, who sat up alone till 5 a.m.– and both cases were without result worth record[11].

Ironically, it was shortly after Procter penned his letter to Stead that one of the most frightening manifestations occurred:

On this occasion the mill was working night and day, when the engine-man, on going into the engine-house at midnight, saw the eyeless woman sitting there. With a wild scream he flung himself out of the window into the Gut, plunged through the mud and water to the opposite side, and never stopped until he reached home at Shields, some three miles off[12].

Around this time a rabbi rented an apartment in the house[13] and this seemed to precipitate an increase in the intensity of the phenomena, although to nothing like the scale experienced by the Procters.

Some may have presumed that as the mill house and surrounding buildings fell into disrepair – the mill house itself was eventually demolished – the ghosts would have dissipated with them. However, this was most certainly not the case.

Notes

1. Richardson, Moses Aaron, *The Local Historian's Table Book Vol. VI* (M.A. Richardson, 1847)
2. *Ibid.*
3. Crowe, Catherine, *The Night Side of Nature, or, Ghosts and Ghost Seers, Vol. II* (T.C. Newby, 1848)
4. Anon, *Ghosts and Legends of Northumbria* (Sandhill Press, 1996), p. 45
5. Stead, William T., *Real Ghost Stories* (Grant Richards, 1897)
6. Davidson, Robert, *The True Story of the Willington Ghost* (Robert Davidson, c. 1886)
7. *Ibid.*
8. Stead, William T., *Real Ghost Stories* (Grant Richards, 1897)
9. *Ibid.*

10. *Ibid.*

11. Letter from Edmund Procter to W.T. Stead, 5 October 1891

12. Davidson, Robert, *The True Story of the Willington Ghost* (Robert Davidson, c. 1886)

13. Stead, William T., *Real Ghost Stories* (Grant Richards, 1897)

Fourteen

KITTY, THE GHOST OF HAGGIE'S MILL

After the failure of Sampson Langdale's soap venture, the mill was untenanted until, in the year 1885, it was taken over by the firm Messrs R. Hood, Haggie & Son. The Haggie family, who lived in nearby Willington Villa, owned a successful rope factory and, when the mill stood vacant, they decided that a golden opportunity was presenting itself to expand their premises at a minimum cost.

There was a ghost at what became known as 'Haggie's Ropery' or 'Haggie's Mill', but there is some dispute regarding whether it was connected with the multitude of spectres that had been said to inhabit the place since its incarnation as a flour mill. The evidence, the authors think, suggests not. One publicaton[1] suggests that 'Kitty', as the ghost became known, was seen long before R. Hood, Haggie & Son took over the mill, and refers to Latimer[2] as substantiation. However, Latimer merely mentions the spectre witnessed by the Mann family discussed earlier, and makes no suggestion that the entity witnessed by them is the one known as 'Kitty'. In fact, the tale of Kitty the Mill Ghost came along much later and seems to have been almost inextricably melded with earlier stories, making it difficult to differentiate between the two.

The first story concerns the ghost of a woman seen on numerous occasions wandering down a road called Burns Closes. The road apparently ran from the mill under the railway viaduct, and is roughly in the same spot as another road still in existence called Millers Bank. However, as Burns Closes was there before the viaduct was built we should not fall into the trap of assuming that the ghost only began to appear after the railway viaduct was constructed. It may well be that the ghost that walked Burns Closes was around before the mill was built, and might possibly be connected with the haunting of the witch's cottage before that.

The real story regarding Kitty the Mill Ghost is of much later provenance[3,4], and during a trip to the mill site itself the authors were told essentially the same tale by a member of staff.

*The mill site
as viewed
from under the
railway arch,
now known as
Millers Bank.
(Darren W.
Ritson)*

Around 1902, a woman called Catherine Devore (or in some accounts Devoire) is said to have started work at the Haggie's rope factory. Aged forty-three[5], Catherine – known as 'Kitty' by her friends – was a larger-than-life character with a robust personality. She was also said to be 'a bit of a gossip', which seemingly caused other workers to keep their distance from her.

Kitty seemingly worked on some potentially highly dangerous machinery. On one occasion, whilst distracted, she leant forward and her long hair became entwined in the rollers. Within seconds her entire scalp was ripped from her head. According to legend she then fell to the floor and received even further injury to her skull. Kitty was, they say, 'deed within the hour' and it is her ghost, apparently, which haunts the mill.

The story of Kitty the Mill Ghost is significant in two respects. Firstly, her spectre is the first anthropomorphic one to our knowledge to become attached to the interior of the mill proper and not the mill house. Secondly, local folklore may already be working to intertwine the true story of Kitty with yet another tale.

When the authors visited the site for the first time they were given a tour of the buildings by Ray Summerson – an employee of Bridon Ropes which still maintains the rope-making tradition to this day. When asked if he'd heard the story of the ghost known colloquially as the Bare-Headed Priest or Ghost Priest. Ray said he had, but had an interesting theory on the apparition's identity.

Ray felt it may not be coincidental that Kitty the Mill Ghost and the Bare-Headed Priest were both said to be without hair or a head-covering. He wondered if, just possibly, they might be one and the same. Was the garment generally identified as a 'priest's surplice' really a dress? Was the 'bare head' or 'bald head' really Kitty minus her scalp? And could those who identify the spectre as of the male gender really be looking at the portly, robust female machine operator?

It's a fascinating idea, but suffers from one, flaw. The ghostly Bare-Headed Priest was around for a long time before Kitty got her hair caught in those rollers.

Ray Summerson thinks he might have seen an apparition on the site once. According to Ray, he happened to glance up at the upper floors of the mill building, which is still standing, and for a fleeting moment saw a woman looking out of one of the windows. Under normal circumstances he might just have assumed that it was a fellow employee – except for the fact that the two top floors of the mill were sealed off and not accessible. Who knows, it's just possible that he might have seen Kitty.

Notes

1. Anon, *The Parish of Willington, Northumberland* (North Tyneside Libraries & Arts Dept, 1986)
2. Latimer, John, *Local Records or Historical Register of Remarkable Events* (Newcastle, The Chronicle Office, 1857)
3. Anon, *The Parish of Willington, Northumberland* (North Tyneside Libraries & Arts Dept, 1986)
4. http://tillysjorn.blogspot.com/2009/01/kitty-mill-ghost.html
5. *Ibid.*

Fifteen

ANIMAL CRACKERS

One of the little-known aspects of the Willington Mill case is the 'mystery animal' conundrum. During the span of the haunting, whilst the Procters lived there, a number of bizarre creatures were seen in and around the premises. To the knowledge of the authors, only two other researchers[1] have investigated this enigma specifically in relation to Willington Mill. However, so peculiar are these incidents that they demand further attention.

As related earlier in this book, on Saturday, 13 November 1841, at about 4.30 p.m., young Joseph Procter was playing in the nursery with his brothers and sisters when he suddenly exclaimed that he could see a monkey. The creature – and we must assume that the children had correctly identified it as a monkey, although we don't know what species – lunged at the youngster and pulled at his bootstrap. For good measure, it also tickled his foot (although how it managed that when the youngster had boots on we do not know). By the time that Joseph Procter senior entered the room (he was only next door) the monkey had disappeared. However, he got there quickly enough to witness the children excitedly looking hither and thither for the creature.

The children at no time seem to have been under the impression that the monkey was a spectral one or in any way 'not of this world'. Edmund Procter said of his brother, 'he did not suppose any other but it was a real monkey'.

Edmund Procter comments, 'Now it so happens that this monkey is the first incident in the lugubrious hauntings, or whatever they may be termed, of which I have any recollection. I suppose it was, or might easily be, the first monkey I had ever seen, which may explain my memory being so impressed that I have not forgotten it. A monkey, and upstairs in the nursery, that is the business'.

Edmund Procter's comment proves that there were two witnesses to the monkey's presence and not simply one.

Edmund further commented, 'My parents have told me that no monkey was known to be owned in the neighbourhood, and after diligent inquiry no organ-man or hurdy-gurdy boy, either with or without monkey, had been seen anywhere about the place or neighbourhood, either on that day or for a length of time'. Had a monkey been living in a small, closely-knit community like Willington Mill, surely everyone would have known about it.

The aforementioned Mrs Hargrave, Elizabeth Procter's sister, also had a mystery animal encounter at the mill. Whilst passing the vegetable garden at the rear of the mill she happened upon a white cat of rather strange countenance. It was seemingly much larger than a domestic feline and had a long snout instead of a nose. Hargrave watched incredulously as the creature ambled through the garden. The animal then walked through the closed garden door (probably a gate) and then through the door leading into the engine house. The text at this juncture is somewhat confusing, and it may be that the creature actually walked through a solid wall. This possibility is interesting in the light of another animal-related incident which we will discuss presently.

Inside the engine house was Joseph Procter. As the creature walked through the door or the wall, Procter also saw it. To his astonishment it ambled into the furnace room and, quite calmly, walked into the fire. Later – although we don't know how much later – the 'cat' was also seen by Hargrave in one of the bedrooms, going through a closed door.

In 1841, Edmund Procter himself saw what he described as 'a funny cat' – an experience which disturbed him for some while. Around the same time, Elizabeth Procter awoke one night and heard the sound of an animal leaping down off an easy chair which stood near her bed.

The first question that has to be addressed is whether the creature could have been flesh-and-blood as opposed to spectral. Certainly the animal resembled nothing that one would normally find scuttling through the Tyneside countryside. Further, there are very few creatures on planet earth at all that bear a likeness to it. There is, however, one. The authors consulted cryptozoologist Richard Freeman, Zoological Director at the Centre for Fortean Zoology, and asked him if the animal described sounded like anything within the conventional world of fauna that he was aware of. Puzzled at first, Richard suggested that the creature might have been something called a moonrat.

The moonrat is found on the Malayan Peninsula and the Indonesian islands of Sumatra and Borneo and is a forest-dwelling insectivore related to the hedgehog. Moonrats can grow up to 19ins in length and weigh up to 3½lbs. Not all moonrats are covered in pure white fur, but some are. The big question is, what on earth would a Malayan insectivore be doing roaming around a flour mill in Willington? The answer is that it almost certainly wouldn't.

It is true that in the nineteenth century a number of travelling menageries toured the UK extensively, carrying with them all manner of exotic creatures to put on display. However, had such a menagerie visited Willington or anywhere nearby then everyone would have known about it and someone would undoubtedly have remembered the moonrat – if the show had one, that is – and put two and two together. Despite extensive enquiries the authors can find no record of a travelling menagerie visiting the area during that period.

Also, it is clear from the behaviour of the creature seen at Willington that it could not have been a flesh-and-blood animal. Twice it was seen to walk through walls, once into a furnace and once through a closed door. This indicates that the creature was more spectral than physical, and probably falls into the category of 'zooform'. Zooforms are entities that superficially look like ordinary creatures, but possess remarkable abilities. They often have glowing red eyes, seem to float rather than walk and – more commonly – can 'shape-shift'. A shape-shifter is a creature that can alter its form at will depending on need and circumstances, and have been mentioned in folklore almost from the dawn of human history. Sceptics believe that the whole concept of zooformic animals is nonsensical, but the authors and many other researchers have seen enough evidence to convince them that, bizarre though they may be, they really do exist. In the following account a couple from Willington had an encounter with a decidedly spectral animal that closely resembled the one seen by Mrs Hargrave. Intriguingly, it provides yet more evidence that there was paranormal phenomena occurring during the tenancy of the Unthank family.

Thomas Davidson was romantically involved with a young woman whom he would later marry, Mary Young, who lived at Willington Mill[2,3,4], although whether she was specifically a resident of the mill house or not we do not know. Davidson was a craftsman employed in the village, but there is evidence he later worked at the mill himself.

Thomas seems to have had an arrangement with Mary to meet her from work and walk her home, or perhaps go courting along the picturesque Willington Gut. Joseph Procter had banned unnecessary visitors from the house by this point because he was worried that they would make up stories about seeing the ghost and 'carry them abroad'. Instead of simply knocking at the back door, then, Thomas waited discretely by a rear window where, upon seeing Mary inside, he 'would give her the usual signal' – perhaps a short whistle, or tap upon the pane – to indicate his presence. On this occasion he successfully let Mary know he was there. All he had to do now was wait patiently till she quickly finished off any last-minute jobs and could leave. Davidson, according to his son's later testimony[5], looked up at the heavens and noted that, 'the night was clear, and the stars beamed forth their light from a cloudless sky'.

Davidson seems to have been standing slightly to the south-east of the mill house rear, adjacent to the wall of the East Mill. This would have placed him not directly in front of the alley or 'cart way' which ran between the house and the East Mill, but close enough so that he could see some way down it. At some point he saw what looked like a 'whitish cat' approach him. For some reason the young man seems to have felt uncomfortable and walked away, but, according to Robert Davidson, it kept 'walking along in close proximity to his feet'. Somewhat unnerved, and, as his son stated later, 'thinking Miss Pussy very cheeky', Thomas took a swipe at the creature with his foot. To his amazement his foot passed right through it as if it wasn't really there. Baffled, he watched as the creature walked on, seemingly oblivious to his attempt to kick it. He then decided to follow it, but the beast suddenly disappeared into the ether. Robert Davidson later said, however, that despite the fact that his father's foot had passed right through the animal, 'still the ghost was not thought of by him'.

Thomas, more puzzled than ever, decided to return to his original position by the mill house window. He then looked back and, to his astonishment, saw the creature appear again, as if by magic. Once again it made towards him, but this time it did not walk but hopped in his direction, like a rabbit, until it was beside his feet for a second time. Again he aimed a kick at it, and, for a second time, his foot passed right through it before it disappeared. Davidson then took a few steps closer to the kitchen window, perhaps to gain the advantage of the light. For a third time the creature appeared, but this time it looked markedly different. According to Robert Davidson, 'it was not like unto a cat or a rabbit, but fully as large as a sheep, and quite luminous'.

Although unnerved on the first two occasions, this time the man became absolutely terrified:

All muscular power seemed for a moment paralysed. On it moved, disappearing at the same place as the preceding apparitions. My father declared that if it was

possible for hair to 'stand on end' his did just then. Thinking for once he had
seen sufficient he went home, keeping the knowledge of this scene to himself.
Next morning he went to the mill and communicated to Mr Procter what he
had seen. Mr Procter thanked him kindly for the information and stated that
he had seen the same thing on another occasion at the front of the house.

A number of questions arise here. Firstly, were the creatures seen by
Davidson one and the same or three completely different animals? The
seemingly ethereal nature of the animal (or animals) he encountered
ostensibly suggests that it (or they) were 'not of this world'. The
authors believed that the only logical conclusion is that Davidson
had encountered what is commonly known as a shape-shifter, but the
slight possibility remains that he actually saw three separate and distinct
animals of zooform origin.

The Spencers[6] hint at a degree of aggression shown on the third
encounter, stating that the beast seemed to be attempting to frighten
Davidson away. Our second question, then, must be, why? This is a
subject the authors will return to presently.

The Spencers also relate[7] the experience of a Mr Wedgwood who saw
a mysterious cat in the furnace room of the mill. Bizarrely, he claimed
that it suddenly began wriggling like a snake before passing through a
wall of solid stone.

Another strange animal encounter involved a 'donkey', which was
seen by two employees[8], Hiram Wedgwood and Walter Middleton.
Whether Hiram Wedgwood was related to the man of the same name in
the above incident we cannot say, although it seems likely.

It seems that Wedgwood and Middleton had just left the East Mill
and were intent upon calling at the mill house to see Joseph Procter
about some business matter. As they turned the corner and entered the
narrow alleyway between the mill and the house, they both saw what
they described as 'a strange-looking donkey'. The creature was, they said,
'quite small with short hair of a sand colour, although somewhat darker'.
They also noticed that its nose 'seemed to bow upwards in the middle,
like a bump'. Apparently oblivious to its human observers, the creature,
according to Middleton, 'several times lowered its head and began as if to
chew grass, but there was no grass in that part, merely stones. As we looked
upon it, the donkey turned and passed through the door leading to the
interior. At no time did it make any sounds that we could discern, not even
the clopping of a hoof or a bray'. This may be the incident involving a
donkey briefly alluded to by the Spencers[9], although we cannot be certain.

The tale about the bizarre shape-shifting cat spread like wildfire through the mill and it is simply impossible to think that they never reached George Unthank's ears.

W.T. Stead relates a cryptozoological incident involving Elizabeth Procter's brother[10]:

> *In November, 1841, Mr Carr paid a visit to the spectral house, when the figure of an animal about two feet high appeared in the window of the blue room. They made a careful search, but found nothing, although Mr and Mrs Mann, who were outside, saw the animal in the window without intermission for half an hour, then it began to decrease in size and gradually disappeared.*

Just what this spectral animal looked like we are not told, but it was obviously supernatural in nature.

Stead goes on to relate that, 'Occasionally the ghost assumed the shape of an animal. A two years' old boy saw it in the shape of a "bonny pussy,".' Likely, this is the same incident described earlier in which Edmund Procter saw a 'funny cat', although we can't be absolutely sure. This experience disturbed him for some while. By 'funny' he no doubt meant odd or strange, which makes it tempting to link this creature with the one saw by Mrs Hargrave.

One peculiar feature of the whole Willington Mill enigma is that certain types of phenomena seemed to present themselves to different families. In the case of the Davidsons, according to Stead, there was the aforementioned 'white towel'-like object – or creature – which suddenly burst into life and gambolled down the stairwell. On another occasion, 'Mr Davidson's aunt [saw an object and] thought it looked like a white pocket-handkerchief knotted at the four corners, which kept dancing up and down, sometimes rising as high as the first floor window'.

On another occasion, 'when his aunt was cleaning boots by the kitchen table, she was suddenly startled by the bark of a dog, and two paws were heavily laid upon her shoulders, so as to make her lay hold of the table for support. Mrs Proctor [*sic*] ran into the kitchen, but no dog could be found, and all the doors were shut, and there were no dogs in the house'.

Just what might have been responsible for this weird menagerie of spectral animals is something the authors will address presently.

Notes

1. Spencer, John & Anne, *The Encyclopaedia of Ghosts & Spirits* (Headline Book Publishing PLC, 1992)

2. *Ibid.*

3. Cohen, Daniel, *The Encyclopaedia of Ghosts* (Avon Books, 1991)

4. Davidson, Robert, *The True Story of the Willington Ghost* (Robert Davidson, c. 1886)

5. *Ibid.*

6. Spencer, John & Anne, *The Encyclopaedia of Ghosts & Spirits* (Headline Book Publishing PLC, 1992)

7. *Ibid.*

8. Anon, *The Willington Quay Ghost* (Privately published, c. 1972)

9. Spencer, John & Anne, *The Encyclopaedia of Ghosts & Spirits* (Headline Book Publishing PLC, 1992)

10. Stead, William T., *Real Ghost Stories* (Grant Richards, 1897)

Sixteen

CATHERINE CROWE
AND WILLIAM HOWITT

Catherine Crowe was born in Borough Green, Kent, in 1798, 1800 or 1803 depending on which you favour.

From an early age, Catherine had a passion for writing. At the age of twenty-four she married an army officer named Crowe and the couple relocated to Edinburgh where, more or less, she remained for the remainder of her days.

Crowe was best remembered for her novels, which included *Susan Hopley*, *Adventures of a Beauty*, *Aristodemus* and *Lilly Dawson*. However, in her twenties she developed a keen interest in the supernatural and investigated a number of heterodox disciplines such as phrenology[1].

Catherine's interest in the supernatural eventually invaded her writing and in 1848 she wrote the book that perhaps brought her more attention than any other, *The Night Side of Nature*[2]. The book, occasionally released in two volumes, contained Crowe's numerous investigations into strange encounters, one of which was the haunting of Willington Mill. In 1859 she penned *Ghost Stories and Family Legends*[3]. Later, the priest Montague Summers included some of these tales in a book he edited entitled *Victorian Ghost Stories*[4].

Crowe was first told of the Willington Mill case by fellow author and investigator William Howitt[5], who was much impressed by it. Howitt, unlike Crowe who heard about the affair too late, was actually able to visit the site at the time. As soon as Crowe heard about the mysterious events in the mill house she wrote to Joseph Procter and asked him for further details. She received the following reply, once again written in the enigmatic third-person pronoun:

> *Josh. Proctor, hopes C. Crowe will excuse her note having remained two weeks un-answered, during which time J.P. has been from home, or particularly engaged. Feeling averse to add to the publicity the circumstances occurring in his house, at Willington, have already obtained, J.P. would rather not furnish*

additional particulars; but if C.C. is not in possession of the number of 'Howitt's Journal,' which contains a variety of details on the subject, he will be glad to forward her one. He would at the same time assure C. Crowe of the strict accuracy of that portion of W. Howitt's narrative, which is extracted from 'Richardson's Table Book.' W. Howitt's statements derived from his recollection of verbal communications, with branches of J. Procter's family, are likewise essentially correct, though, as might be expected in some degree, erroneous circumstantially.

J.P. takes leave to express his conviction, that the unbelief of the educated classes, in apparitions of the deceased and kindred phenomena, is not grounded on a fair philosophic examination of the facts, which have induced the popular belief of all ages and countries; and that it will be found by succeeding ages, to have been nothing better than unreasoning and unreasonable prejudice.

11 Willington, near Newcastle- on- Tyne,
7th mo. 22, 1847[6].

It is interesting that although Procter in no way rebuffs Crowe's attempt to solicit information from him, and is actually quite helpful to a degree, he nevertheless refuses to 'furnish additional particulars'. This can only mean that Procter, as he already admitted, knew of other incidents that had taken place which were not entered into his diary or detailed elsewhere. We can only wonder at what these might have been.

William Howitt related his own experience at Willington Mill in his book[7], which Crowe copied in her own:

These singular circumstances being at various times related by parties acquainted with the family at Willington, I was curious, on a tour northward some time ago, to pay this haunted house a visit, and to solicit a night's lodgings there. Unfortunately the family was absent, on a visit to Mrs Procter's relatives in Carlisle, so that my principal purpose was defeated; but I found the foreman and his wife, mentioned in the foregoing narrative, living just by. They spoke of the facts above detailed with the simple earnestness of people who had no doubts whatever on the subject. The noises and apparitions in and about this house seemed just like any other facts connected with it as matters too palpable and positive to be questioned, any more than that the house actually stood, and the mill ground. They mentioned to me the circumstance of the young lady, as above stated, who took up her lodging in their house, because she would no longer encounter the annoyances of the haunted house; and what trouble it had occasioned the family in procuring and retaining servants.

The wife accompanied me into the house, which I found in charge of a recently married servant and her husband, during the absence of the family. This young woman, who had, previous to her marriage, lived some time in the house, had never seen anything, and therefore had no fear. I was shown over the house, and especially into the room on the third storey, the main haunt of the unwelcome visitors, and where Dr Drury had received such an alarm. This room, as stated, was, and had been for some time, abandoned as a bedroom, from its bad character, and was occupied as a lumber-room.

William Howitt, the Victorian author and researcher who tried, but failed, to solve the Willington Mill enigma.

At Carlisle, I again missed Mr Procter; he had returned to Willington, so that I lost the opportunity of hearing from him or Mrs Procter any account of these singular matters. I saw, however, various members of his wife's family, most intelligent people, of the highest character for sound and practical sense, and they were unanimous in their confirmation of the particulars I had heard, and which are here related.

One of Mrs Procter's brothers, a gentleman in middle life, and of a peculiarly sensible, sedate, and candid disposition, a person apparently most unlikely to be imposed on by fictitious alarms or tricks, assured me that he had himself, on a visit there, been disturbed by the strangest noises. That he had resolved, before going, that if any such noises occurred he would speak, and demand of the invisible actor who he was, and why he came thither. But the occasion came, and he found himself unable to fulfil his intention. As he lay in bed one night, he heard a heavy step ascend the stairs towards his room, and some one striking, as it were, with a thick stick on the banisters, as he went along. It came to his door, and he essayed to call, but his voice died in his throat. He then sprang from his bed, and opening the door, found no one there, but now heard the same heavy steps deliberately descending, though perfectly invisibly, the steps before his face, and accompanying the descent with the same loud blows on the banisters.

My informant now proceeded to the room door of Mr Procter, who, he found, had also heard the sounds, and who now also arose, and with a light they made a speedy descent below, and a thorough search there, but without discovering anything that could account for the occurrence.

The two young ladies, who, on a visit there, had also been annoyed by this invisible agent, gave me this account of it: The first night, as they were sleeping in the same bed, they felt the bed lifted up beneath them. Of course, they were much alarmed. They feared lest some one had concealed himself there for the purpose of robbery. They gave an alarm, search was made, but nothing was found. On another night, their bed was violently shaken, and the curtains suddenly hoisted up all round to the very tester, as if pulled by cords, and as rapidly let down again, several times. Search again produced no evidence of the cause. The next, they had the curtains totally removed from the bed, resolving to sleep without them, as they felt as though evil eyes were lurking behind them. The consequences of this, however, was still more striking and terrific. The following night, as they happened to awake, and the chamber was light enough for it was summer to see everything in it, they both saw a female figure, of a misty substance, and bluish grey hue, come out of the wall, at the bed's head, and through the headboard, in a horizontal position, and lean over them. They saw it most distinctly. They saw it as a female figure come out of, and again pass into, the wall. Their terror became intense, and one of the sisters, from that night, refused to sleep any more in the house, but it is remarkable that this hoisting of the bed-curtains is similar to an incident recorded in the account of the visit of Lord Tyrone's ghost to Lady Beresford.

... It would be too long to relate all the forms in which this nocturnal disturbance is said by the family to present itself. When a figure appears, it is sometimes that of a man, as already described, which is often very luminous, and passes through the walls as though they were nothing. This male figure is well known to the neighbours by the name of 'Old Jeffrey!' At other times, it is the figure of a lady also in gray costume, and as described by Mr Drury. She is sometimes seen sitting wrapped in a sort of mantle, with her head depressed, and her hands crossed on her lap. The most terrible fact is that she is without eyes. [Regarding the ghost of 'the woman with no eyes', which was regularly seen at Willington mill house, Stead comments, 'The Ghost children, however, were the chief ghost- with-eyeholes seers, No one was allowed to tell them anything about the ghost, and any servant who told a fairy tale in Willington Mill was instantly dismissed. No conspiracy of silence, however, would prevent the children from seeing the ghost. On one occasion one of the little girls came to Mrs Davidson and said, 'There is a lady sitting on the bed in mamma's bedroom. She had eyeholes, but no eyes; and she looked so hard at me.' On one occasion a little girl told Mrs Davidson that on the previous night a lady had come out of the wall and looked into the glass; she had something tied over her head; she had eyeholes, but no eyes']⁸.

To hear such sober and superior people gravely relate to you such things, gives you a very odd feeling. They say that the noise made is often like that of a paviour with his rammer thumping on the floor. At other times it is coming down the stairs, making a similar loud sound. At others it coughs, sighs, and groans, like a person in distress; and, again, there is the sound of a number of little feet pattering on the floor of the upper chamber, where the apparition has more particularly exhibited itself, and which, for that reason, is solely used as a lumber room. Here these little footsteps may be often heard as if careering a child's carriage about, which in bad weather is kept up there. Sometimes, again, it makes the most horrible laughs. Nor does it always confine itself to the night. On one occasion, a young lady, as she assured me herself, opened the door in answer to a knock, the housemaid being absent, and a lady in fawn-coloured silk entered, and proceeded up stairs. As the young lady, of course, supposed it a neighbour come to make a morning call on Mrs Procter, she followed her up to the drawing-room, where, however, to her astonishment, she did not find her, nor was anything more seen of her.

Such are a few of the 'questionable shapes' in which this troublesome guest comes. As may be expected, the terror of it is felt by the neighbouring cottagers, though it seems to confine its malicious disturbance almost solely to the occupants of this one house. There is a well, however, near to which no one ventures after it is dark, because it has been seen near it.

It is useless to attempt to give any opinion respecting the real causes of these strange sounds and sights. How far they may be real or imaginary, how far they may be explicable by natural causes or not; the only thing which we have here to record, is the very singular fact of a most respectable and intelligent family having for many years been continually annoyed by them, as well as their visitors. They express themselves as most anxious to obtain any clue to the true cause, as may be seen by Mr Procter's ready acquiescence in the experiment of Mr Drury. So great a trouble is it to them, that they have contemplated the necessity of quitting the house altogether, though it would create great inconvenience as regarded business. And it only remains to be added, that we have not heard very recently whether these visitations are still continued, though we have a letter of Mr Procter's to a friend of ours, dated September 1844, in which he says, 'Disturbances have for a length of time been only very unfrequent, which is a comfort, as the elder children are getting old enough (about nine or ten years) to be more injuriously affected by anything of the sort.'

Over these facts let the philosophers ponder, and if any of them be powerful enough to exorcise 'Old Jeffery,' or the bluish-grey and misty lady, we are sure that Mr Joseph Procter will hold himself deeply indebted to them. We have lately heard that Mr Procter has discovered an old book, which makes it appear that the very same 'hauntings' took place in an old house, on the very same spot, at least two hundred years ago.

Catherine Crowe, fascinated by the Willington Mill case, then added her own thoughts:

To the above information, furnished by Mr Howitt, I have to subjoin that the family of Mr Procter are now quitting the house, which he intends to divide into small tenements for the work-people. A friend of mine who lately visited Willington, and who went over the house with Mr Procter, assures me that the annoyances still continue, though less frequent than formerly. Mr P. informed her that the female figure generally appeared in a shroud, and that it had been seen in that guise by one of the family only a few days before.

A wish being expressed by a gentleman visiting Mr P. that some natural explanation of these perplexing circumstances might be discovered, the latter declared his entire conviction, founded on an experience of fifteen years, that no such elucidation was possible.

Even though Crowe, and Howitt, from whom she drew much of her information, maintained an extensive interest in the case, it was, as we know, never solved.

In many respects, Catherine Crowe was an unsung hero in regards to the Willington affair. Guy Lyon Playfair, the author of *This House is Haunted*[9] and many other works on the paranormal, when told the authors were writing a book on the Willington Mill case, said he was, 'delighted to hear that Catherine Crowe is not forgotten. She deserves to be remembered as one of the first serious researchers as well as a damn good writer'.

The authors of this book both heartily agree with this sentiment. Howitt is to be commended for his writing up of the case, whilst Crowe is also to be lauded for raising the public consciousness regarding it and taking research into it a step further where Howitt left off. Were it not for these two writers, our knowledge of what transpired would be immeasurably less.

Notes

1. Routledge (Creator), *A Historical Dictionary of British Women* (Routledge, 2003)
2. Crowe, Catherine, *The Night Side of Nature, or, Ghosts and Ghost Seers, Vol. II* (T.C. Newby, 1848)
3. Crowe, Catherine, *Ghost Stories and Family Legends* (T.C. Newby 1858)
4. Summers, Montague, *Victorian Ghost Stories* (Simpkin, Marshall Ltd, 1936)
5. Howitt, William, *Visits to Remarkable Places; Old Walls, Battle Fields, and Scenes Illustrative of Striking Passages in English History and Poetry* (Longman, Orme, Brown, Green & Longman, 1840)
6. Crowe, Catherine, *The Night Side of Nature, or, Ghosts and Ghost Seers, Vol. II* (T.C. Newby, 1848)
7. Howitt, William, *Visits to Remarkable Places; Old Walls, Battle Fields, and Scenes Illustrative of Striking Passages in English History and Poetry* (Longman, Orme, Brown, Green & Longman, 1840)
8. *Ibid.*
9. Playfair, Guy Lyon, *This House is Haunted* (Souvenir Press, 1980)

Seventeen

THE VISIT

On Friday, 19 June 2009, Michael J. Hallowell boarded a train to North Shields. As the train passed through numerous stations on its way to its destination, Mike checked his camera. He had a photograph to take at one precise spot, and only a window of several seconds in which to do it. He wanted to be ready. 'Make sure you sit on the right-hand side of the carriage', co-author Darren had told him. 'Just after Hadrian Road if you look out of the window, you'll see Willington Mill and the river called Willington Gut. If you want to take a picture you'll have to be quick'.

Just after the train pulled out of Howdon station Mike switched his camera on and waited. There was shrubbery on the side of the track which obscured his view, but after a minute or two it thinned out and there, up ahead, was the mill. Mike had never seen it before, but

A high-elevation view of the mill site from the nearby rail bridge. This would have been the view as seen by 'Jane' during her singular trip as she drew near to the factory. (Thunderbird Craft & Media)

recognised it from Darren's description. He quickly lifted up his camera and took two shots.

Before long the train arrived at Howdon and Darren boarded.

'Did you get your picture?'

'I got two, actually,' replied Mike. 'One is really poor, but the other is just salvageable'.

At North Shields, the authors alighted. First on the agenda was a trip to the Central Library to dig out as much information as they could about Willington Quay and, of course, the haunted mill. They were not disappointed. Mike had rung the library two days earlier and asked if any material relating to the site could be made available. The librarian had been as good as her word, and when they arrived the file was on her desk waiting for them. She then directed the authors to a number of tomes which contained detailed accounts of Willington's history. They made copious notes.

Next, the authors visited the site of Willington Mill at Willington Quay. The site, once possessed by Haggie's Ropery, is now owned by Bridon Ropes. On the left were a number of prefabricated, hangar-type buildings with pointed roofs. Slightly to the right was a large office block of indeterminable age. Further to the right again was an imposing edifice that had been built during the reign of George III; the mill, or what was left of it. In front of the factory was a large car park for employees.

Inside the foyer of the main entrance an employee, seeing us looking around as if lost, came out to greet us with a smile and the words, 'Can I help?' Mike explained who they were and what they were doing there.

'Basically, we're after two things. Firstly, we'd like any information we can get about the site, the alleged hauntings … anything really. Also, if it's not too cheeky or presumptuous, could we have a look around? If we could talk to the Site Manager or Operations Manager and get permission we'd really appreciate it'.

'Ah … that might be difficult. He's in a meeting right now, and …', but before the employee had a chance to finish his sentence the Operations Manager, Colin Pratt, came down the stairs. Not realising who we were, and seeing that we were in the capable hands of his colleague Ray Summerson, he smiled politely and entered the main office.

Ray grinned, and said, 'Hey, you're in luck! That's the Operations Manager! Give me a minute and I'll see what I can do.' Ray promptly returned to the office. 'No problem! Please … come into the office.'

Inside, the authors were formally introduced to Colin Pratt, who made it clear that he'd be glad to help in any way he could.

*Ray Summerson, of Bridon Ropes,
who kindly gave the authors an
all-access tour of the site. (Darren W.
Ritson/Thunderbird Craft & Media)*

'Come this way,' he said, 'I've got something I'd like to show you.'

At the far end of the office, two paintings of Willington Mill hung upon the wall. Colin told the authors about their history, gave his thoughts regarding what exactly they depicted, and explained that Willington Gut, which could be clearly seen in the paintings, had subsequently been rerouted so that the car park could be built. Colin then told the authors quite a bit about the history of the mill – including some points they had hitherto been unaware of.

'Have any of your employees seen the ghost?' both authors asked simultaneously.

Colin looked a little sceptical, but Ray related the incident when he'd seen the apparition of a woman on one of the upper stories of the mill.

Colin had to return to his meeting, but said that Ray was at the authors' disposal and would take them wherever they wanted to go. It goes without saying that the first place they wanted to visit was the mill. Within two minutes the trio had walked past the old mill house site to the distal end near the Gut and were looking at the stout wooden door which led inside.

Nowadays the old mill is used as an office and meeting centre where seminars and other events can be held. On the ground floor, where at one time heavy plant would have been stationed, there now sat rows of red upholstered chairs upon a bright blue carpet. The old, cast-iron

Left: *The upper floor of the mill, rarely accessed by members of the public, as it is today.* *(Thunderbird Craft & Media)*

Right: *The authors in the old mill building next to the original sign for R. Hood Haggie & Son Ltd, former owners. (Thunderbird Craft & Media)*

pillars had been painted sky blue and the iron girders supporting the roof were coloured dark brown, giving off a faint echo of Tudor-style beams. The entire effect was quite pleasant. Mike, with Ray's permission, took some photographs.

Walking up the stairs, Ray took the authors into another long room that ran the length of the entire mill. On the right were numerous offices and meeting rooms, the doors of which were separated by iron pillars identical to those on the ground floor. On the right were windows and vertical beams. Looking down the length of this corridor towards the other end of the mill was a breathtaking experience. It was very easy indeed to imagine what it must have looked like in the days of George Unthank and Joseph Procter. Mike took several more snaps before Ray showed them around the offices. On the walls hung magnificent portraits – some in oils, some photographs – of past owners and managers of the mill. Ray then asked if they wanted to see a picture of the mill hanging on the wall in the corridor.

The picture was one that Darren and Mike had seen on several occasions in books, but this was a far better copy. Ray lifted it from its hook and placed it upon a table where Mike could photograph it.

'Here,' said Ray, 'let me show you something else.'

At the far end of the corridor on the left, in between two windows, were two framed sheets of glass. They looked like – and probably were –

panes of glass that had once themselves sat within window frames. Now they were displayed as pieces of history, some may even say works of art.

Upon the top pane were the words R. HOOD HAGGIE & SON LIMITED, and on the smaller one, underneath, STEEL WIRE ROPES. The words had been expertly laid upon the glass with the finest gold leaf.

'That's from the days when Haggie owned the mill … it's a piece of history.'

Finally, Ray asked Darren and Mike to accompany him into the garden where there was something he wanted to show them. Ray took the authors over to an outgrowth of shrubbery and pointed at something.

'There … crawl in and take a look at that. Just be careful.'

From the outside, peering in between the branches, foliage and flowers, Darren and Mike could see a circular stone wheel lying horizontally. It was raised from the ground approximately one foot in height and supported by what looked like worn blocks of stone. The wheel was obviously an old millstone which had survived from the Procter days. Darren crawled under the shrubbery and gently laid his hand upon it.

'Look,' said Darren, there's something on the top of the wheel. It's a plaque of some kind.' Darren then took his camera and began snapping.

'What does it say?' asked Mike.

'Don't know … can't make it out.'

Darren extricated himself from the bushes to allow Mike a chance to examine the artefact for himself. As he pushed the branches to one side in an effort to get closer, he noticed a series of spoke-like grooves running from the perimeter of the wheel to the hole in the centre. He knew what these were. In old flour mills the wheat was crushed between the stone and the spindle, and the raw material would fall into the grooves and slowly make its way to the centre of the wheel where it would be crushed before falling onto the milling table below for collection.

What really interested Mike, however, was the plaque. On closer inspection it wasn't ornate. Rather, it was plain, functional and had absolutely no adornment whatsoever. It had been attached to the spindle sticking through the centre of the millstone with four bolts, the heads of which were now somewhat rusted. As he stared at the stone in the undergrowth, the sun dipped behind some clouds momentarily and the sky darkened. He peered at the words upon the plaque, and slowly they came into focus:

KITTY'S STONE
THIS MILL STONE WAS FOUND DURING EXCAVATIONS
FOR A NEW BOILER HOUSE, JUNE 1952, ON THE SITE OF
THE OLD WEST MILL. IN THIS AREA FORMERLY STOOD A
FLOUR MILL OWNED BY MR. JOSEPH PROCTER, FAMED
AS AN EARLY STEAM DRIVEN MILL AND HAUNT OF THE
WILLINGTON GHOST.

Someone, it seems, had taken the story of Kitty seriously enough to create a touching memorial to her. Neither of the authors had seen this tribute to Kitty referred to before in any literature relating to the mill. On returning to the front of the reception entrance, the authors asked Ray Summerson and Colin Pratt, who had briefly rejoined us, if they knew exactly where the mill house had stood before it was demolished.

'That's easy,' said Colin, 'look; it stood right there where the car park is now.'

Ray took Darren and Mike over to the car park until they found themselves in pretty much the same position as the photographer who had first snapped an image of the mill over one and a half centuries ago. It was eerie, looking at the remainder of the old mill, and recalling its past.

When Darren and Mike had convinced themselves that they were in the right place, they started taking pictures – dozens of them, all from slightly different angles. There was a very good reason for this. Later,

Left: *One of the original mill grinding stones, now completely obliterated by undergrowth, which bears the strange plaque about 'Kitty the Mill Ghost'. (Darren W. Ritson)*

Right: *The strange plaque erected as a memorial to Kitty the Mill Ghost. (Thunderbird Craft & Media)*

Mike would attempt to digitally reconstruct the mill house on one of the new photographs to illustrate not only where it had stood, but also what it would have looked like had it still been standing. Both Darren and Mike looked at a the old picture of the mill they had with them, and saw with their own eyes for the first time what Ray had told them. The mill that was still standing had been reduced by two or three stories and was nowhere near as tall as it had once been. The windows had been enlarged, too, which only served to enhance the smaller look of the place. Still, the substantial part was still there; enough for a positive identification to be made regarding the exact location of the mill house itself.

Eighteen

PHENOMENA

Researching the history of Willington Mill and the fascinating story of the ghosts which haunted it, was, for the authors, an incredible experience. Their exhaustive research threw up much detail concerning what really happened back then, enabled them to dispel several myths and inaccuracies and, crucially, allowed them to gain a much clearer picture of the strange events which fuelled so much discussion and bewilderment. Of course, intriguing though these things were, there was still one unanswered question which tantalised them; just what did happen at Willington Mill?

The authors always accepted that, hypothetically at least, hoaxing, over-active imaginations or misattribution might have caused the entire panoply of seemingly paranormal phenomena. However, from an early stage in the investigation it became clear that these were very difficult ideas to sustain. The truth is that there were simply too many witnesses – and credible witnesses at that – who had admitted that they had seen things for which there was simply no rational explanation. Even the initially sceptical Edward Drury left the mill house believing that the place was well and truly haunted. Commendably, he had the courage to say so, although his co-investigator Thomas Hudson later entertained some doubts.

Each reader will have to make his or her mind up, of course, whether anything truly supernatural did go on at the mill house, but for the authors' part they are convinced. To begin our look at the nature of the phenomena that occurred, we need to make a list of the different types. Taken in their entirety, the phenomena at Willington Mill can be divided into four basic categories. Under each category heading are the specific phenomena which fall within them.

Witchcraft
Cursing
Possible appearance of 'familiars'

Haunting
The appearance of transparent and/or glowing anthropomorphic figures
Shadows and/or 'shadow people'
Anomalous sounds or disembodied voices
Music or musical sounds, such as bells
The appearance of seemingly disembodied heads
Pressure on face, eyes, coldness, or other physical symptoms
Appearance of seemingly conventional animals but which act like
  apparitions

Poltergeistry
Shaking of windows, floors and walls
Appearance of strange objects
Moving of small household objects
Moving of large household objects, such as beds
Disturbed bedclothes, as if moved by 'invisible hands'
Indentations on bedclothes and pillows, as if made by an invisible person
Anomalous sounds and noises, including music, bell-ringing, etc.
The appearance of seemingly disembodied heads
Pressure on face, eyes, coldness, or other physical symptoms
Instances of solid matter passing through matter

Cryptozoology
Appearance of seemingly conventional animals but which act in a
  bizarre manner
Appearance of bizarre or unconventional animals collectively known as
  zooforms

Witchcraft at Willington
Perhaps the least prevalent phenomena were those that can essentially
be placed under the banner heading of witchcraft. In fact, this category
initially seemed so weak it was in danger of fading from the authors'
radar altogether. However, some research carried out by the authors
has, for the first time that they are aware of, enabled them to tentatively
identify the Willington Witch.

We know as a historical fact that there was a cottage of the site on the old mill, and that it had a reputation to be both cursed and haunted. We also know that the tenant was, by all accounts, a witch. At the very least we can say that witchcraft, whether in reality or just by reputation and rumour, was present on the old mill site in some shape or form. Crowe[1] states that Joseph Procter, despite his protestations to the contrary later, had evidence to suggest that the witch had lived 'about two hundred years ago'. As Crowe was writing in 1848, then the witch in question must have flourished around 1648.

One of the peculiar things about the 'Willington Witch' stories is that although just about everyone believed the old woman was a witch and that her home and the area around it was haunted, the authors cannot find a single record of the lady having actually done anything untoward to her neighbours. Although Summers denounced the woman as a 'notorious witch'[2], it seems to be that her reputation at Willington was gained by things that happened around her, not because of her. Ghosts were seen in or near the cottage, and the place – not the person living there – was said to be cursed. If the witch had gained her 'notorious' reputation by actively practising witchcraft, then she surely must have done this before arriving at Willington Quay.

Seemingly, after the woman's death a local priest bragged about how he had refused to give the woman a deathbed confession before she passed away. It seemed odd to the authors that a dying follower of Wicca would want to confess her sins to a Christian priest. The only scenario in which this would make sense would be one in which the person was, in some bizarre way, practising both Roman Catholicism and witchcraft at the same time. If we are to try and identify the witch in question, then we need to look for someone who lived in the mid-seventeenth century, practised both Roman Catholicism and Wicca at the same time and had gained for herself a 'notorious' reputation. Although witchcraft wasn't exactly rare in those times, there would have been few witches who would have fitted all these criteria. But there was one; a well-known character who went by the curious epithet of Mrs Pepper.

On Tuesday, 3 February 1665, Mrs Pepper – sometimes called Miss or Mistress Pepper – was interrogated before Sir Francis Liddle, the mayor of Newcastle-upon-Tyne. Pepper had been a successful midwife in the city, but unfortunately midwifery was often seen as synonymous with witchcraft. Despite her good reputation, a number of incidents conspired to bring about her professional downfall.

As well as midwifery, Pepper was also consulted by sufferers of various ailments. One patient, a mineworker called Robert Pyle, had been feeling ill for some time and the symptoms may indicate that he was suffering from migraine. Pyle's physician suggested that his patient consult Mrs Pepper with a sample of his urine for her to analyse, which is indicative of the fact that she was not seen by more orthodox medics as either dangerous or eccentric. Pepper later made a house visit to see Pyle and, in the presence of his wife, Margaret, asked him to go to the door at the rear of the premises. Almost immediately Pyle seems to have had some sort of seizure and lost the use of one of his legs[3]. Pepper gave the man a cup of water to drink which, one presumes, had been imbued with herbal or other medicinal substances. Almost immediately the pitman suffered another seizure. Whether this was merely coincidental or had been caused by the 'water' he'd been given to drink we may never know, but Margaret Pyle certainly found it suspicious. To try and rectify the situation, Pepper brought two of Pyle's children to his side and 'layd them to his mouth'. By doing so she claimed that the breath of the children would suck the demons or evil spirits out of their father. We are not told exactly what the outcome was, but we must presume that it was somewhat less than successful. Elizabeth Pyle was the first to testify against Pepper during her arraignment.

A second woman, Elizabeth Rutherford, said that her husband, a tailor, had been ill and also went to see Mrs Pepper. During the consultation the midwife discovered a 'red-hot spot' on the back of one of Richard Rutherford's hands and demanded that 'holy water' be sprinkled upon it, after which she placed a crucifix across the very same area. Pepper then seems to have reached some diagnosis but without voicing forth exactly what it was. Next, she took the crucifix from Rutherford's hand and placed it in his mouth.

Pepper was found to be innocent of witchcraft, and, seemingly, left Newcastle-upon-Tyne.

The rather odd rituals which Pepper used to treat her patients, such as the use of a crucifix, have caused some researchers to speculate that the midwife may have practice a strange mixture of both Christianity and witchcraft. Bath, for example, says that she was probably a follower of Roman Catholicism and utilised Roman ritual with other, more unorthodox healing methods[4].

It was around the time of her appearance before Sir Francis Liddle, and subsequent discharge, that the mysterious Witch of Willington is first mentioned as living in the cottage provided for her by her son-in-law Mr Oxon. Both women were said to practise witchcraft, both were 'notorious' and both, despite their Wiccan tendencies, seemed to have some sort of affinity with Roman Catholicism. It is the authors' contention that Mrs Pepper and the Willington Witch may have been one and the same person and that the midwife relocated from Newcastle to Willington Quay in an effort to escape the hue and cry surrounding her inquisition.

There may also be a connection between the 'mystery animals' discussed earlier and the labelling of Mr Oxon's mother-in-law as a witch. Witches are said to possess 'familiars'; that is, spirits in animal form who act as guardians, protectors and agents of their owner. Curiously, the most popular form by far that a familiar will take upon itself is that of a cat. It may not, then, be coincidental that the most common mystery animal seen around Willington was that of a cat or cat-like creature. Thomas Davidson claimed that the creature he encountered changed shape three times. Witches' familiars are said to have the ability to shape-shift – that is, change from one animal to another (or even from an animal into a human) – and by tradition could be sent forth by their owners to wreak havoc in the lives of those who the witch felt deserved it. These facts led the authors to an almost irresistible conclusion; that the bizarre animals seen in the area even before the mill was constructed would almost certainly have been perceived as familiars working on behalf of the 'notorious witch'.

It is intriguing that familiars were (and are) said to sometimes take on the shape of an animal which has no known taxonomical identity; in other words, they are not of any known species. The strange creature seen by Mrs Hargrave – which looked tantalisingly like a Malaysian moonrat but almost certainly wasn't – would certainly fit into this category comfortably.

Marsden Bay in South Shields – on the other side of the River Tyne to Willington Quay – was long thought to be populated by 'elementals' created as 'helpers' by local occultists in the eighteenth and nineteenth centuries. To the authors' knowledge they were seen as recently as 1992.

On 14 October 1992, Christine Carolle-Dick, a sales assistant from Newcastle, was walking along the beach at South Shields when she suddenly saw something 'scuttle' amongst the rocks. Clambering over the boulders and rockpools towards what she suspected to be a large crab, she was astonished to see a small, perfectly-proportioned 'little man' – about nine inches in height, standing on top of a large rock. He was staring at her. He was dressed in a pair of green trousers and a matching jacket, and sported a bright red pointed cap on his head. After Christine and the man made eye contact they stared at each other for several seconds. Then, the diminutive, snazzily-dressed pixie – or whatever he was – scampered towards the cliff face and disappeared through a crack in the rock.

Christine did not subsequently mention her experience to anyone other than a few close friends and the authors, knowing full well that if she did she would either be ridiculed or pronounced mad.

'But I know what I saw,' she said with conviction. 'Stupid though it sounds.'

If 'familiars' – in whatever guise they come in – are able to exist independently of their human companions and even survive their death, then the bizarre creatures seen at Willington Mill could, theoretically, have been 'familiars' conjured up by the Willington Witch in the seventeenth century. Far-fetched though it may seem to some, it is an intriguing thought.

Haunting

There can be little doubt that Willington Mill and the mill house itself was haunted in some sense of the word. There are simply too many eyewitness testimonies to the fact for them to be either dismissed or ignored. The symptoms of a haunting are not easy to define. There is a perception amongst the general public that a haunted building is simply one in which a ghost has been seen, but the reality is that the situation is far more complex than that. In most haunted locations other symptoms present themselves beside the classical glimpses of opaque or semi-transparent anthropomorphic spirits. Some symptoms are nigh-identical to those identified in cases of poltergeistry, making it hard or even impossible to work out exactly what the phenomenon at work is or even whether there may actually be more than one phenomenon present. At Willington Mill a number of apparitions were spotted, but witnesses also testified to seeing 'shadows' that sometimes had a broadly human appearance, hearing anomalous sounds and voices, and catching a glimpse of ghosts that were not human-shaped but actually animal-like.

Just what or who are the ghosts of Willington Mill? Some, perhaps, are the spirits of people who lived, worked or died on the site, although as far as the authors know none of them have been conclusively connected with historically verifiable persons. Some have suggested that the 'grey lady' who so traumatised Dr Edward Drury may, in fact, have been the Willington Witch. As we shall see, there may be some substance to this argument.

Poltergeistry

The word poltergeist frightens many people, for they believe that a poltergeist is an evil spirit or demon who has chosen to wreak havoc upon the inhabitants of its dwelling place. The authors have written two books on the poltergeist phenomenon, and have been forced to take a far different view. This is not the correct place to engage in a full examination of the poltergeist enigma, but the authors believe that the poltergeist is a form of disruptive energy seated within a human host which can sometimes externalise itself. Upon doing so, it can move household objects, create bizarre sounds and, on occasion, even mimic human voices. All of these symptoms were witnessed at Willington Mill. However, a degree of caution needs to be exercised. There is a difference between symptoms which have their origin in poltergeistry and those which are merely poltergeist-like. To differentiate between the two, some researchers have begun to use the phrase 'pseudo-poltergeistry'. Pseudo-poltergeistry is where phenomena occur that superficially look like the work of a poltergeist but may not be.

The authors can say with confidence that there were certainly poltergeist-like phenomena occurring at the mill, but are not able to say with complete conviction that they were precipitated by a genuine poltergeist.

Cryptozoology

Cryptozoology is the study of unknown animals. Cryptids generally fall into three categories:

- Conventional flesh-and-blood creatures which have not yet been taxonomically classified.
- Conventional flesh-and-blood creatures which have been taxonomically classified but which appear in locations where they are not supposed to be (often called pseudo-cryptids).
- Bizarre creatures whose behaviour and nature are so odd that they demand to be viewed as something 'supernatural'.

The weird creatures seen at Willington Mill – putting to one side the 'witch's familiar' theory for a moment – could be slotted into all three categories, but the important question is, of course, what are they doing there?

The authors know for certain that witchcraft, ghosts, poltergeists and cryptozoological animals do exist. Over the decades they have investigated literally hundreds of cases in which these and other paranormal phenomena were present.

A Theory

When the authors started to investigate the Willington Mill case, their primary thoughts were upon the vigil carried out by Drury and Hudson well over a century ago. This was because that single incident, more than any other, captivated the media and raised the public consciousness regarding the whole affair. When people think of Willington Mill, they think of the doctor and the chemist sitting on the upper landing waiting pensively for the ghost to show itself.

As time went on, however, a larger, more complex picture started to take shape. Contrary to popular belief, it was not just the mill house that was haunted but also the mill itself and the surrounding environs. It seemed to the authors that the entire place was infected by a wide range of paranormal phenomena, not just one house playing host to one ghost.

Stead notes[5]:

> *Again it was like a donkey galloping round the room overhead; at another time it was as if a shovelful of scrappy iron had been thrown upon the fireplace and fender. It was very difficult to get servants to remain in the house. Heavy footsteps were heard going up and down stairs, door handles turned, doors creaked as if they were opening, occasionally the room would be filled with bluish smoke. Sticks would crackle as if they were burning, but when the closet door was opened no fire was to be seen. At other times it was as if newspapers were being crumpled and trampled about football fashion. On one occasion Mr Davidson's mother counted 120 taps on the wash-table, as if some one were striking it with a pencil.*

What was it about Willington Quay, then, and particularly the site of the mill, that could be responsible for the presence of so much paranormal activity?

Window Areas

The idea that certain places can be 'hot spots' or 'window areas' of paranormality is not a new one. Back in the 1970s, for example, the town of Warminster in Wiltshire became a veritable Mecca for UFO enthusiasts. In fact, so many sightings of peculiar aerial objects were made that the place gained the epithet of 'the UFO capital of the world'. Marsden Bay in South Shields is another such area, playing host to ghosts, sea monsters, elemental spirits and other weird phenomena to a breathtaking degree.

Richard Freeman is the Zoological Director of the Centre for Fortean Zoology in Devon, and one of the UK's leading experts on paranormal phenomena. He has a special interest in cryptozoology and has written several books about dragon lore.

The authors, therefore, decided to contact Richard and ask him whether he believed that the site of Willington Mill could perhaps, like Warminster, Marsden and elsewhere, be considered as a 'window area' of paranormality. We also took the opportunity to ask Richard to spell out exactly what a 'window area' is:

Firstly, we must ask ourselves if 'window areas' are creations of those who observe them. For example, at Warminster the UFO wave was well publicised and doubtless brought many interested people to the area; but those people would have come expecting to see something weird. Hence, eerie lights in the sky became flying saucers in the minds of those who saw them, just as every boat-wake or water bird on Loch Ness becomes a monster in the eyes of observers (although that is not to say there is not a genuine cryptid in the Loch).

This explanation would be popular with knee-jerk sceptics, but it falls down upon closer inspection. Many window areas are in places where the general public know nothing of odd events. As Mike and Darren have mentioned, Marsden Bay is once such place and plays host to a sea dragon, faeries, monster lobsters, poltergeists and ghosts to name but a few.

Another area is Falmouth Bay (note the association with water). Here we have Morgawr the sea serpent, the infamous Owlman, mystery big cats, ghosts, UFOs and other stuff that makes the works of Stephen King look like an episode of The Care Bears.

We can also mention other places, such as the Pine Barrens of New Jersey and the Nullabor Plain of Australia. In non-English speaking countries, too, there are probably many 'window areas' which Western researchers have never even heard of.

One thing I look out for in a potential window area is the occurrence – cheek in jowl – of two or more creatures of the 'global monster template'. These are animals that are repeatedly reported from all cultures around the world. They include dragons (sea serpents and monster snakes fall into this category, as well), hairy giants, little people, monster birds, monster cats and monster dogs. When you have two or more of these monsters manifesting alongside other Fortean phenomena, you have a window area.

But just what is a widow area? One idea is that it is an area were the barriers between dimensions are at their thinnest, allowing 'things' – as the late Ivan T. Sanderson would have called them – to slip through into our world.

Could the key to other dimensions be speed? We know that atoms vibrate at a certain rate. Could other worlds – or at least, other 'things' – occupy the same space if their atoms had a vibrational rate faster or slower than what we term as 'normal'? In a window area, the rate of oscillation might be speeded up or slowed down, allowing us to see 'things' in that other world and, inversely, the 'things' in that other world may well be able to see us.

Another idea is that a window area is a place that has a direct physical influence on the brain. The brain is essentially an electrochemical computer, and if some kind of energy field or other force can effect it, causing it to 're-boot' like a real computer, we might find ourselves going back to a primitive state and raising 'things' up from our collective subconscious or race memory.

Several million years ago, humans were small, hairy hominids on the plains of East Africa. They had to contend with predators like crocodiles, pythons, martial eagles, Cape hunting dogs, lions and leopards. They were in direct competition with other hominids – some larger, some smaller – and primates such as giant baboons. Volcanoes were also very active at that time. Think of it; monstrous beasts, giants and little people as well as disturbing fiery lights in the sky! Could some Fortean phenomena be age-old terrors from our primitive past? It has been suggested that the association of black with evil is due to our ancient fear of the dark when early humans were at a disadvantage against predators with night vision. Today, we have our bedrooms upstairs. Is this a hang-over from sleeping in trees to avoid the teeth and claws of flesh-eating beasts?

Maybe the 'window area' is a type of time machine; not a physical one like the Tardis in that wonderful programme Doctor Who, but a place that, at certain times, takes us back in time mentally, to an age when life was a savage struggle against nature.

Although it is generally recognised by paranormal researchers that 'window areas' or 'hot spots' exist, their nature is not particularly understood. Perhaps the best that can be said is that they are locations where clusters of paranormality occur. One common feature seems to be that witnesses often describe a complete change in the landscape around them. Typically, they will describe features that are no longer there, such as houses or farms, or assert that trees across the landscape seem to disappear. Even a cursory examination of such cases flags up the possibility that the experients might, as Richard Freeman postulates, have been seeing the landscape not as it now is, but as it once was, as though they had gone back in time.

Many years ago, Mike was firmly of the opinion that ghosts were not spirits or discarnate, sentient people, but simply moving images from the past that had somehow been captured by their environment and which could, under the right conditions, be 'replayed' to a modern audience. Further research, however, has shown that this 'one size fits all' solution does not explain a number of hauntings in which the witnesses actually interact with the ghosts and even – on rare occasions – have conversations with them. There are numerous cases in which the ghosts seemed to interact comfortably with the landscape or environment as it is now. The ghost of the Black Horse pub in West Boldon, Tyne & Wear, is a classic example.

The Black Horse is a delightful pub-cum-restaurant which has stood on its current location since the seventeenth century when it was built as a coaching inn. For years the pub has had a reputation for being haunted by a 'cavalier' with a pockmarked face who dresses in black clothes, knee-length leather boots, a wide-brimmed hat and a somewhat ostentatious ruffle. Mike detailed the story of the ghostly cavalier in his book *Ales & Spirits*[6], and in 2009 both Darren and Mike investigated the case further in their book *Ghost Taverns*[7]. The cavalier has been seen sitting, bizarrely, on a barstool with his elbows on the bar itself! It is as if the ghost is capable of interacting with our modern environment as well as his own. Perhaps the best we can say, then, is that sometimes our own time seems to collide with another period on the historical timeline, causing the two to temporarily interact with each other and thus precipitating some bizarre results. Could such 'time-slips' be responsible for the bizarre phenomena at Willington Quay? The evidence suggests that they very well might.

At Willington Mill, the apparitions almost always seemed oblivious to the presence of the flesh-and-blood residents. As detailed earlier, Mrs Hargrave saw an apparition uncommonly similar to that seen by Dr Edward Drury during the by-then infamous 'vigil'. She described the ghost as, 'the figure of a woman in a grey mantle, which came through the wall' of her room from the adjacent one. According to Mrs Hargrave the apparition drifted towards her bed before fading away. Curiously, she noticed that the feet of the ghost seemed to be about 3ft above the level of the floor.

It was as if the ghost was walking upon a floor that no longer existed. It is tempting to think that Mrs Hargrave had been granted a glimpse of a person who had lived and died many years previous to her encounter.

On 3 February 1837, Joseph Procter's sons were disturbed by what they described as 'a loud shriek', which seemed to come from the foot of the bed. Later, Joseph said his bed moved backwards and forwards and a voice by the foot of the bed said 'Chuck' twice. Other snippets of conversation and odd words, such as 'Never mind' and 'Come and get', were heard by young Joseph and other experients. As with the experience of Gerald Connor, it was as if odd words and phrases, dislocated from their original context, were being replayed at a later time.

The most common phenomenon which presented itself at Willington was that of anomalous sounds; footsteps walking across a floor in the room above, the sound of someone poking the fire, the typical kitchen noises made by the cook even when she wasn't there ... all of which could possibly be 'echoes' of real sounds made days, months or even years earlier.

Perhaps the most fascinating examples of potential timeslips at Willington can be found in the mystery animal or cryptozoological stories. When Mrs Hargrave saw the cat-like creature with a long snout at the rear of the mill she could not recognise it. According to one account, it actually walked through the wall of the mill into the machine room where it was also seen by Joseph Procter. Procter, stunned, gazed at the creature as it walked into the furnace room and quite literally disappeared into the flames.

The Procter children, as we know, on one occasion saw a monkey. Monkeys do not naturally inhabit the British Isles and there were none in private residences, zoos, circuses or menageries in the area. And yet, they saw it.

A 'donkey' was also seen by two employees[8]. The creature was, they said, 'quite small with short hair of a sand colour, although somewhat darker'. They also noticed that its nose, 'seemed to bow upwards in the middle, like a bump ... as we looked upon it, the donkey turned and passed through the door leading to the interior. At no time did it make any sounds that we could discern, not even the clopping of a hoof or a bray'.

What the men saw was obviously not a donkey, but they labelled it as such because a donkey may have been the nearest thing in size and shape that they could liken it to.

Earlier, the authors drew attention to the fact that the 'strange cat' seen by Hargrave and others looked uncannily like the Malaysian moonrat. The small, donkey-like creature seen grazing on grass that wasn't there by the two mill-workers sounds not unlike the prehistoric proto-horse merrychippus, some species of which had a convex snout similar to that sported by the creature spotted by Wedgwood and Middleton.

Merrychippus lived in the Miocene Period, between 11 and 18 million years ago.

Millions of years ago, before the advent of Homo sapiens on planet earth, our globe was teeming with myriad species of animal that are now extinct. For all we know, something akin to the moonrat may have inhabited our land in prehistoric times. It is not impossible that a large variety of merrychippus may have lived in what is now northern England.

The authors think it is significant that the vast majority of the phenomena experienced at Willington could fit into the 'timeslip' category comfortably; visual and auditory encounters with the near or distant past. Although some phenomena may be genuine hauntings and even demonstrations of poltergeistry, there is a very real possibility that many of the witnesses were seeing our world as it was in times gone by.

Before we leave the subject of the phenomena which presented themselves at Willington, it is important to detail what Joseph Procter thought about them. The authors do not dismiss out of hand his conclusions, although neither do they entirely agree with them. We have already seen how, in his diary, the mill owner asserts:

> *Those who deem all intrusion from the world of spirits impossible in the present constitution of things will feel assured that a natural solution of the difficulty will soon be obtained on further investigation; whilst those who believe with the poet 'that millions of spiritual creatures walk the earth unseen' and that, even in modern times, amidst a thousand creations of fancy, fear, fraud or superstition, there still remain some well-attested instances in which good or evil spirits have manifested their presence by invisible tokens, will deem it possible that this may be referred to the latter class – especially when they learn that several circumstances tending to corroborate such a view are withheld from this narrative.*

There is a strong hint here that Procter was seriously considering the idea that the phenomena at the mill house were being precipitated by demons. This seems to be supported by Edmund's comment:

> *My father never made any attempt to open up communication in this way; his experiences were prior to the time when modern developments of spiritualism made the lingo of the séance familiar to the public ear, and although he took an earnest interest in the subject, he never attended a séance and laid stress upon the application of the well-known text about 'seducing spirits and doctrines of demons'.*

According to his son Edmund, on one occasion, Procter, when witnessing some extraordinary phenomena in his own room, cried out, 'Begone! Thou wicked spirit!' – a clear indication that the man believed that the entity confronting him was demonic in nature. As Stead and others have recounted, the entity within the mill house would sometimes generate 'the most horrible laughs', which would also have made Procter think that it was demonic in nature.

As detailed earlier, Joseph Procter was said by Crowe, Howitt and others to have found 'an old book' in which he discovered the story of the Willington Witch. Crowe, we know, took a substantial portion of Howitt's work, with his permission, and wove it in to the text of her own work whilst clearly referencing Howitt as the source. Procter had read everything written by Crowe and Howitt on the 'Mill Ghost', and in February 1853 penned a letter to the editor of *Spiritual Magazine* in which he stated, 'In reply to thy inquiry about the accuracy of the narrative in the work referred to, I may state that the portion of it from p. 125 to p. 137 taken from *Richardson's Table Book*[9], a local antiquarian publication, was written by the late Dr Clanny, of Sunderland, and revised by myself before being printed, and is perfectly true and correct. In that other portion, derived from William Howitt's personal inquiries, there are trifling inaccuracies, yet not such as materially affect the nature of the facts referred to'.

Procter's other letters published in the *Spiritual Magazine* (*see* p. 89–90, 92, 98, 99, 200, 203, 204, 206, 209, 222, 224), show that three times, to the authors' knowledge, Procter acknowledges the accuracy of what Crowe and Howitt had said, but then he has a mysterious change of heart and alleges that the statement by Howitt regarding the witch's cottage was completely wrong. So concerned was Procter about this that he demanded a correction or retraction. 'It wasn't the witch's house, it was another house,' he said in essence. 'There was no house built on the same site as the mill – it never existed,' he argued.

On the surface it seems puzzling that Procter should have changed his mind so radically and become upset at such a trifling detail. Whether there was a house built on the site previously or not was an issue which had no impact upon the veracity of the haunting of the mill during Procter's lifetime. The answer, the authors believe, lies in part in Joseph Procter's deep-seated religious convictions and his conclusion that the entities inhabiting the site were of a demonic or devilish nature. It has already been pointed out earlier that witches were believed to have 'familiars'; spirits in animal guise who went about the bidding of their master or mistress. Procter, the authors think, felt uncomfortable about admitting to the presence of the witch's cottage on the exact location of the mill, for such an idea only served to strengthen what he was already being coerced to believe; namely, that the strange animals seen on the site were quite literally devils in disguise.

William Stead reiterates this[10]:

> *On another occasion the spirit made itself so fearfully palpable in Mr Proctor's bedroom, that he adjured it in the following words: — 'If thou art a good spirit, why not stay in thy own place? If thou art a bad spirit why torment me and my house?'*
>
> *With a great noise the spirit took its departure for that night. Next night, however, it was as busy as ever.*

It seems that the miller found this notion too horrible to contemplate, and, quite simply, engaged in an exercise of self-delusion. He denied the truthfulness of Howitt's statement not because it was inaccurate, but because it troubled him deeply to think it might be true.

Even today there are authors who seem to mirror Procter's concern that sentient entities might have actually been consciously attempting to let the householders know that they were there. Perhaps they were. Liddell, for instance[11], states that, 'In 1800, when the mansion was built, the ghosts *tried harder* to make their presence known' (italics ours). How, though, can we know they 'tried harder' from 1800 onwards, when there is a complete dearth of information regarding how hard they supposedly tried before? Unfortunately Liddell doesn't give us any contextual material to work with and his statement goes completely unsupported.

Veteran researcher Harry Price, on the other hand, rigorously avoids subjective interpretation and leans towards the idea that the phenomena at Willington were essentially demonstrations of poltergeistry[12]. Although Price's account is brief, he carefully draws attention to both the similarities and differences between the Willington case and others such as Borley Rectory and Ballechin House.

The evidence suggests overwhelmingly that it was not just the mill house that was haunted, but also the mill itself and the surrounding grounds. Gauld and Cornell[13] state that, 'the case is commonly, but somewhat misleadingly, referred to as that of "Willington Mill". This is likely because the vast majority of available material on the Willington case deals exclusively with the supernatural phenomena within the house itself, but as the authors have ably demonstrated it is simply not the case that the house alone was affected.'

Some of the phenomena at the mill house were so bizarre that they defy categorisation. The following example, recounted by Stead[14], although somewhat poltergeist-like, is a good example for it could also be seen as a cryptozoological incident:

> *Mr Davidson's sister-in-law had, as the authors have already detailed, a curious experience on one occasion: 'One evening she was putting one of the bedrooms right, and looking towards the dressing-table, she saw what she supposed was a white towel lying on the ground. She went to pick it up, but imagine her surprise when she found that it rose up, and went up behind the dressing-table over the top, down on the floor across the room, disappeared under the door, and was heard to descend the stairs with a heavy step. The noise which it made in doing so was distinctly heard by Mr Proctor [sic] and others in the house.*

Was the object an animated towel, or had the woman had yet another encounter with the mystery cat-like animal seen by Mrs Hargrave?

Stead[15] relates a circumstance which might lend support to the poltergeist theory:

> *The last time the apparition was seen was quite recently, and I well remember the story being told at Sunday School by my scholars. It was long after the Proctors [sic] had left the mill, and the manifestations, it was noticed, were always worst when a member of the Proctor [sic] family was on the premises.*

Darren laments the dearth of factual information regarding the Willington Mill case[16], even in published works specifically dealing with the affair, but adds the caveat that, 'although they do not relay the full story … they give a good idea of the types of phenomena witnessed at the mill house at Willington'.

Much, it seems, is yet to be said about the ghosts of Willington Mill.

Notes

1. Crowe, Catherine, *The Night Side of Nature, or, Ghosts and Ghost Seers, Vol. II* (T.C. Newby, 1848)
2. Summers, Montague, *The Geography of Witchcraft* (London, 1926)
3. *Country Folk-Lore*, Vol. 4 (The Folk-Lore Society, 1903)
4. Bath, Jo, *Dancing With the Devil and Other True Tales of Northern Witchcraft* (Tyne Bridge Publishing, 2002)
5. Stead, William T., *Real Ghost Stories* (Grant Richards, 1897)
6. Hallowell, Michael J., *Ales & Spirits – The Haunted Pubs & Inns of South Tyneside* (Peoples Press, 2001)

7. Ritson, Darren W. & Hallowell, Michael J., *Ghost Taverns* (Amberley Publishing, 2009)

8. Anon, *The Willington Quay Ghost* (Privately published, *c.* 1972)

9. Richardson, Moses Aaron, *The Local Historian's Table Book Vol. VI* (M.A. Richardson, 1847)

10. Stead, William T., *Real Ghost Stories* (Grant Richards, 1897)

11. Liddell, Tony, *Otherworld North East: Ghosts and Hauntings Explored* (Tyne Bridge Publishing, 2004)

12. Price, Harry, *Poltergeists Over England* (Country Life Ltd, 1945)

13. Gauld, Alan & Cornell, Tony, *Poltergeists* (Routledge & Kegan Paul, 1979)

14. Stead, William T., *Real Ghost Stories* (Grant Richards, 1897)

15. *Ibid.*

16. Ritson, Darren W., *Supernatural North* (Amberley Publishing, 2009)

Nineteen

THE STONE IN
THE CELLAR

Some of the untruths told by Unthank and Procter are understandable and have already been explained. Unfortunately, as we shall see, some of the things they covered up really mattered.

The Cellar that Never Wasn't

In his work *The Local Historian's Table Book*[1], Moses Richardson comments:

> *We have visited the house in question, which is well known to many of our readers as being near a large, steam corn-mill, in full view of Willington viaduct, on the Newcastle and Shields Railway; and it may not be irrelevant to mention that it is quite detached from the mill, or any other premises, and has no cellaring under it.*

Crowe[2], Howitt[3] and others – some using Richardson as their source, others not – all consistently state that the mill house did not have a cellar. Even the *Journal of the Society for Psychical Research*[4], in an article on the Willington affair, has Richardson's words quoted above as an appendix.

Neither Unthank nor Procter ever contradicted this notion. Of course, they wouldn't have had any need to contradict it had it been true, but the simple fact is it wasn't true at all. The mill house did have a cellar. Procter, we know, kept well up to date with everything written about the Willington haunting, and from his writings it is clear that the works of the above authors – apart from Stead's, which were written after Procter's death – were well-known to him. Why, then, did he not put the record straight? We do not know where Richardson and others got the idea from that there was no cellar in the mill house, but it is obvious that someone must have told them that. The likelihood is that it was Procter himself.

At some point, Procter called in a team of labourers and, as Stead[5], relates, 'caused excavations to be made in the cellar'. Alas, according to later reports, including those written by Stead, 'they found nothing'.

Stead's words are illuminating, however, for they tell us something about Procter's motive. Had the excavation been something to do with renovation or internal remodelling, then there would be no conundrum. But to say that the builders 'found nothing' implies that the purpose of the excavation was to look for something. Just what this might have been is something we will discuss presently.

However, within days, word spread around Willington that the labourers had found much more than 'nothing'. Stead explains that, 'when the men dug down to a certain depth they came upon a huge stone or slab, beneath which they believed the mystery lay'.

At no point immediately after this strange excavation did Procter ever deny that it had taken place. If no such excavation had taken place, then surely Procter would have denied it. Procter consistently refused to promote or even allow tittle-tattle within his own household about the haunting and dismissed staff on the spot for doing so. We have seen that although admitting to the haunting freely, he continually rebuffed requests for further information other than that he had already divulged, 'feeling averse to add to the publicity the circumstances occurring in his house, at Willington, have already obtained, J.P. would rather not furnish additional particulars'[6]. Later, however, the rumours became so bad that Procter was forced to make a denial after all, although he seems to have done so in couched terms: 'I have an impression,' says Stead[7], 'that Mr Proctor denies the truth of this story. If so, there is not even a shadow of a clue to the solution of the mystery'.

Just why Procter would have wanted to deny he had a cellar in the first place, then excavate it anyway, is something that the authors were determined to find out.

It seems that at some point in the excavation the labourers found what they were looking for; a 'stone slab' undoubtedly buried under the cellar floor. One would imagine that Procter would at this point have urged the workers on and asked them to remove the slab itself so that they could find 'the mystery' beneath the stone. But Procter did not. As soon as the slab was laid bare he asked the labourers to down tools. Suddenly, the miller had a revelation that to carry on excavating further would, as Stead puts it, 'endanger the foundation of the mill'.

This latter fact only adds to the mystery, as the cellar the labourers were excavating was not under the mill at all – which was a separate building, divorced from the mill house by a 'cartway' – but under the mill house.

When the authors first read about this incident, they concluded a number of things. Procter, they believe, knew all along what was under the stone, and never had any intentions of allowing the labourers to remove it. All he wanted them to do was make it accessible. The authors still believe that this was the case. Procter's claim that further excavation might 'endanger the foundations of the mill' was merely an excuse to explain his sudden desire to end the exercise abruptly. However, evidence would subsequently come to light that there might actually have been some truth in the miller's assertion, although this would only serve to make an already baffling enigma even more complex.

What was the 'mystery' hidden beneath the stone slab? Stead, like others, eventually tired of trying to 'join up the dots' and concluded, 'and so the mystery remains unsolved to this day'[8]. As already stated, Stead added, 'I have an impression that Mr Proctor denies the truth of this story. If so, there is not even a shadow of a clue to the solution of the mystery'.

Somehow, Stead seems to be suggesting that solving the mystery depended on Procter admitting that he (a) knew about the stone slab in the cellar, and (b) had indeed attempted to have the cellar excavated.

Before we focus upon 'the mystery' under the stone in the cellar and just what it might have been, we need to return momentarily to the issue of who first occupied the flour mill at Willington. In Chapter Three, the authors demonstrated that it was the family of William Brown who occupied the mill house in the year 1800. The Unthank family did not move into the mill until the year 1806, meaning that for at least five years others lived there before them. We now know who it was that 'warned' Joseph Unthank that the house was haunted; it was none other than his business partner, William Brown.

Throughout this book the authors have insisted that, despite all protestations to the contrary, George Unthank simply must have experienced supernatural phenomena himself at the mill house.

Davidson, in fact, claims that the haunting phenomena at the mill house were so bad that the Procters and the Unthanks came to an arrangement whereby, every four years, they would swap homes to give each family a respite from the disturbing occurrences. This seems strange indeed. If the phenomena were that intense, then four years would seem like an eternity. Nevertheless, Davidson's assertion is not without support. Stephenson Haggie, whose family owned the nearby rope factory, commented that the Unthank and Procter families 'occupied the mill house turn and turn about' because of the 'manifestations, whether of sound or sight'[9].

For just how long this arrangement went on we do not know. The almost unanimous perception of historians is that the Unthanks lived at the mill house for twenty-five years without intermission, and both George Unthank and Joseph Procter made statements that would lead one to think that that had indeed been the case. However, Davidson offers an intriguing clue that the arrangement may have continued for quite some time, even after Joseph Procter officially moved into the residence in 1831.

Procter, we know, married in the same year that he and his new bride moved in to the mill house. However, Davidson states, 'While living in *North Shields*, Mrs Procter [Elizabeth, Joseph's wife] engaged a new servant named Mary Young. This girl *came with the family to Willington*, and remained in the service of Mrs Procter eight years' (italics ours).

Davidson was in a good position to know, as Mary Young was his own mother. It is clear then that for at least one period whilst the Procters were supposed to be living at Willington they were actually living in North Shields. What makes this so interesting is that neither the Procters nor the Unthanks, to the authors' knowledge, ever admitted to this arrangement and few writers other than Davidson and Haggie seem to have been aware of it. Of course, this arrangement could also explain why there are curious gaps – sometimes lengthy ones – in Procter's diary of events. Likely, he simply wasn't there to see what was going on.

Although this four-yearly exchange arrangement seems to have been utilised occasionally, it is unlikely that it was adhered to strictly. Had it been, then between 1806 and 1847, when the Procters vacated the premises, there would have been no less than ten 'swaps' between the two families. This would have put George Unthank in the ridiculous position of having to argue that during his five stays in the building nothing paranormal occurred, whilst during the five stays of the Procter family there were ghosts leaping out around every corner! Had this been the case, then Procter would have realised far earlier that his cousin was lying to him when he said that he had no personal knowledge of any supernatural occurrences.

Having established that the very first residents of the mill were members of the Brown family, we can now return to our examination of just what the 'mystery' was under the stone slab in the cellar. We have already seen how, from the time the mill was first built, it had a reputation for being haunted. We also know that there were rumours that a murder had been committed on the site, possibly within the mill house itself. After some time a second rumour took hold; specifically that the murder had been committed by 'a worker' who had been engaged in the building of the mill and mill house. Curiously, no victim was ever identified or found, and no perpetrator, alleged or real, ever arrested. In fact, nothing was ever brought forth to indicate that such an event had ever taken place in the first place.

But there's no smoke without fire, as they say, and it seems to the authors that something must have precipitated these stories. At this juncture the authors would like to propose an interesting hypothesis. Supposing that a murder had been committed at the mill house, then the absence of a body would indicate that it must have been hidden somewhere. Could it be that the murderer hid his victim's body in the cellar under the aforementioned large, stone slab? In a way, this would have been the ideal place. The authorities would have been extremely reluctant to embarrass three influential families like the Browns, Unthanks and Procters by tearing up the cellar floor of the mill house whilst searching for a body that might not even be there.

At some point, however, we know that, during his residency, Joseph Procter became aware of the stone in the cellar and the fact that it covered up, quite literally, a grisly secret. This, the authors are sure, is why he decided to have it excavated. But several questions present themselves here. If Procter, an outstanding, devoutly-religious citizen, eventually came to realise that there was a body buried in his cellar why didn't he immediately declare what he knew to a local magistrate? After all, he wasn't (and couldn't have been) the murderer. Surely his Quaker conscience would have overridden any fears he had about bad publicity and a media frenzy? And yet Procter remained suspiciously silent about what he knew, even to the point of denying that there was a cellar in his home at all. Before we focus upon just why Procter tried to keep what he knew hidden, we can take the opportunity to see how his desire to do so explains some rather strange things about his behaviour in the years he lived at the mill house.

We know, for example, that he was unusually touchy about the idea that there had been a witch living in a cottage on the very same site as his home 200 years previously. At first he admitted it, but then he came to deny it. Of course, if Procter knew that a body was buried in the cellar this becomes perfectly understandable. It is just possible that, deeply troubled by what he knew, he wanted to deflect as much attention as possible away from his home and what lay beneath it. The last thing he would have wanted is for his house to become an even larger centre of curiosity – something that juicy stories of 'notorious' witches and curses would guarantee.

We also know that Procter omitted many accounts from his diary – even ones that strongly supported the veracity of what eyewitnesses were seeing. As we shall see in a later chapter, these missing accounts may well have drawn attention to the family and its home in a way that even the sturdy Procter would have had trouble coping with.

But why, then, did the miller openly admit that he lived in a haunted house? Surely, history testifies that this brought upon him all the attention and more that he was so desperately trying to avoid? This is not so puzzling as it may seem. Procter admitted that no less than thirty witnesses had seen apparitions or experienced other bizarre phenomena in his home. Later he revised this figure to forty. Denying that his house was haunted would have been a fruitless task. It would have been ludicrous for Joseph Procter to deny something that dozens of upright acquaintances would be willing to testify to. He had no choice, then, but to admit to living in a haunted house, but, having done that and graciously accepted the degree of publicity that went with it, he then made sure he did nothing that would exacerbate the situation even further.

As far as the authors can see, there is only one reason why Joseph Procter would have desired to keep the 'mystery in the cellar' a secret: the murderer was not a 'workman' engaged with the building of the mill house at all, but someone very close to the Procter family. It may even have been one of the Procters or Unthanks themselves, although as the Browns were living on the premises they would be more logical suspects. This is only a hypothesis, however, and the authors do not want to cast aspersions of homicide towards people who may well have been entirely innocent. Perhaps the best we can say is that a murder seems to have taken place at the mill on or around the year 1800, and that someone closely connected to the mill house may have been responsible for it.

Another question that arises is why Joseph Procter decided to have the cellar excavated. We know that he suddenly told the workmen to 'down tools' as soon as the stone slab was uncovered. Procter did not need them to lift it up to see what was underneath it. He already knew. Likely, he wanted the stone excavated so that, at some future time, he could lift it up himself and, perhaps, dispose of the body underneath. This would not assuage his guilt at having covered up what he knew, but it would relieve him of the burden of worrying that, at some future time, the body could be discovered by others. What would have happened then? Could allegations have even been levelled against Procter himself that he might have murdered someone and hid the corpse under the slab? It isn't

Site of the mill house and its cellar – a possible burial site for at least one murder victim. (Darren W. Ritson)

A view of the potential burial site from the window of the mill factory, upper floor. (Darren W. Ritson)

impossible. Probably, then, Procter disposed of the body – perhaps even giving the victim a decent but anonymous burial.

Much of what the authors have presented in this chapter is hypothetical, and they would be the first to admit it. However, these hypotheses are the only ones that seem to make sense of so much of the Willington mystery; the absence of any detailed historical information about the first tenants of the mill house, the weird references to stone slabs, hidden cellars and rumours of murder most foul … all of these things, when put together, paint a largely hypothetical scenario, but one which, like no other, seems to fit the facts.

But there is one, final enigma regarding the stone in the cellar. As previously noted, Stead explained that, 'when the men dug down to a certain depth they came upon a huge stone or slab, beneath which they believed the mystery lay'[10].

It is tempting to believe that the 'mystery' was a cryptic reference to the alleged body underneath, and that what would be solved would be the 'mystery' regarding whether or not a murder had really taken place on the site when the mill house was first built. However, the 'mystery' may have encompassed far more than a nineteenth-century 'whodunnit'. It may have been intrinsically tied up with the entire panoply of paranormal phenomena presenting themselves at Willington Mill.

Soon, the authors would discover evidence that their hypotheses regarding the alleged murder at the mill carried far more weight than anyone had hitherto realised.

Notes
1. Richardson, Moses Aaron, *The Local Historian's Table Book Vol. VI* (M.A. Richardson, 1847)
2. Crowe, Catherine, *The Night Side of Nature, or, Ghosts and Ghost Seers, Vol. II* (T.C. Newby, 1848)
3. Howitt, William, *Visits to Remarkable Places; Old Walls, Battle Fields, and Scenes Illustrative of Striking Passages in English History and Poetry* (Longman, Orme, Brown, Green & Longman, 1840)
4. *Journal of the Society for Psychical Research* (December, 1892)
5. Stead, William T., *Real Ghost Stories* (Grant Richards, 1897)
6. Crowe, Catherine, *The Night Side of Nature, or, Ghosts and Ghost Seers, Vol. II* (T.C. Newby, 1848)
7. Stead, William T., *Real Ghost Stories* (Grant Richards, 1897)
8. *Ibid.*
9. Davidson, Robert, *The True Story of the Willington Ghost* (Robert Davidson, c. 1886)
10. Stead, William T., *Real Ghost Stories* (Grant Richards, 1897)

Twenty

REVELATIONS

During their investigations, Darren and Mike made efforts to accumulate as much information about Willington Mill as they could. At the end of June 2009, Darren rang the newly-rebuilt Newcastle-upon-Tyne Central Library and asked them if they kept a file on Willington Quay. The librarian said they didn't have much on Willington Quay, but they were in possession of a book by Robert Davidson called *The True Story of the Willington Ghost*[1]. This got the two authors excited, for they knew that Robert Davidson was none other than the son of Mary Young and Thomas Davidson, both of whom had endured very close encounters with the entities at the mill.

The book was 19cm in length and 8cm in width and not much larger than a pocket diary. On the jet-black cover, in gold lettering, were the words, *The True Story of the Willington Ghost* – Robert Davidson.

On the inside cover was simply a piece of white pasteboard covered in paper, opposite which was a black page. Upon it was glued a small, yellowing piece of paper bearing the printed words, 'WILLINGTON GHOST By Robert Davidson, Rosehill.'

Rosehill, for those who do not know, was the area in North Tyneside in which Davidson lived. Each page thereafter contained portions of columns cut from copies of the *Newcastle Leader* which had been carefully glued in place. This was not a printed tome so much as it was a scrapbook of cuttings. Nevertheless, it contained the complete testimony of Davidson regarding what he knew about the Willington haunting – and much more.

The authors began to re-examine the evidence surrounding the potential murder. Both realised that they seemed to be missing something. There was the historical puzzle regarding the supposed killing, and then there were the supernatural ones involving ghosts, mystery animals and other bizarre occurrences. It seemed to the investigators that the two enigmas were essentially separate, and yet a nagging feeling that both were inextricably intertwined just refused to go away.

The authors re-examined the testimonies of Thomas Hudson and Dr Edward Drury who had carried out the vigil. What had it all meant? Working on the reasonably safe presumption that the former hadn't mesmerised the latter, and that Drury really had seen a ghost, who was it? And why was she clutching her breast? Further, why had she pointed at Hudson and attempted to place her hand upon his head before pointing to the floor itself?

What if the apparition was that of the murder victim? What if she was trying to communicate something to the two men, particularly Hudson? This startling realisation immediately made the authors scrutinise Drury's account once again for clues.

The first clue seemed to be connected to the fact that the woman was clutching her breast with her hand and seemed to be in pain. Was she attempting to communicate something about the manner in which she had died? Had she been shot, or more likely stabbed?

The difficult question was why she seemed to focus more upon the dozing chemist Hudson instead of the doctor. Was there something about the chemist – his life, his beliefs, his circumstances – that made him the natural target of her attention? Despite hours of deliberation, there seemed to be nothing of relevance in any of them. Then the authors wondered if it was simply Hudson's personality that had attracted her. If she was attempting to communicate something of importance, did she believe that Hudson was the better option between the two men? We may never know.

The final clue, the authors concluded, came with the fact that the woman seemed to be pointing down towards the floor, possibly indicting that she was buried beneath the building.

It was an intriguing thought that the ghost of a long-dead murder victim may have been calling out for justice from beyond the grave. More, the victim's body may literally have been lying under that stone slab in the cellar whilst Hudson and Drury were carrying out their vigil several floors above.

Could the other female apparitions seen at the mill house have been of the same woman? What about the woman without eyes who had been seen sitting on a bed, in a chair and in a number of other places? They could, of course, have been different personages, but it was also possible that they had been one and the same.

The old tales of a murder being carried out on the premises, the evidence that a dark secret had been buried under a slab in the cellar, the behaviour of the apparition towards Drury and Hudson ... all these things and more pointed clearly to a solid link between the historical enigma and the supernatural one. However, the authors felt they needed supportive evidence; but how on earth could they get it? How could they prove that over two centuries ago the ghost of an old flour mill was also the spirit of a homicide victim? Before long, an answer was to come echoing down the corridors of history.

Notes

1. Davidson, Robert; *The True Story of the Willington Ghost* (Robert Davidson, c. 1886)

Twenty-One

MAKING CONTACT

Eleanor Mildred Balfour came into this world, and more precisely West Lothian, in Scotland, in the year 1845. She grew to be witty, forthright, a social campaigner and an educationalist. Eleanor could afford to be outspoken, as her family was one of the most influential in the UK. Her brother, Arthur, went on to become Prime Minister.

Eleanor's younger brother Frank Maitland Balfour was killed tragically whilst attempting to climb Mont Blanc. Frank had been a genius; a gifted biologist, many believed he was the one to inherit the mantle of none other than Charles Darwin. To what degree Frank's death influenced his sister to take an interest in psychical research, the supernatural and the concept of 'life beyond the grave', the authors cannot say.

Eventually Eleanor fell in love with Henry Sidgwick, and the two eventually married. Sidgwick convinced Eleanor to become a champion of women's rights, a cause which she took up with gusto. She also went on to become a leading light in the Society for Psychical Research (SPR), her husband, of course, having been one of its founders. Eleanor was also destined, although she did not realise it at the time, to play a pivotal part in the outworking of one of England's most notorious hauntings – that of Willington Mill.

There lived, in Durham City, 16 miles south of Willington, a family. We know nothing about its members save two things; the father was a pitman and the mother, Jane, was an insomniac with incredible abilities as a clairvoyant. Also operating out of Durham City at that time was a doctor, whose identity was kept secret by the Society for Psychical Research. In subsequent writings he is simply called, 'Dr F'. Before we go on to examine the doctor's part in the affair, the authors think it appropriate to state, for the first time in over a century, just who 'Dr F' really was. Although efforts were made to maintain his anonymity in SPR publications, it is little recognised that he was actually identified in Volume 7 of the *Proceedings of the Society for Psychical Research*, p.88.

John Trotter was born in 1796, the son and only child of John and
Margaret Trotter. On reaching maturity John Trotter Jr married
Marianne Fawcett of Newton Hall, who was the daughter of the
distinguished Revd John Fawcett, MA. In 1819 he entered Edinburgh
University to study medicine, and left that establishment very well
qualified indeed, although curiously he never became an 'MD', and
only had that distinction conferred upon him honourably in 1863. After
distinguishing himself as a skilled physician in numerous Edinburgh
hospitals, Trotter moved to Durham City where he took up a senior
post at the Durham Infirmary (later to become the Durham County
Hospital). He soon became the senior doctor at the hospital as well as
running his own practice at 53 Old Elvet, also in Durham City.

When Trotter passed away on 3 October 1875, the entire city went
into mourning and the cathedral bells were tolled in his honour. The
Durham Directory for 1875 lamented:

> *In the death of Dr Trotter, the city has lost one who, during a long and useful
> professional career, did a large amount of good, more particularly among the
> poorer class, by whom his medical skill both as a physician and surgeon, was
> held in the highest repute. The greater part of his life was spent in our midst,
> doing good wherever and whenever called upon, alike in the daytime as at night.*

Jane was a 'poorer class' patient of Dr F., and in the year 1845 consulted
him about her inability to sleep soundly. Dr F. decided to hypnotise Jane
in an effort to treat her condition, and it was during these sessions that
her clairvoyant abilities came to the fore.

Now it so happened that Jane had 'one or two relatives' who had
been employed as domestics by a local family. The family is never
specifically identified in contemporary literature, but we know that
in the familial group were several prominent figures, including the
Revd C. Green. Within this family was none other than the Revd T.
Myers, of Twinstead Rectory, Sudbury, who happened to be a cousin of
Frederic Myers – another founding member of the SPR. Tales of Jane's
clairvoyancy eventually filtered back to Myers, who was intrigued. With
the collaboration of Dr F. Myers, Revd Green and others, a log was kept
of the visions Jane had experienced whilst mesmerised.

Seemingly, Jane had little or no recollection of her clairvoyant
experiences when brought back to consciousness and therefore
had discussed them with only a handful of people. However, when
hypnotised she would begin to talk in a childlike manner and, with

a little encouragement, 'travel' to places near and far. Whenever the elements of her psychic wanderings were compared with the known historical facts, they invariably turned out to be accurate. Whatever he might have initially thought about Jane's psychic abilities, Frederic Myers had no doubts about the woman's integrity. Of this he commented, 'This good woman never received any fee, and never made any exhibition of her powers, fearing to be suspected of being a witch'[1].

Eventually her clairvoyant talents impressed him just as much, for he also said, 'How many rare and invaluable talents have thus been lost to the world! Dr F. mesmerised her for sleeplessness, and discovered that, when in the mesmeric state, she was wonderfully clairvoyant'[2].

Myers, during his investigations, found no evidence whatsoever that Jane was play-acting: 'There was,' he said, 'an entire absence of the motives which may often prompt to the simulation of clairvoyance; and although the fragmentariness of these records is very unsatisfactory, it may be remarked, on the other hand, that it would be difficult to imagine a case in which the faculty was less desired by its possessor, or less wondered at by its observers'.

Stead describes Jane as, 'a remarkably refined woman, sweet and gentle-looking, with delicately cut features, and wavy dark hair. She was very religious, conscientious, and resigned'[3].

With each passing session, Jane increasingly engaged in something that modern parapsychologists would probably term 'remote viewing'; that is, the ability to go into an altered state of consciousness and mentally 'journey' to anywhere in the world. Some of the places Jane 'visited' were, according to Stead[4], 'the interior of St Paul's, the building of St Peter's in Rome [and] the tent of Dr Livingstone in Africa'.

To some, Stead's comment would seem almost laughably naïve. Even in the mid-nineteenth-century images of the interior of St Paul's Cathedral and St Peter's Basilica were easy to come by, and the appearance of the interior of 'the tent of Dr Livingstone', would be something impossible to verify. However, Jane also demonstrated an ability to accurately describe other, obscure places of which she almost certainly had no knowledge.

According to Stead, Jane, 'when liberated by the mesmeric sleep, was quite a different personality. She always spoke when in trance of her body as "we's girl", regarding her as something quite distinct from herself, who troubles her to give her pains in her side and face, for Jane suffered from very bad health. Her body was without feeling when in the sleep. She could read the thoughts of those present, and, when tired, would read what she saw in the mind of the mesmeriser instead of taking the usual journeys to which he was wishing her'.

Just how Jane came to psychically 'visit' the inside of Willington Mill, and the adjacent mill house, is an intriguing story in itself.

During one experiment[5], Dr F. was interrupted when a man called at his surgery and asked to see him. Dr F. recalls, 'At this stage I was called out, and Mr P., a gentleman belonging to the Society of Friends, wished me to accompany him to see his son, who had returned from Carlisle after taking chloroform during the extraction of some teeth'.

At this juncture the doctor left the consulting room after asking a female observer to stand in for him till he returned. As soon as Dr F. had departed, Jane complained angrily to his assistant about his leaving her, and insisted in 'following him' clairvoyantly.

We are not told whether the son of 'Mr P.' was located nearby, or whether Dr F. arranged to visit him later, but in any event it seems that he returned to the consulting room in a short while. Jane then started to tell the doctor what she had 'seen' as, psychically, she had accompanied him and Mr P.:

> She [had] found me, she said, with a gentleman with a broad-brimmed hat who was remarking, 'thou knowest it'. She next described the young gentleman [Mr P's son] ill from the effects of some stuff which had been given to him by a person along a railway, a long way off, which had done him harm, and that the person fancied himself a great man, but was not one, and should not meddle with such things. She saw the room, and one lady standing over him, and recognised two other young ladies she had before seen, asking how she had got there. This was all correct, except I do not remember Mr P. using the expression above named.

A close reading of the doctor's account throws up some facts which are, to put it mildly, quite extraordinary.

Firstly, anyone who has read this book carefully so far will have realised that the 'Mr P.' who dropped into Dr F.'s surgery that day was none other than Joseph Procter.

Secondly, although Jane never left the consulting room, she clairvoyantly ascertained information about the incident involving Procter's son that she simply could not have gained by conventional means.

However, the third and most telling point is that Jane had, at the point where the youngster was being treated by a dentist 'along a railway, a long way off', journeyed there clairvoyantly and actually observed his teeth being extracted. The most mind-boggling aspect of this is that the dental treatment on Procter's son had been carried out before the miller even arrived in Durham. Jane, then, seems to have gone back in time to the point where the operation took place and actually watched it happen! If this wasn't breathtaking enough, she states that in the room there was a woman 'standing over him [the boy] and two other ladies she had before seen'.

It seems likely that the person 'standing over' the child was one of the dentist's assistants, whereas the other two were relatives who had accompanied him back from Carlisle. These latter two women, Dr F. asserts, could actually see Jane and promptly asked her 'how she had got there'.

Apart from the sentence supposedly uttered by Procter in the doctor's presence – 'Thou knowest it' – Dr F. asserts that everything seen by Jane was 'all correct'. We can deduce from this that the doctor must have subsequently checked – probably with Procter – (a) whether Jane's account was true, and (b) whether, when his son was having his teeth extracted, a mysterious woman had suddenly appeared in the room. It is hard to see how such an extraordinary event could have been faked.

The one troubling aspect of the account is the fact that Jane candidly admitted that she recognised the 'two young women' accompanying the young Master Procter on his journey from Carlisle. This indicates, at least superficially, that she had personally met with members of the Procter family previously. For some reason this does not seem to have troubled the SPR researchers, but we cannot imagine that they would not have been aware of it. Seemingly, they must have discussed the matter and subsequently discounted it. There may be a good reason for this, even if we cannot now fathom it, for the later testimony of the researchers is unanimous that she had no knowledge of the Procter family or their residence at Willington Mill. Perhaps Jane had 'seen' the women previously not in the flesh, but in another one of her clairvoyant trances. Readers will have to make up their own minds as to what degree this aspect of the story impacts upon its veracity, if at all.

It seems that Dr F., obviously impressed by all of this, also knew of the notorious haunting at Willington Mill and wondered if Jane's clairvoyant abilities could again be put to the test. He arranged for another session to be held on 14 July 1853, during which she would be 'mesmerised'. What follows is a transcript of the dialogue which took place between them both. According to the doctor, he 'was determined on this occasion to give her no leading questions and at the same time in no manner to cheat or deceive her'. Dr F. then put Jane into a hypnotic trance and initiated what would prove to be an incredible dialogue[6]. Doctor Trotter is hitherto referred to by his pseudonymous F, and Jane simply as J:

F: We are on a railway, and can see a large building like a mill; where is it?

J: Is it a mill for grinding food?

F: Yes. Can you find by what means the mill is made to work? Is it a wind-mill?

J: No.

F: Is it the water that turns the mill?

J: No. It is a steam-mill.

F: May we go into the mill?

J: [The doctor interjects here, 'Upon my giving her leave, she described the noise of the machinery, the flour-dust falling like snow, the miller, in white, standing by a 'poke', and was proceeding in her account of the interior of the building when I stopped her, and told her to leave the mill and enter the house near it'.]

J: Is it a small house?

F: No. [Dr F. then tells her it is 'the larger house' he wishes her to look into'.]

J: Is it this with the garden in front?

F: Yes, with the large garden.

J: No, the garden is a small one, and just in front of the house. May we go in? [The doctor here clarifies, 'I was [then] under the false impression that the garden was of considerable size'].

F: [The doctor adds, 'She said a gentleman lived in the house, but directly afterwards corrected herself, and remarked that he was not a gentleman, but that a gentleman had formerly lived in it. She now seemed very much puzzled, her face accurately expressing the perplexity of her mind.'].

F: Why did the gentleman leave this pretty house?

J: There is something very strange about this house. I can't understand this. Can we not tell we what it is that is so strange here?

F: Can we not tell we why this gentleman went away?

J: Oh, yes; it is something about a lady. Can it be this gentleman's wife who died here, and thus caused him to leave it?

F: [Dr F. notes, 'All these questions she asked rapidly and in an excited manner, very different from her ordinary, calm bearing when in the mesmeric state'].

J: Now we see it is not this gentleman's wife, for she is alive; it was a vision that frightened him away. The lady was only a vision. Do we believe in

visions? We don't like to believe in visions, do we? Tell we why the vision
came to the gentleman. Had he done anything wicked to the lady?

F: [Dr F. interjects, 'I now told her that I brought her to that house for
the purpose of finding out why the lady haunted that house, and she
must not be lazy, but find out the cause'.]

J: We are not lazy, but the lady is not there now, but if we will tell we
where to find her, we will go and look for it.

F: ['As this was a request with which I had no means of complying,
I said she had better go back to the time when the gentleman lived
in the house'.]

J: Yes we will. Now I see the gentleman has a wife and a family, and I see
the vision standing before him; but why does it make these noises? Why
does it now frighten them all? And why does it frighten the servants in
that way so that the gentleman is forced to leave? She thinks he has no
right to be there, but why has he no right to be there? It cannot be an
angel of light, can it? It must be an angel of darkness, and to find out an
angel of darkness we will have to go a long way, to a bad place.

F: ['I said she had better find out the gentleman for himself'.]

J: Shall we go again upon the railway? Now we have come to a large
town. Shall we go up the road to this little village?

F: ['Finding by her description that she had passed the house, I replied,]
No, you must go back again the same road, you are a little too far.

J: Then may we go into this house, with a little lodge and a garden?

F: ['I again told her she was too far, for the house I recognised by her
description is one a few hundred yards beyond the one I wished her
to go to'.]

J: Now we have got to the right house, and we see the gentleman, but
why does he wear his hat that way? And what a wide brim it is, and
he is saying, 'We are much obliged to thee, friend', and, 'We hope thou
art well'. Why is he saying thee and thou? We don't like that way of
speaking, do we? But he looks a kind gentleman. I don't see why the
vision should have come to him.

F: ['She continued her description of a member of the Society of Friends,
and so accurately described the peculiarities of the gentleman that no
one who knew him could doubt who was meant, but as she seemed
now tired, I stopped her for the present and she fell into a short sleep'.]

This session with Jane does not seem to have been resumed, but Dr F.
arranged for a further to be carried out on 21 July of the same year, 1853.
At 8.55 a.m. precisely, Jane was hypnotised by another accomplished

mesmerist, Mrs Frazer, of whom Dr F. said, '[she] has been in the habit of doing it for some years, and her lucidity and rapidity of utterance were very strikingly increased compared with the uncertain, slow manner with which she spoke when under my influence'.

In the following dialogue, Jane is again denoted by the letter J, whilst Mrs Frazer is denoted by the letters Fz.

Fz: Is that we's light? Can we see well with it?

[Although the session had just begun, almost immediately Jane went into a deep sleep. After she awoke the still-hypnotised woman was again questioned].

Fz: What are we thinking of now?

J: Where shall we go? Shall we come back again?

Fz: Yes, we promised to come back to this place same sun [same day], so we must keep our promises.

J: Shall we look at it?

Fz: What is it? What do you call it? Is it a vision?

J: No, that is not the name. We don't like it. Why can't we get hold of the word, of we's own we's word? It is a haunted house. What an ugly word. Why do we want to look again?

Fz: We said that we would go into it.

J: We don't care for it, do we? It looks like a vision. It is a lady.

Fz: What is it like?

J: It has a face, but not like we's face. It is very white, but she moves about so quick; she has eyes, but there is no sight in them. She is like a shadow.

Fz: Has it a name in its head?

J: No, she has no name and no brains; she is just like a shadow, and flits about so quickly from place to place. We don't care about the lady. We want to go into the house and downstairs. We want to go into the cellar. Is there a way to the sea in this house? We will go downstairs into the lowest part and take a candle. We are not a coward. We will examine and find a place to the sea. Let us look – there is a cellar. Could not the gentleman examine the cellar? He must have stronger than we to look into them, we are too weak. We can't see any place of concealment. Tell him to bring somebody to look down. There must be a place of concealment. Like it ran down to the sea, and people came up for some bad purpose. It seems like something about the sea. We'll tell the gentleman with the broad hat about this. We're not afraid, there must be something concealed there, and it might be found out in this cellar, and we will come and help him. Let us go to the gentleman.

Fz: Would he like to see we's sleep?

J: We want this place looked into, and, mind, not a slight examination, for something will be found there.

Fz: Are they real people, then?

J: Well, she is a strange one, and walks about so quietly.

Fz: Has it spoken?

J: Yes, it has spoken. But there are so many, there are two or three kinds of animals. We's only a coward after all.

Fz: What are the animals like?

J: We won't be afraid. Do we like to look? One is a monkey, and the other like a dog. Had the lady dogs and monkeys? They go all about the house. She has got funny things, has she not? We don't like her. What is that other one? Do we know what we call it? It is not a pussy, it runs very fast and gets amongst feet. It is a rabbit, but a very quick one.

Fz: Are they real animals?

J: We do not touch them to see. We would not like a bite. What a violent woman she is. She wants to stay all alone in that house, but we can't see in to her, she is so strange. We have never seen her eat any supper nor anything else.

Fz: Has she a name in her head?

J: No, she has no brains. She is now going upstairs, and it is so dark. She has no light with her, but we have light.

Fz: Are the animals with her now?

J: No, they are not. She is all white: it is loose, not a dress like we's, but something loose thrown over her. She disturbs everybody.

Fz: Why don't they catch her?

J: Because she moves so quickly. But the mischief is in the cellar, and tell the gentleman to look there.

At this juncture Jane seemingly became tired and took a short nap before the session resumed.

J: We won't have her for ours.

Fz: Is she always like that?

J: We will look. Now she is coming downstairs again to go her rounds. She makes we feel cold. Now she is as dark as the devil. It is very strange; we don't like her.

Fz: Look and see what her dress is like.

J: We will. It is not like we's, for it is all dark. Where have we seen anything like it before? It is not like we's English ladies' dress. Where

has she got that? It is like the dress we saw in foreign countries – a
Spanish lady kind of dress. They are rich things she has on. It rustles
like silk. Is it not strange? She is just like a devil.

At this point the session was brought to an abrupt end for reasons
not disclosed, but likely because Jane was becoming exhausted. The
following session was arranged for 28 July, one week later.

After Jane was hypnotised, she was again taken back to 'the haunted
house' where she saw a man who troubled 'we's'. Mrs Frazer wanted to
know whether it was a 'real man she saw'.

Fz: Could it not be the person who now lived here?
J: No, it is a vision; he has no brains in his head; he looks very fierce, his
   eyes flash like a tom-cat's, like a tiger's; he has a white dress on like a
   surplice. Oh, how angry he is! He is so indignant at being disturbed.
   He does not want the gentleman to find out what he is there for. It is
   the man who makes the noises in the house. He goes stamping about.
   We did not like the woman, but the man is far worse. Oh, how angry
   he is! What a commotion there is in the cellar! They have not made the
   hole large enough. It is not close enough to the wall. They must make a
   wide, deep hole close to the wall, and they should take down the wall.
Fz: But perhaps the house will fall if they take the wall down.
J: Never mind, if they only find it out. The woman walked about with
   her hands upon her breast, as if in pain, but the man is very angry. Oh,
   how indignant he is that the gentleman is digging in the cellar!

At this point the third (and as far as the authors know, final) session came
to an end.

Perhaps it would be useful at this point to recap on exactly what Jane
managed to discover during her psychic or clairvoyant journeys.
• A Quaker 'gentleman' who lived at the mill house at Willington Quay
had a 'vision' of a woman or ghost and was subsequently frightened away
from the premises by it with his family.
• A woman, not married to 'the gentleman', died in the house. She was
of the opinion that the 'gentleman' mentioned above had no right to be
there, and might have 'done something wicked' to her. Jane states that
the woman died at the mill house.
• A lady with white skin also haunted the mill house. She flits around
quickly, and has 'eyes but no sight'. This woman is connected to the cellar,

and concerning her Jane says, 'the mischief is in the cellar, and tell the gentleman to look there'. The woman has a violent temper, and is in some way connected to strange animals seen at Willington Mill. Of her, Jane asks, 'Had the lady dogs and monkeys? They go all about the house. She has got funny things, has she not?' In some way Jane seems to be implying that the animals actually belonged to the woman. This same woman wanted to stay alone in house, never eats and wears a loose cowl or dress.

• A third woman haunted the mill house. She wore dark, expensive clothing and jewellery. This lady was of foreign extraction, possibly Spanish, and was of a foul, bad-tempered disposition.

• There was also a male ghost at the premises who was of even worse disposition than the above-mentioned female. This ghost wore a priest's surplice.

• That there was a cellar under the mill house at Willington Quay, and that something was seemingly buried in it that needed uncovering. Jane also suggests that there is 'a place of concealment' in the cellar that leads to the sea.

• That there were some very strange animals on the site, including a monkey, something that looked 'like a dog', and a third creature that she at first thought was a cat but then tentatively identified as a rabbit.

Although not stated explicitly, Dr F. hints strongly that the Quaker gentleman seen by Jane is none other than Joseph Procter. However, we must remember that Jane herself does not make such an identification, and that Joseph Procter's father, grandfather and other ancestors were devout Quakers too. The authors believe that the angry, bitter woman seen in the vision could well be the murder victim and the Quaker gentleman she despised so much, to the point of wanting him off the premises, could, just possibly, be the perpetrator of the crime. However, there is a second ghost seen in Jane's visions; a man dressed in a priest's surplice who seemed to be of a positively evil disposition and who was most reluctant to see the cellar excavated. Could he have been the perpetrator, and was his reluctance to see the cellar explored based upon the fact that to do so would unearth the woman's body and possibly expose him posthumously to ignominy?

Stephenson Haggie[7] made the comment, 'If the spirits of those who in the flesh have played a part in dark and bloody deeds do indeed "revisit the glimpses of the moon" then, as appears abundantly in the course of these articles, the phantoms of the dead might well jostle the living along the whole course of the Tyne'.

There is a clear inference here that at least one of the ghosts at the mill house may, whilst in the flesh, have carried out a murder. From this we know that the notion that the murderer or victim was already being identified as one of the spectres had gained currency at a very early stage in the affair. Even Procter admitted as much when he said, in his letter to *Spiritual Magazine* on 2 September 1853, 'I have never shrunk from the avowal of undoubting assurance of these appearances, noises, &c., being made by the spirit of some person or persons deceased, notwithstanding that the who and the wherefore have not hitherto been ascertained'.

Procter, we know, knew quite a bit more about 'the who and the wherefore' than he was letting on, but his admission that the spectres within the mill house could have been the spirits of the dead and not, as he customarily thought, demons, is telling indeed.

When one looks at the visions of Jane collectively, they powerfully support the assertion that a murder was carried out on the premises and that the victim's body was buried under a stone slab in the cellar, and that, subsequently, the ghosts of both victim and killer came back to haunt the mill house.

Jane also spoke of the spectral woman clutching her hands to her breast and looking as if she was in great pain. This, we must remember, is exactly the way Dr Edward Drury described the ghost that he saw at the mill house in 1840.

The simple fact is that Jane was either an astonishingly gifted medium, or a charlatan of the first order. We need to address the question, then, which was she?

We have already seen the testimony of Jane's physician, Dr F., who had known her since a child and had not the slightest doubts about her sincerity. In addition to this, we have that of the Revd T. Myers, who stated[8], 'She was very religious and conscientious, and even when mesmerised and under the influence of others, could never be induced to read letters or pry into things, which she knew the person visited would wish to keep secret. On one occasion I remember taking her in the sleep to see a young lady; she said, "She is writing to her lover." "What is she saying to him?" Indignant answer; "We will not look; would we like anyone to look over we's shoulder when we write love letters?"'

Going by character references alone, then, the weight of the testimony decidedly goes in favour of Jane. But of course it is just possible that, despite her high moral standing, she could have been faking it all.

The first thing we need to address is whether Jane could have 'cold-read' those around her and surreptitiously picked up information about the Willington case from them without them being aware of it. It's possible, of course, and we must acknowledge that the doctor certainly didn't help any. He claimed at the outset that he would avoid asking her any leading questions, but the truth is he failed miserably. Instead of opening the first session by simply asking Jane what she could see, he enquired, 'We are on a railway, and can see a large building like a mill; where is it?'

Immediately, then, Jane would have known that the doctor wanted her to (a) visit a 'large building', (b) that it was likely a mill, and (c) it was by a railway track. Jane, unfortunately, is then allowed to ask her own leading question, which she probably did in all innocence: 'Is it a mill for grinding food?' The doctor then compounds matters by asking Jane to ascertain by what means the mill works. This could have provided her with a hint that there was something unusual about the mill and its method of operation.

How likely is it though, that she could have already known about the mill and its history? The truth is that it was very likely indeed. The story, as we know, had been written up in a number of magazines, journals and newspapers all of which but three were circulated in the Durham area. Many of the facts brought forth by Jane whilst hypnotised could have easily been gleaned from such publications.

However, on the flip-side there are things which, apart from her upright character, suggest strongly that Jane may have been genuinely clairvoyant and picked up from the psychic ether things that she could not have known.

Firstly, there is the context in which the sessions with Dr F. were held. From the testimony of the physician, it seems almost certain that he had given Jane no prior warning of what he was going to question her about whilst she was mesmerised. This means that when he asked her his admittedly loaded questions, Jane, to impress those in attendance, would have had to possess through sheer luck a detailed knowledge of the mill, its environment and history. In effect, she would have needed to recognise almost immediately that the doctor was talking about Willington Mill and no other. How likely is this? It is true that Willington Mill was the first steam-powered mill in the north east of England when it was built in 1800, but by 1853, when Jane was mesmerised, there were dozens. However, could Dr F's statement that it was beside a railway have given Jane an extra advantage? It's possible, but unlikely. As Stead points out[9], 'Jane, I should mention, had never heard of the haunted mill; she had once passed over Willington Bridge by rail, but knew absolutely nothing about the story which she was wished to unravel'.

Of course, the doctor only had Jane's word for that. She may well have heard of the tale in passing, but it is unlikely that she would have given it much thought and even if she did hear of it she may well have forgotten about it. Without at all being deprecatory towards working-class women of the mid-nineteenth century, the truth is that they had far less access to reading material of the day even if it was circulated in the areas where they lived and, probably, less of an incentive to read it. As previously related, Mike photographed the site from the Metro train when he arranged to meet Darren in June 2009, but it is only visible for a short while, and its geographical location diminishes its impact greatly. It sits in the centre of a deep hollow, and even when the entire mill was standing it would not have unduly drawn the attention of commuters. On balance, then, the authors think that Jane was unlikely to have possessed a detailed enough knowledge of Willington Mill to enable her to pass off a hoax as spectacularly as she allegedly did.

Another thing in Jane's favour is that she seemed to have knowledge of as many obscure bits of mill lore as she did the well-known ones. As we have seen, her testimony fits in perfectly with what we now know to be the truth, even though the perception in 1853 was radically different. Jane, for instance, accurately placed the ghosts she saw in her vision in their correct place on the historical timeline. She insisted that the mill house had a cellar, even when Joseph Procter was denying it. Critics may suggest that Jane claimed there was a cellar only because she'd heard the rumours circulating that there was one. However, to insist on something that could have later turned out to be untrue would have run the risk of destroying her mediumistic or clairvoyant reputation considerably.

The members of the SPR, Jane's own doctor and a number of prominent clergymen all became convinced of Jane's authenticity. Her credibility is not exactly watertight, but rationally it is easier to accept her story than to believe she was a fake.

Professor Henry Sidgwick later wrote about Jane and included Hargrave's recollections of how an 'eminent clairvoyant' from Newcastle visited the mill personally. She, too, was called Jane and the suspicion naturally arises that the two 'Janes' may have been one and the same. Again this is unlikely, as one hailed from Durham and was by no means 'eminent', whilst the other was from Newcastle and seemingly very well known indeed. Besides, Hargrave and others would have known immediately if they were one and the same as they were obviously acquainted with both.

Dr F.'s notes eventually found their way into the possession of Elizabeth Procter's sister, the aforementioned Mrs Hargrave, who was then living in Southport. She copied them, after which they were sent to Eleanor Sidgwick who then penned her lengthy piece on Jane in the *Proceedings of the Society for Psychical Research*. Had she not done so, the story of Willington Mill would not have survived in anything like its present form.

The bigger question, though, is whether the spirits of the murder victim and the perpetrator were ever really put to rest.

Notes

1. *Proceedings of the Society for Psychical Research*, Vol. 7, p. 53
2. *Ibid.*
3. Stead, William T., *Real Ghost Stories* (Grant Richards, 1897)
4. *Ibid.*
5. *Proceedings of the Society for Psychical Research* Vol. 7, p. 60
6. *Proceedings of the Society for Psychical Research* Vol. 7, p. 82
7. Davidson, Robert, *The True Story of the Willington Ghost* (Robert Davidson, c. 1886)
8. *Proceedings of the Society for Psychical Research* Vol. 7, p. 54
9. Stead, William T., *Real Ghost Stories* (Grant Richards, 1897)

Twenty-Two

THE DAVIDSON ACCOUNT

During one of the Procter family's four-year absences from Willington Mill, whilst they were living at North Shields, they employed a servant girl by the name of Mary Young. When the Procters returned to Willington, after their four-year stint was over, Mary, who had proved herself a valued and trustworthy employee, went with them. After eight years Mary married a mill employee called Thomas Davidson and terminated her own employment with the Procters. This was an amicable arrangement, and both Mary and the Procters remained on good terms. The newly-married couple continued to live on the site in a cottage. Both Mary and Thomas, we know, had strange experiences at Willington Mill.

The couple had a son whom they named Robert. What is not well-known is that although Robert went on to write the first complete account of Willington Mill other than the Procter diary, he drew his material from an even older document compiled by Thomas and Mary Davidson, his parents. Robert makes reference to this in his own work, where he states, regarding the supernatural events, that, 'they are facts recorded by my father and mother'. The versions of many stories recounted by Davidson differ markedly in style and content to those in common currency, which also led the authors to suspect that an earlier, written document had been utilised as source material. Alas, this document is now lost to us and is unlikely to still be in existence. However, Robert Davidson seems to have made a conscientious effort to keep his own account faithful to that of his parents.

The Old Book

One of the first assertions made by Davidson in *The True Story of the Willington Ghost*[1] is that, 'two hundred years ago a cottage stood on the site now occupied by the mill house, and is said to have been occupied by a curious old woman, but I cannot give any further particulars concerning her, save that she had dealings with his Satanic Majesty, and was gifted in fortune-telling'.

One fascinating aspect of Davidson's account is that it furnishes us with two new details about the 'witch'. Firstly, we are told that she was 'gifted in fortune-telling'. Whether this was by scrying (using a crystal ball, mirror or a bowl of water in which to see visions), reading tea leaves (tasseomancy), palmistry or by some other process of divination we do not know. Tasseomancy was popular from the mid-seventeenth century onwards, particularly near trading waterways like the River Tyne, where European sailors frequently visited.

The second point of interest is that Davidson says of the witch that she, 'had dealings with his Satanic Majesty'. It is difficult to determine from the context in which this sentence is placed how literally it should be taken. On face value, it could suggest that the 'witch' was not so much a practitioner of Wicca, but actually a Satanist. This would, of course, explain how she came to be condemned by Montague Summers[2] and others as 'notorious'. On the other hand, to Davidson and other devoutly religious folk, anything other than the practice of Christianity automatically labelled one as a follower of Beelzebub. As the authors have already shown, it was likely that the witch practised a strange mixture of Wicca and Roman Catholicism.

A number of researchers, including the authors, have drawn attention to the fact that Joseph Procter initially claimed to have seen evidence of the witch's existence in 'an old book' which he had read. (Although Procter later changed his tune and consistently denied this.) What book this was is unclear as unfortunately the only reference Procter made to it is his diary was an unfinished quotation which read, 'An infirm old woman, the mother-in-law of R. Oxon, the builder of the premises, lived and died in the house, and after her death the haunting was attributed-----'.

Davidson seems to have been aware of this book and drawn from it. Like Procter, for instance, he refers to the witch as an 'old woman' and even supplies supplemental details about her that Procter does not. As the authors have not been able to find these details in any other publications, despite exhaustive searches, then it is likely that the 'old book' was not only Procter's source of information on the witch, but also Davidson's. Unfortunately, also like Procter, Davidson does not identify the publication, its author or its year of publication.

However, in the copy of *The True Story of the Willington Ghost* held within Newcastle Central Library, some curious annotations have been added in ink by an unknown hand. On the inside front cover, for example, are the words:

> *Mr Anthony Hails, the Son of a Shipwright at Willington dock became a Methodist Local Preacher under Wesley influence. In 1798 became a Schoolmaster at Newcastle and as the Years went by was a student of Science, Oriental language and general scholarship. Earned his place in [unintelligible] of [unintelligible]. Died August 30. 1845 aged 79 years.*

Hails, we know, was both an able scholar and a mild eccentric. An accident at the age of four severely retarded his education and he was unable to attend school until he was eleven years old. Although his education was supplemented by his father at home, when he left school he gained employment, with his father's assistance, as a shipwright.

Hails developed a thirst for knowledge and seems to have desired to make up for time lost during his school years. He made a study of ancient languages – including Hebrew, Aramaic, Latin and Classical Greek – as well as dabbling in others such as Sanskrit and Mandarin Chinese. The self-taught scholar eventually turned his hand to writing, and by the age of sixteen had already penned a number of contributions for Valpy's Classical Journal. Afterwards, he wrote for well regarded publications such as the *Gentleman's Magazine*, the *Weekly Chronicle*, the *Monthly Chronicle* and the *Monthly Magazine*, and penned several books and pamphlets[3].

Hails was also a devout Methodist, and as the annotator in Davidson's book testifies, became a local preacher on the Methodist circuit. He died on Saturday, 30 August 1845.

The puzzle is just why the person who annotated Davidson's book should have included a potted biography of him in his or her notes. Although the man visited Willington Quay and knew of the mill, there is no mention made of him throughout the text. What, then, could his connection have been with the contents of Davidson's book?

The authors do not know for certain whether Hails wrote abut the Willington Ghost specifically (although if he did we're sure someone will tell us), but it is possible that he may have written about earlier episodes in the village's history.

In the back of Davidson's book there is another series of annotations:

> *The 'Haunter & Haunted' by [unintelligible] 1925. Mills & Boon quote as its authorities*

Tomlinson's Guide
Richardsons of Cleveland [unintelligible]
Journal of Psychical Research' 1892
Howitt's Journal 1847
Real Ghost Stories Stead 1897
Davidson article in Leader [unintelligible] 1886
'The Umanian Magazine' 1782
'The Monthly Chronicle' 1887

Someone had apparently gone to some effort to list eleven publications dealing with the Willington Mill enigma. We know that the list must have been composed after 1925, for the latest publication on the list was issued in that year. To ascertain whether there is anything of specific interest to us in this list we need to go through it line by line.

The first publication, seemingly released in 1925, is entitled 'Haunter & Haunted', and is probably a reference to Sir Edward Bulwer Lytton's work, *A Strange Story and the Haunted and the Haunters*, first published in 1857. There is a footnote stating that, 'Mills & Boon quote as its authorities'. Mills & Boon, the popular fiction publishers, was founded in 1908 by Gerald Rusgrove Mills and Charles Boon, and, according to the annotator, must have utilised Edward Bulwer Lytton's work as a reference source in one or more of their publications.

The second work is referred to simply as, 'Tomlinson's Guide' and refers to William Weaver Tomlinson's travel guide, *A Comprehensive Guide to the County of Northumberland*[4]. Edmund Procter made reference to this work in his commentary on his father's diary.

The next publication in the list is called 'Richardsons of Cleveland', and refers to the book, *Records of a Quaker Family: The Richardsons of Cleveland*[5], which details much of the history of the Procter family.

The following publication listed is 'The Journal of Psychical Research, 1892'. This would seem to be a reference to the *British Journal of Psychical Research*, which was published by the national Laboratory of Psychical Research in London. However, this publication was only launched in 1926. The suffix 1892 strongly suggests that the publication is actually the *Journal of the Society for Psychical Research*, specifically the issue that carried Joseph Procter's diary.

'Howitt's Journal' is a reference to *Howitt's Journal of Literature and Popular Progress*, which William Howitt, one of numerous famous 'mill investigators', edited between 1847 and 1849.

'Real Ghost Stories Stead 1897' is patently William T. Stead's book, *Real Ghost Stories*[6] which contains a detailed account of the Willington Mill enigma.

'Davidson's article in Leader' obviously refers to Robert Davidson's series of articles published in the *Newcastle Weekly Leader* in 1888[7], and which he subsequently published in book form later that year.

'The Monthly Chronicle "1887"' could refer to the June issue of that year[8] which contained the story of the Willington Ghost, or, although unlikely, the November issue,[9] which detailed the role that Thomas Hudson played in the 'Harriet Martineau affair'.

There was, in fact, only one publication mentioned in the entire list which the authors had not been able to track down; the penultimate reference to the curiously titled 'Umanian Magazine'.

Despite extensive Internet searches, there seemed to be no reference to an 'Umanian Magazine' or indeed the word 'Umanian' other than in a context where it was obviously an artificial construct with no real meaning. To get to the bottom of the mystery, the authors started with the hypothesis that the word 'Umanian' might in some way be connected to 'Romanian' as they are phonetically similar. Mike spoke to Ionela Flood from the Romanca Society, a cultural organisation dedicated to supporting the social integration of Romanian citizens within the UK. Ionela is a former Director of the Mihai Eminescu Centre in Bucharest, and was the founder of *Enigmaticul Magazine*. After examining the handwritten text in Davidson's book, Ionela said that she believed the word Umania to mean something like 'humanity', although she couldn't be certain exactly what language or dialect it represented. It was a good start, though, and eventually the authors managed to find the home of this obscure term.

Lingua Franca was a pidgin language that was popularly spoken in parts of coastal Europe until the mid-nineteenth century, although its use in England was rare. It was made up of elements of numerous other languages, including French, Catalan, Croatian and Arabic. Umania, in fact was a Lingua-Francan word which, as Ionela Flood had correctly stated, meant 'humanity'. So far so good; the publication listed in Davidson's book had a title which was a mixture of English and Lingua Franca and essentially meant 'Humanitarian Magazine'. Presumably, the content would appeal to someone who had an interest in humanity and, it seems, languages; someone just like Anthony Hails, the authors thought.

But what could the connection be between Hails, the *Umanian Magazine* – which despite the title was obviously printed in English – and the Willington mystery? The authors came up with a tantalisingly plausible hypothesis; what if Hails had written an article for the *Umanian Magazine* about Willington, or at least some aspect of its history, that touched upon the subject?

At Willington there was a Wesleyan Chapel known locally as 'the College', for here many famous Methodist preachers first cut their oratorial teeth, including Bishop John Trotter, the Fijian missionary George Fryar and the Revd Robert Cooke. It is unthinkable that Anthony Hails, himself a devout Methodist and well-known local preacher, would not have delivered sermons here. Likely, then, Hails would have heard stories about the 'old witch in the cottage' and may have been inspired to write about her. Hails would have been just seventeen when the article appeared, but we know that he had already had several articles and papers published even at such a tender age.

The haunting of Willington Mill could not have begun, obviously, until the place was built in 1800. Hence, anything that Hails had to say on the matter must have concerned things that happened before then, as the issue in question had been published long before then in 1782. The only piece of Willington history that could possibly be related to the haunting before the mill was built was that which concerned the cottage that stood upon the same site two centuries earlier. Even though the authors had never seen the issue of *Umanian Magazine*, they became almost convinced that Hails might well have written an article for it which detailed the story of the witch in the cottage. If this was the case, then it allowed the last piece of the jigsaw to fall perfectly into place; The 'old book' which Joseph Procter had read, in which it was stated that there had indeed been a cottage on the site of the mill in the seventeenth century, must have been the issue of *Umanian Magazine* that had contained Hails' article. Hails, then, was Joseph Procter's source for the existence of the cottage, the old woman and the haunting. Further circumstantial proof comes from the fact that in the quotation Procter makes from 'the old book', there is no mention of the mill at all; only the old woman, her home, its builder Mr Oxon and the haunting. The article by Hails couldn't have mentioned the mill, of course, because it hadn't even been built when the piece was published. By the time Procter read the article by Hails then the issue of *Umanian Magazine* which contained it would have indeed been 'old'; possibly over half a century.

Why, though, would Procter refer to an issue of a magazine as a book? Mike thinks that the magazine may have been a large publication with a great many pages, therefore making the calling of it a 'book' perfectly reasonable. Darren leans towards the idea that by the time Procter read it, the issue may have been bound together with others into one volume, thus making it truly a book as opposed to a magazine. Either theory is perfectly plausible.

A search with all local libraries and the British Library drew a blank, so it is likely that the *Umanian Magazine* was a small-circulation publication issued in the Tyneside area, and no copies are now in existence.

Whit Monday

Stead alleges[10] that Mary Young/Davidson, during her eight years' service with the Procters, 'saw something on three occasions'. Robert Davidson, Mary's son, argues for only two. The two accounts recorded specifically by Davidson, and which only appear rarely elsewhere, are particularly interesting.

One Whit Monday, Mary was at the mill house washing dishes in the kitchen. She had planned to finish promptly as she'd organised a visit to her mother who lived in North Shields, intending to have what she described as a 'holiday' there for several days. Suddenly she heard footsteps in the hallway. Her immediate reaction was that someone must have been coming to visit Mrs Procter. This annoyed Mary, for she knew that if visitors had come to stay her holiday leave would be immediately cancelled. At that moment she also saw a young woman walk past the kitchen door and ascend the stairs. Davidson[11] says that his mother then tip-toed across the floor and peered up the stairwell just in time to see the woman, sporting a fashionable lavender-coloured dress, turn off the top step onto the first-floor landing and enter one of the bedrooms.

Both shocked and irritated that someone should have entered the house so rudely and without knocking, Mary went into the lounge and asked Elizabeth Procter if she knew about their new 'guest'.

'No, Polly [Mary's nickname], but I have heard a great noise in that room. I will not stay here any longer, but will go with thee to the kitchen'.

Davidson then goes on to recount the experience his father had with a bizarre mystery animal at the mill, which the authors have already outlined in great detail earlier.

One of the consistent things the authors have noted throughout this book is the way in which Joseph Procter candidly admitted his house was haunted, but skilfully played down anything which would unduly increase the amount of publicity the situation was attracting or dramatise it in any way.

Davidson[12] details an event which supports this theory. When Thomas Hudson gave his version of events to the *Newcastle Weekly Chronicle*[13], he noted how the children in the household displayed an uncommon lack of fear at the paranormal phenomena they witnessed. To many researchers this would have seemed odd to say the least, and may have precipitated allegations that the youngsters might even have been responsible for faking some of the incidents. Elizabeth Procter seems to have pointed out this potential anomaly to her husband and word was put around that, contrary to popular opinion, the children were very frightened indeed. When Robert Davidson was compiling his book, *The True Story of the Willington Mill Ghost*[14], he spoke to his mother about this matter. Mary, who was a devoted employee and close friend of the Procters, told the truth whilst simultaneously making a desperate attempt to avoid accusing Joseph Procter of lying[15]. According to Mrs Davidson, Procter was wrong when he claimed the children were all frightened:

This, my mother considers, an error. Mr Procter must have been misunderstood, as the greatest fear seized all the occupants of the house, save, perhaps, the infantile portion. So great was the terror of one of the sons that he had to be sent away to Carlisle to escape the troubles at home.[16]

According to Mary Davidson, then, most of the children weren't frightened at all, and only one severely.

To be fair, the evidence does suggest that one of the Procter children was indeed subjected to more supernatural occurrences than the rest, although whether to the degree portrayed by Mary Young is debatable. A subsequent event made the perpetuation of any denial on the part of the Procters untenable. Davidson relates[17]:

Mr Procter had a son who was very much tormented with the ghost. His bed was in Mr and Mrs Procter's room. This boy had always to have a hand bell on a table by his bed-side, in order to call some of the family to his help. On one occasion, a gentleman was visiting Mr Procter. The boy had gone to bed, and shortly afterwards the bell was rung. Mr Procter left the room, and on his return explained the cause of his absence to the gentleman, who thereupon disputed the boy had heard anything, and asked if Mr P would allow him to conceal himself in the room. Leave was granted, and he took up his position behind the bed-curtains, quite unknown to the boy. He remained in the room about an hour and a half, and twice during this period Mr Proctor was summoned to the room by the ringing of the bell. The second time the gentleman retired from his hiding place, and he assured Mr Procter that he was thoroughly changed in his views concerning those mysterious noises. This was the boy previously referred to as having been sent to Carlisle to get freed from the trouble at home.

Falling Stones

One of the later members of the Wesleyan Chapel that Anthony Hails almost certainly preached at was an engineman at Willington Mill. Davidson's paternal grandfather, Tommy Davidson, was also a member of the church. The engineman held Bible classes at the chapel, which the grandfather attended. Whenever he had occasion to visit the mill, he would pop into the engine room to pass the time of day with his Bible teacher. Davidson takes up the story[18] of what happened one evening when his grandfather was on his way home after having one such discussion whilst the mill was working a 'double shift':

> My grandfather was not at all a believer in the existence of the ghost. He was under the impression that whatever was heard or seen could be accounted for; but on one occasion, he was returning homeward, when between the house and the mill he was brought to a sudden stop, as if he had come against some barrier. At the same moment he heard a great noise. He described it thus: 'I heard a great noise, and suddenly stopped. My first thought was that the house and mill gables were falling together. I quite naturally raised my hands as it were to save my head from the falling debris. I stood for a few seconds, when all was calm, and nothing out of its usual'.
>
> When he got home, a neighbour entered, who with himself had been an unbeliever. The first salute from my grandfather was, 'Well, Sally, do you believe in the existence of the ghost yet?' 'No Tommy', said Sally, what makes thee ask such a question as that?' 'Well then', replied my grandfather, 'thou and I change opinions from this time', and much to her consternation he repeated the above incident, and expressed his belief that no human agency could produce the noise, and more particularly the peculiar sensations which he experienced at the moment. He lived many years after this event, and continued to believe in the existence of the mystery.

Intriguingly, the very spot where Tommy Davidson had his bizarre encounter was the same one where Hiram Wedgwood and Walter Middleton espied their 'strange donkey'[19].

A Riveting Experience

Davidson's father, Thomas, despite his encounter with the strange, cat-like creature, maintained a fascination with the Willington Mill enigma and from time-to-time made efforts to get to the bottom of it. One summer, according to Robert Davidson, the Procters were all going to

Carlisle for a holiday and the mill house was destined to be standing empty for the duration. Thomas – who according to his son had nerves of steel – asked Joseph Procter if he could spend a night in the house whilst they were away to see if the ghost would appear. Procter had consistently refused to allow others to do the same thing (apart from the Drury-Hudson vigil, during which he was actually in the house) but said, 'as thou art a young man of the village, and for whom I have very great respect, I will give thee the permission thou asks, and should she pay thee a visit, I hope thy courage won't fail thee'.

It was the habit of the Procters to have two employees sleep in the house whenever they were away, essentially to act as security guards. Several days after the family had departed, Davidson turned up to spend the night and was allowed to class himself as a 'relief' for one of the men already there.

What happened next is a little confusing. It seems that the remaining guard in the house was a man called John Ridley. Ridley appears to have agreed to join Davidson in his 'ghost watch', and at 9 p.m. precisely the mill foreman arrived to 'escort them to their bedroom'. Just why this was necessary is a mystery, but even stranger is the fact that the foreman then proceeded to lock the door and, as Robert Davidson explains, make 'them prisoners during his pleasure'. Why would the foreman have taken the bizarre step of incarcerating the two men in such a manner? Well, for one thing, it would have prevented either Thomas or his colleague John 'Jack' Ridley exploring the house, and in particular the cellar.

Both men got into bed. Ridley fell asleep almost immediately, after which Davidson made himself comfortable in a sitting position and extinguished the candle. He later explained, perhaps with some justification, that if 'her ladyship' was going to appear she would 'carry sufficient light to render herself visible'.

Shortly after midnight, Davidson heard a noise. As detailed in an earlier chapter, it lasted for approximately fifteen minutes and steadily got louder. He later described it as being like the sound of, 'rivetters [*sic*] rivetting [*sic*] a boiler'.

Eventually the noise became so deafening that Davidson couldn't figure out how Ridley was managing to stay asleep. He nudged Jack with his elbow and shouted his name, and at that very moment the noise abruptly stopped.

'What's the matter?' said Jack. 'Hast thou seen something?'

Thomas explained as best he could what he had heard, but as the room was now silent his experience doesn't seem to have captivated Ridley's imagination, and he promptly fell back asleep. Another thirty minutes passed by without incident, and then the noise started again – only worse. According to Davidson, 'the building seemed to shake to its very foundations, the bed curtains shook, the rings rattled, and this continued for a very long period'.

Once again, Thomas shouted, 'Jack!' in an effort to wake his slumbering companion. For a second time, as he did so, the noises abruptly ceased. Nothing more transpired until the foreman arrived at six o'clock in the morning to release them.

Another incident mentioned by Robert Davidson concerned his aunt and Bessy Mann, wife of the mill foreman Thomas Mann.

Both women saw what they described as a 'whitish figure' glide down the stairs from the top floor until it got to the landing of the first floor. It then entered the nursery and disappeared into a closet. Less than an hour earlier they had heard groaning noises coming from within the same cupboard. It is interesting that Dr Drury saw his ghost appear from a closet, and there are numerous other incidents recorded in mill lore of apparitions entering and leaving closets on both the first and second floor.

On another occasion, Joseph Procter Jr managed to give his nursemaid the slip and ran off to play with some other boys from Willington. Not long after he burst into the house and started shouting for Mary Davidson, commonly known as 'Polly':

'Polly! Polly! The boys in the village say there is a ghost in our house. Come Polly, let me see the ghost. What is it like, Polly?'

Joseph Procter had placed restrictions upon his children mixing with youngsters from the village in an effort to curtail the rumours that were starting to circulate. Davidson suggests that this was also done to keep the existence of the ghost hidden from the youngsters themselves. This may have been Robert's sincere perception, but it is hard to see how it could be true. All the children in the house knew of the ghost, and most if not all of them had personally experienced the strange phenomena that accompanied its presence. For this reason this incident must, the authors think, have occurred before the affair had really reached its apex and early on in the Procter residence.

Polly answered young Joseph and tried to pacify him: 'The boys have been telling you nonsense. Your mamma will be very vexed at you going out. You mustn't do it again'.

Not to be dissuaded, Joseph persisted: 'Oh, but Polly, I want to see the ghost. They say it is such a funny thing. Is it that which makes all the noises in the house?'

Feeling uncomfortable, Polly ended the conversation there and then.

The Davidson account is in many ways superior to the Procter diary. Its layout is more logical, the incidents described in more detail and the narrative much easier to follow. Without it, our knowledge of what transpired all those years ago would be immeasurably impoverished.

Notes

1. Davidson, Robert, *The True Story of the Willington Ghost* (Robert Davidson, *c.* 1886)
2. Summers, Montague, *The Geography of Witchcraft* (London, 1926)
3. Latimer, John, *Local Records or Historical Register of Remarkable Events* (Newcastle, The Chronicle Office, 1857), p. 204
4. Tomlinson, William Weaver, *A Comprehensive Guide to the County of Northumberland* (Walter Scott, 1909)
5. Boyce, Anne Ogden, *Records of a Quaker Family: The Richardsons of Cleveland* (Thomas Harris & Co., 1889)
6. Stead, William T., *Real Ghost Stories* (Grant Richards, 1897)
7. Davidson, Robert, *The True Story of the Willington Ghost* (Robert Davidson, *c.* 1886)
8. *Monthly Chronicle, June* 1887
9. *Monthly Chronicle,* November 1887
10. Stead, William T., *Real Ghost Stories* (Grant Richards, 1897)
11. Davidson, Robert, *The True Story of the Willington Ghost* (Robert Davidson, *c.* 1886)
12. *Ibid.*
13. *Newcastle Weekly Chronicle,* 20 December 1884
14. Davidson, Robert, *The True Story of the Willington Ghost* (Robert Davidson, *c.* 1886)
15. *Ibid.*
16. *Ibid.*
17. *Ibid.*
18. *Ibid.*
19. Anon, *The Willington Quay Ghost* (Privately published, *c.* 1972)

Twenty-Three

TONY STOCKWELL

In January 2007, Mike received an e-mail from an agent asking him if he'd like to interview one of their clients, the well-known psychic medium Tony Stockwell. Tony was giving a demonstration of mediumship at the Sunderland Empire Theatre the following month, and Mike thought it would be a good story to write up in his WraithScape column.

Tony Stockwell was born in the East End of London and belonged to a closely-knit family. At the age of sixteen a friend invited him to attend a meeting at a local spiritualist church. 'From the moment I set foot in the door I knew that this was what I wanted to do with the rest of my life,' he recalled.

Now, Tony Stockwell is one of the UK's most highly regarded mediums. Every week, legions of viewers tune in to watch programmes such as *Psychic Detectives* and *Tony Stockwell's Psychic Academy*, where they can watch Tony demonstrate his skills.

After an interesting and informative interview, Mike, impressed by what Tony Stockwell had said and his apparent talent as a medium, decided to e-mail Tony's agent a picture of his long-dead great-grandfather, John 'Jack' Robinson IV – a fascinating and somewhat eccentric character but one who had not been mentioned in print anywhere. As far as Mike could tell, it would have been impossible for Tony to find out anything about him through conventional research. The point of the exercise was to see whether Tony could 'read' the photograph and tell Mike anything about the person. So, how did he do? Well, look at Tony's statements below and judge for yourself.

TONY: This man travelled a lot. He was born abroad, I think in America. (FACT: Mike's great-grandfather was born in the USA and came to England when he was 18 months old.)

TONY: Smoking … pipes … did this man have a collection of pipes? (FACT: Mike's great-grandfather had a large collection of briars and other pipes which he kept in a cupboard in his room.)

TONY: There's a very strong connection with Canada ... a family connection. (FACT: There are relatives of Mike's great-grandfather who live in Canada to this day.)

TONY: The letter A is important. Someone close to this man. (FACT: His wife was called Ann.)

TONY: The name Albert is also important – twice. (FACT: John Robinson had a son-in-law called Albert. It was also the name of his best friend, Albert Grimes.)

TONY: He was close to someone called William. (FACT: William was his son-in-law.)

Of course, cynics would say that some of Tony's responses could have just been lucky guesses, but the authors think not. He told Mike many other things – obscure details about his family – that all proved to be perfectly true. Some of those things Mike didn't even know himself until he verified them later.

How did he also know about John Robinson's love of horses, his overly-generous nature and flamboyant dress sense? Altogether, Mike counted twenty-seven separate verifiable facts in Tony's reading and not a single inaccurate statement. At worst, there were a couple that may well have been true but simply couldn't be verified.

Darren and Mike wanted to see if they could re-create the event involving the medium 'Jane' who, after being hypnotised by Dr John Trotter, gave an astounding description of the mill and its ghosts. They decided to ask Tony if he could pick up anything psychically or

Medium Tony Stockwell, who, without any prior knowledge of which case the authors were working on, verified both crucial aspects of their research and messages given through the medium 'Jane' in the nineteenth century. (Blonde Sheep Events)

spiritually regarding Willington Mill and possibly verify what they knew. To recreate the event properly it would be necessary for the medium to work 'remotely' – that is, whilst not physically present at the mill itself. The only allowance that needed to be made was for the fact that each medium has his or her own technique for contacting the spirit world. It would be no good having a modern-day medium hypnotised if that was not their normal means of getting in touch with the world beyond our senses; they would have to use a method that they felt comfortable with. With Tony, one of those methods was obviously the psychic reading of photographs.

It was agreed that the picture of 'a building' would be sent to Tony Stockwell and an interview would take place at 11 a.m. on Wednesday 22 July. Tony was told absolutely nothing about the building, except that the geographical location was in the north east of England.

At the pre-arranged time, Mike telephoned Tony. 'Right,' said Tony, 'let's see what I can gather from the picture …'

Mike heard a faint but distinct exhalation at the other end of the line as Tony began to concentrate. What follows is the conversation between Mike and Tony Stockwell. Mike is designated by the letter M, and Tony by the letter T.

T: The first thing I'm getting is that this is a house … but it's not just a house. Its connected with a business of some kind … I'm not sure what … but there was commerce or business carried out there. It was a house, but in some way connected with a business, does that make sense?

M: Yes.

T: It's as if there was a business nearby, but some of the transactions actually took place in the house.

M: Yes.

T: The house … I get the feeling its no longer there. It's been demolished.

The cropped photograph sent to Tony Stockwell and Philip Solomon, hours before they provided startling information to the authors about the Willington Mill haunting. (Courtesy of Bridon Ropes)

M:Yes.

T: I get the feeling of a dock or dockyard nearby … as if the place is by a river … a dock.

M:That's correct.

T: But there are other buildings – buildings connected with the house in some way that are still standing. They are really close by.

M:That's correct.

T: I think that although the building has been knocked down there may still be a small part of it standing – maybe a bit of a wall, or something.

M:That may be true, but I can't be sure.

T: I don't think I like this house. I don't like it at all. It's really strange. It's as if the people who lived there were having to put up with very difficult circumstances.

M:Yes?

T: I can see lots of people … they're working there – working very hard … maybe factory workers of some kind.

M: Okay.

T:You know, even though the place is demolished now there's still a presence there. It's not just the building, it's the whole place. There's a bad aura around it. It's as if there are a lot of layers to this house in some way … its difficult to understand, but it's as if its in layers …

M: I understand.

T:There's a lot of stuff going on in this house, and there's a man … he isn't comfortable with it. I can hear banging … lots of banging, particularly upstairs and on the stairwell. There's really loud banging. Also loud footsteps upstairs …

M:That's interesting.

T: At the top of the house there are rooms. I'm seeing rooms. These rooms are odd, and there's a disturbing feeling to them. These rooms aren't used … they're empty

M: Okay.

T: I'm actually seeing a young woman. I think she lost her life there in some way. She doesn't like that house at all. Actually, there was a murder committed in that house.

M:That's interesting, too.

T: You know, there's something else. This place … I know the house was haunted, but I get the feeling the place was actually haunted before the house was even built, from a long time ago. People said it was haunted … it was known to be haunted.

M:You mean the place or land around the building?

T:Yes. Before the building was there ... there were slaves. People treated like slaves ... maybe black people.

M:Working there?

T:Yes, but not at the buildings ... they were working there before they were built.

M: Okay.

T: I'm also sensing the presence of children – lots of them. There were definitely children living in this house. There's a connection between children and up above ... the attic.

M:When you say the attic, do you mean the loft or the top floor ... where?

T: Up ... at the top, up and above. The attic ... upstairs rooms ... the children are connected in some way. Those rooms are really odd.

M: Okay, that's interesting.

T:There's also a man who haunts this place; in fact, he's the dominant personality. The thing is, he's really very, very aggressive. I'm sensing lots of aggression and anger ... and bitterness. This man is violent. I get the feeling that he wielded a lot of power over people, and not always in a good way. He was prominent in the community ... he had influence and wasn't afraid to use it. He was also obsessed with money – he had something to do with money or commerce.

M: I understand.

T: I also feel that someone committed suicide there; maybe a man ... he might have actually committed suicide sitting at his desk.

M: I honestly don't know anything about that, although that doesn't mean it didn't happen. I'll have to check into that.

T: I get the feeling there was a fire connected to this place ... I think there was a fire there at some time.

M: A fire in the building?

T: Not necessarily ... but connected to it.

M: Okay.

T:Are there pubs around this place?

M:Yes.

T: I'm getting the name of two pubs. The first one is called The White Hart. Is there a White Hart pub connected to the area?

M: Not to my knowledge, but it's possible. I'll check.

T:The second pub ... I'm not getting the full name, but the first word is 'Jolly', as in 'Jolly Sailor', 'Jolly Cavalier'... that type of thing. Do you know a pub by that name in the area?

M: No, but again I can check.

T: Oh, I'm also sensing the presence of a man. His first name is William.
  I don't know if that is relevant to you in any way?

M: Can you give me anything else about him?

T: Yes, his surname begins with the letter B.

M: Okay, that could be relevant, yes.

T: This man was closely connected with the place, and it's as if he has a
  story to tell about something and he's desperate for it to be heard. He's
  in the world of spirit now, but he definitely wants people to know the
  truth about something … about something that went on there.

M: Anything else?

T: There's a man … You know, he actually knew that the place was
  already haunted. He knew that. He'd been warned that it was already
  haunted.

M: Anything else?

T: Just one other thing. I'm seeing an animal. It's a goat. Actually, it
  might be a lamb … I can't tell. It's strange. To be honest I can't tell
  what it is … whether it's a goat or a lamb … it's really odd.

At this point the interview drew to a close. Tony said that he'd be
interested in visiting this place as he was intrigued by it. Mike told him
that the current owners of the premises had been very co-operative and
had already agreed that the authors could visit the site with a medium if
they wished.

To assess the value of Tony Stockwell's reading – and its accuracy – we
need to compare the information he provided with the known historical
facts and the multitude of stories surrounding the mill and the people
who lived, worked and died there. A point-by-point analysis seems best.

'The first thing I'm getting is that this is a house … but it's not just a
house. Its connected with a business of some kind … I'm not sure what
… but there was commerce or business carried out there. It was a house,
but in some way connected with a business, does that make sense?' We
know that the mill house was connected to the Willington Mill and was
in many respects the centre of gravity of the entire operation.

'It's as if there was a business nearby, but some of the transactions
actually took place in the house.' We know that much of the 'mill
business' was carried out by Joseph Procter at the residence.

'The house … I get the feeling its no longer there. It's been
demolished.' This, of course, was correct.

'I get the feeling of a dock or dockyard nearby … as if the place is by
a river … a dock.' The very name of the village – Willington Quay –

verifies Tony's assertion. Shipbuilding, marine trade and fishing were all crucial aspects of local life.

'But there are other buildings – buildings connected with the house in some way that are still standing. They are really close by.' Although the mill house was long ago demolished, the adjacent East Mill building is still standing.

'I think that although the building has been knocked down there may still be a small part of it standing – maybe a bit of a wall, or something.' Ostensibly there are no parts of the mill house building still standing, but it is entirely possible that the sub-surface aspects of it – such as the cellar – may still be partially intact although buried.

'I don't think I like this house. I don't like it at all. It's really strange.' Tony Stockwell's statement provides a fascinating parallel to something that the mediumistic Jane told Dr John Trotter: 'There is something very strange about this house. I can't understand this. Can we not tell we what it is that is so strange here?' Willington Mill was, we now know, a very strange place indeed.

'It's as if the people who lived there were having to put up with very difficult circumstances.' Jane, we know, picked up on exactly the same sense of discomfort: 'And why does it frighten the servants in that way so that the gentleman is forced to leave? She thinks he has no right to be there, but why has he no right to be there?' Both Jane and Tony Stockwell, then, sensed that the previous occupants were living in the house under uncomfortable conditions and were finding it difficult to stay there.

'I can see lots of people … they're working there – working very hard … maybe factory workers of some kind.' The mill, of course, was teeming with 'factory workers' day and night.

'You know, even though the place is demolished now there's still a presence there. It's not just the building, it's the whole place. There's a bad aura around it.' This statement of Tony's is intriguing too, for it echoes what others already knew and what Joseph Procter latterly came to deny; that the area upon which the mill was built was reputed to be haunted and possibly even cursed. We also know that the apparitions and other bizarre phenomena continued to manifest themselves even after the mill house was demolished.

'It's as if there are a lot of layers to this house in some way … it's difficult to understand, but it's as if its in layers …' Tony genuinely seemed to struggle when he tried to articulate his feelings to Mike here, as if he knew what he wanted to say but just couldn't find the right words. It was possible that Tony was picking up on the fact that there was a 'hidden' layer to the house – the cellar – and a 'haunted' layer – the top floor. Perhaps he sensed that each level of the house seemed to have its own particular 'feel' to it. However, the authors also wondered if the 'layers' Tony was sensing were metaphorical ones, and that it was simply another way of saying that there were 'hidden' aspects to the house that had been kept secret, covered with a blanket of contrived innocence. However one interprets Tony's words, though, they provide food for thought.

'There's a lot of stuff going on in this house, and there's a man … he isn't comfortable with it.' This, of course, could well describe the feelings of Joseph Procter, who bravely endured the paranormal phenomena in the house but certainly wasn't comfortable with them.

'I can hear banging … lots of banging, particularly upstairs and on the stairwell. There's really loud banging. Also loud footsteps upstairs …' We know that one of the most frequent displays of paranormality at the mill house were the anomalous noises, which did indeed include bangs, thumps and 'loud footsteps'. We also know that these often occurred on the stairwell and the landing. Jane also alluded to such anomalous sounds when she said, 'Now I see the gentleman has a wife and a family, and I see the vision standing before him; but why does it make these noises?'

'At the top of the house there are rooms. I'm seeing rooms. These rooms are odd, and there's a disturbing feeling to them. These rooms aren't used … they're empty.' It seems obvious to the authors that what Tony Stockwell was seeing here was the top level of the house which contained the 'disturbed room' and the adjacent bedrooms. Mike was intrigued by Tony's statement that, 'These rooms aren't used … they're empty', for it verified what the authors had deduced circumstantially but was not directly admitted in any written record; that there were times when not just the 'disturbed room' was unused, but actually the entire floor.

'I'm actually seeing a young woman. I think she lost her life there in some way. She doesn't like that house at all. Actually, there was a murder committed in that house … You know, there's something else. This place … I know the house was haunted, but I get the feeling the place was actually haunted before the house was even built, from a long time ago. People said it was haunted … it was known to be haunted. Jane also said something similar; 'It is a haunted house … Why do we want to look again?'

'Yes. Before the building was there … there were slaves. People treated like slaves … maybe black people … they were working there before they were built.' Although there is no historical proof of slavery at Willington Quay before the building of the mill, there were several thousand black people treated as slaves in the UK in the seventeenth and eighteenth centuries, although their exact legal status was unclear. Most were used as domestic slaves or servants, but it is not impossible that some were sent into forced labour.

'I'm also sensing the presence of children – lots of them. There were definitely children living in this house. There's a connection between children and up above … the attic.' We know that the Procters had several children who lived at the mill house, and that other youngsters from the Procter, Carr and Unthank families visited there on a regular basis. There was, we know, even a schoolroom upstairs for the children to use. Although to the authors' knowledge there was no direct connection between the attic and the children of the household, there most certainly was a connection between the children and the upper floor of the house where their schoolroom was.

'There's also a man who haunts this place; in fact, he's the dominant personality. The thing is, he's really very, very aggressive. I'm sensing lots of aggression and anger … and bitterness. This man is violent. I get the feeling that he wielded a lot of power over people, and not always in a good way. He was prominent in the community … he had influence and wasn't afraid to use it. He was also obsessed with money – he had something to do with money or commerce.' This is one of the most intriguing of Tony Stockwell's statements, especially when compared to something that Jane told Dr Trotter back in 1853: 'No, it is a vision; he has no brains in his head; he looks very fierce, his eyes flash like a tomcat's, like a tiger's … Oh, how angry he is! He is so indignant at being disturbed. He does not want the gentleman to find out what he is there for. It is the man who makes the noises in the house. He goes stamping about. We did not like the woman, but the man is far worse. Oh, how angry he is!' It is difficult to resist the notion that both Jane and Tony Stockwell were talking about the same person here.

'I also feel that someone committed suicide there; maybe a man … he might have actually committed suicide sitting at his desk.' This is something that the authors have as yet been unable to verify.

'I get the feeling there was a fire connected to this place … I think there was a fire there at some time.' In 1865, Joseph Procter closed the flour mill for good. It stood empty for two years, until a ferocious fire consumed another mill in Newcastle, and Joseph Procter agreed to rent a portion of his own mill and the adjacent mill house to the company whilst their own premises were rebuilt. This could well be the fire that Tony felt was 'connected' to the mill in some way, but it is possible – even likely – that there was also a fire at the mill itself. Flour mills were particularly vulnerable to fires, and in 1871, when Joseph Procter relinquished his business entirely and sold it to Sampson Langdale, the latter employed a highly dangerous procedure to make soap from partially-crushed olives. Whether this resulted in an actual fire we do not know.

'I'm getting the name of two pubs. The first one is called The White Hart. Is there a White Hart pub connected to the area?' There is no White Hart public house in Willington, or even near it. However, there is a village in Bedfordshire called Willington which does have a White Hart Inn. Although it was 'the wrong Willington', it could well be that this slight error stands as a testimony for Tony's mediumistic abilities and not against them.

'The second pub … I'm not getting the full name, but the first word is 'Jolly', as in 'Jolly Sailor', 'Jolly Cavalier' … that type of thing. Do you know a pub by that name in the area?' There is a public house nearby, in Wallsend, called the Jolly Bowman.

'Oh, I'm also sensing the presence of a man. His first name is William. I don't know if that is relevant to you in any way? … His surname begins with the letter B.' There were several 'Williams' that were connected to the Willington mystery, including William T. Stead. However, the only person called William whose surname began with the letter B was William Brown, one of the first three partners in the milling business at Willington.

'This man was closely connected with the place, and it's as if he has a story to tell about something and he's desperate for it to be heard. He's in the world of spirit now, but he definitely wants people to know the truth about something … about something that went on there.' As William Brown was, as we now know, the first resident in the mill house when the murder took place, Tony Stockwell could well be right. Again, that he should get the first name of the man correct and the second name by abbreviation is quite extraordinary. William Brown is virtually unknown to even dedicated mill historians, and to the authors' knowledge is only mentioned in one obscure nineteenth-century volume.

'There's a man … You know, he actually knew that the place was already haunted. He knew that. He'd been warned that it was already haunted.' This statement is fascinating, because we know from historical testimony that when the Unthanks moved into the mill house in 1806 they were 'warned that the mill was already haunted'. The person who warned Joseph Unthank was almost certainly William Brown.

'I'm seeing an animal It's a goat. Actually, it might be a lamb ... I can't tell. It's strange. To be honest I can't tell what it is ... whether it's a goat or a lamb ... it's really odd.' This statement is highly significant, for it parallels the incidents in which witnesses such as Mary Young, Mrs Hargrave and Thomas Davidson saw animals that they found difficult to identify. We also know that others saw 'funny monkeys' and 'funny cats', and that two employees saw a 'strange donkey' that was more like a prehistoric merrychippus.

Again we are forced to recall the words of Jane, who commented, 'We won't be afraid. Do we like to look? One is a monkey, and the other like a dog. Had the lady dogs and monkeys? They go all about the house. She has got funny things, has she not? We don't like her. What is that other one? Do we know what we call it? It is not a pussy, it runs very fast and gets amongst feet. It is a rabbit, but a very quick one.'

What is intriguing is the way in which Tony picked up on incredibly obscure bits of mill lore that took the authors months to track down and are only accessible to members of the public by great effort – and then only if you know the place you're researching. Tony didn't even have that advantage. All he had was a cropped photograph of an old house in the north of England that is only available in a small number of local history publications. It could have been anywhere. The photograph was only sent to Tony's agent the day before the interview, so any suggestions that he had time to research the picture and somehow establish the identity of the building is highly unlikely.

Tony Stockwell knew nothing about the mill house or its history – and yet, against all the odds, he provided startling proof of much that the authors already knew.

Twenty-Four

PHILIP SOLOMON

Philip has been described as 'one of the finest Spiritualist mediums in the world', and has given consultations to many household names over the years. The late Professor Hans Holzer, one of the world's leading authorities in the field of psychical research, once described Philip Solomon as 'the greatest medium of our time'; praise indeed.

Like all good mediums, Philip has come in for some criticism from rabid sceptics who seem terrified at the idea that there could be more to this universe than what we can see. He seems to just take it all in his stride.

Philip has written a column for *Psychic News* for years now, and as well as being upbeat his writings betray a great deal of insight. He has a good sense of humour, and even when recalling psychic incidents from his childhood which obviously moved him deeply, he finds himself able to interject a dose of wry humour.

It struck the authors that Philip could add his own contribution to the Willington Mill enigma. Mike rang Philip to ask whether he might be able to pay a visit to the Willington site. Unfortunately, Philip's schedule was booked up long in advance and, although he was willing, he simply wasn't able. As with the image sent to Tony Stockwell's agent, Mike simply named the picture file 'Building' so that it wasn't even possible to determine whether it was a house or place of business. The following day, Philip replied.

Hi Mike,

The picture itself is not very clear, but one thing I do seem to be picking up with this is, was there an association to a situation where someone was murdered, perhaps even a serial killer?

I also picked up something to do with large barrels and something to do with a workhouse.

The names of John, Mary, David or Davis.

Hope this might be of some help to you. I would need to come and walk the site to really get its vibe.

Kindest regards,

Philip

The reference to a murder made perfect sense, of course, as, since 1800, there had been rumours that someone certainly was made the victim of a homicide at the mill house. Tony Stockwell had also mentioned this in his reading of the photograph, and the authors found it intriguing that both men had picked up on this fact independently of each other.

But Philip also made reference to the possibility that the perpetrator was not simply a murderer, but a serial killer. The authors hadn't come across anything in their research that had even remotely flagged up the possibility that the anonymous killer could have murdered two or more victims. However, given Philip Solomon's track record for accuracy, they decided to go back over the evidence and double check. Indeed, it was true that one of the difficulties the authors had encountered was working out just who the victim and the murderer had been. They had accumulated circumstantial information about both, but some of it left the authors more confused than ever.

We know that from 1800 onwards there were rumours that someone had been murdered at the mill, but absolutely no detail is available about their circumstances or even their gender. As the authors speculated earlier, it is possible that the victim may have been an itinerant person or tramp, which would explain why they were never listed as missing. Had the victim been an influential person or even simply someone of good standing in the community, it is likely that their absence and death would have drawn much attention.

We know that the Brown family was the first to inhabit the mill for a number of years. If – and we can only speculate – the perpetrator was a member of the Brown family then they would fit in perfectly with the men seen by Jane who wore wide-brimmed hats and spoke archaic English; in other words, they would be Quakers. There is some circumstantial evidence that William Brown may have been implicated in the murder in some way; that is not to suggest he committed it, necessarily, but he may have had some knowledge of the deed and kept it secret. Perhaps it was his involvement with the killing, however peripheral, that soured the relationship between himself, Joseph Unthank and Joseph Procter.

Jane, whilst mesmerised, received a vision of, '… something about a lady. Can it be this gentleman's wife who died here, and thus caused him to leave it?'

However, Jane then determines that the woman concerned was not the gentleman's wife, but another, unnamed woman:

Now we see it is not this gentleman's wife, for she is alive; it was a vision that frightened him away. The lady was only a vision. Do we believe in visions? We don't like to believe in visions, do we? Tell we why the vision came to the gentleman. Had he done anything wicked to the lady?

Although we are unable to positively identify this woman, Jane provides some tantalising clues about her. She was, Jane said, 'as dark as the devil. It is very strange; we don't like her'. She also describes in some detail the woman's dress: 'It is not like we's English ladies' dress. Where has she got that? It is like the dress we saw in foreign countries – a Spanish lady kind of dress. They are rich things she has on. It rustles like silk. Is it not strange? She is just like a devil'.

Whoever the woman was, it seems highly likely that she was of foreign extraction and of some bearing – to quote Jane's own description, 'rich'. If this woman was also a murder victim, it is highly unlikely that she was synonymous with the person murdered in 1800, whose disappearance seems to have precipitated no official investigation and was subject to nothing more than a few wild rumours and bits of juicy gossip. This leaves open the possibility, then, that there were at least two murders carried out at the mill, and not merely one.

On reviewing the evidence further, the authors noticed something that they had previously glossed over; Jane had actually seen no less than three women haunting the mill house in her visionary trances. A clinical dissection of the text enables us to separate the three as follows:

Woman 1: This woman was connected to a 'gentleman' who lived in the house, but was not his wife. The woman was of the opinion that the 'gentleman' had no right to be there, and Jane asks if he might have 'done something wicked' to her. Jane states that the woman died at the mill house.
Woman 2: This female apparition had milk-white skin, flitted around quickly and had 'eyes but no sight'. This woman was also connected to the cellar, and concerning her Jane says, 'the mischief is in the cellar, and tell the gentleman to look there'. The woman has a violent temper, and

is in some way connected to strange animals seen at Willington Mill. Of her, Jane asks, 'Had the lady dogs and monkeys? They go all about the house. She has got funny things, has she not?' In some way Jane seems to be implying that the animals actually belonged to the woman. This same woman wanted to stay alone in the house, never eats and wears a loose cowl or dress.

Woman 3: This apparition, discussed above, wore dark, expensive clothing and jewellery. This lady was of foreign extraction, possibly Spanish, and was of a foul, bad-tempered disposition.

We know that Woman 1 may have been a murder victim for reasons already stated, but what about Woman 2? Jane refers to some 'mischief' concerning her, and states that, 'it is in the cellar'. This too implies that the woman may have been murdered and buried under the cellar floor. Woman 3 may also have been the victim of foul play, although there is no evidence that the authors are aware of to directly support the idea.

Jane also mentioned something about one of the female apparitions; that she was attached to an extremely violent male ghost who wore a priest's surplice. Actually, it is possible to work out with a high degree of probability which one it was. Jane says of the man, 'We did not like the woman, but the man is far worse'. Of the three female apparitions seen by Jane, only two of them had personalities disagreeable to her; Woman 2 and Woman 3. Of the female apparition connected to the male ghost in the surplice, Jane states, 'The woman walked about with her hands upon her breast, as if in pain.' Readers will no doubt recall what the apparition seen by Dr Edward Drury looked like years earlier:

> *[I] saw also the figure of a female attired in greyish garments, with the head inclining downwards, and one hand pressed upon the chest, as if in pain, and the other, viz., the right hand, extended towards the floor, with the index finger pointing downwards.*

Drury, then, clearly saw the same ghost as Jane did in her vision. As it was obviously not the woman dressed in black, Spanish-style clothing, it can only have been the second woman seen by Jane, then, of whom she said, 'the mischief is in the cellar, and tell the gentleman to look there'.

The final piece of evidence comes from both Jane and Drury. Jane testified that there was 'mischief' surrounding this woman's demise 'in the cellar'. The ghost seen by Drury, you will recall, pointed down towards the cellar when seen by the good doctor. Because of this the authors had already suspected that she may have been identifying herself as a murder victim buried there, but Philip Solomon's seemingly outlandish statement regarding a serial killer had made them go over the evidence yet again. What he had said was not outlandish at all, and was actually supported by the testimony of another medium one and a half centuries earlier. Conversely, Philip Solomon's testimony supported something that Jane had alluded to but no other researchers had picked up on – that there may have been several murder victims and not just one in the mill house.

Having identified the three potential murder victims, we now have to turn our attention to the possible suspects.

Suspect 1: Woman 1 was connected to a 'gentleman' who lived in the house who had a 'wife and family'. The woman was not his wife. The 'gentleman' was later troubled by the ghost of this woman and forced to leave the premises. One obvious candidate, then, must be William Brown, the first resident at the mill house, who did have a wife and family and did subsequently leave the premises. The authors have speculated that Brown may have known something about the murder that took place there in 1800 even if he did not actually commit it, and that this may have precipitated the fracture of his relationship with Procter and Unthank. However, it is also possible that Brown may have been forced to leave the premises due to the paranormal activity going on there. Could Brown have actually committed the murder? It is possible, but we simply can't be certain. However, if he was the perpetrator it could explain why the ghost of the victim seemed to have came back to haunt him.

The question, of course, is just what might have caused the suspect – Brown or someone else – to murder the woman in the first place. We know that the 'gentleman' was connected with the woman in some way even though she was not his wife. Had he been having an illicit affair with her, and had she subsequently threatened to expose their dirty little secret to the world? If so, then the suspect may have killed her to keep her quiet. Jane, you will recall, asks whether the 'gentleman' might have 'done something wicked' to her. We also know that the woman actually died at the mill house, further supporting that she was synonymous with the first victim who died there in 1800.

Suspect 2: The female spectre we have called Woman 2 had milk-white skin and had 'eyes but no sight'. As the authors have already stated, the woman was also connected to the cellar, and concerning her Jane says, 'the mischief is in the cellar, and tell the gentleman to look there'.

Before we attempt to identify who might have killed this woman, if indeed she was a victim of homicide, it will pay us to look a little closer at the woman herself.

Firstly, we know that she had a bad-tempered disposition. The old witch who lived on the site in the nineteenth century was described by Montague Summers as 'notorious', and Robert Davidson accused her of being in league with 'His Satanic Majesty'. Whether she was actually bad-tempered or not we do not know, but she certainly doesn't seem to have been very popular. However, there is one intriguing piece of information given to us by Jane about this woman that the authors have already touched upon but demands further elaboration.

The authors have suggested that the bizarre animals seen on numerous occasions at Willington Mill may have been 'familiars' created by the witch to do her bidding, and it is true to say that they certainly displayed some of the classical characteristics of familiars, such as shape-shifting. It may not be coincidental, then, that Jane says of Woman 2, 'Had the lady dogs and monkeys? They go all about the house. She has got funny things, has she not? What is that other one? Do we know what we call it? It is not a pussy, it runs very fast and gets amongst feet. It is a rabbit, but a very quick one.'

When Jane asks, 'Had the lady dogs and monkeys', her words imply a sense of ownership, as if the animals belonged to the woman. Jane's subsequent words reinforce this view, when she says, 'She has got funny things, has she not?'

Tentatively, then, the authors would suggest that the second potential murder victim mentioned by Jane may actually have been the old witch of Willington. Intriguingly, when we look at the potential suspect for that crime, what we discover does fit the known facts, however scant they may be.

Whilst she was on her deathbed, the witch seemingly called upon a Catholic priest to give her confession. The priest subsequently bragged later that he had refused to accede to her wish. It is odd that a witch would want confession from a Catholic priest, and the authors have already suggested that the woman may have been following a bizarre mixture of Roman Catholicism and Wicca at the same time. However, just as odd is the priest's refusal to give a dying woman confession. This implies that there must have been a great deal of enmity between the two, or at least an intense dislike of the witch on the part of the priest. Could things have deteriorated to such a point where the unthinkable happened, and the priest actually murdered the old witch?

This is not such an outrageous idea as it may first seem. Remember, the seventeenth century was a time when followers of witchcraft were persecuted terribly, and 'witches' were still being executed up until 1682. If the Willington witch was as 'notorious' as Montague Summers states, then her murder, although illegal, might not have precipitated any sympathy for her at all. In fact, the local populace might well have been pleased to get rid of her.

Having put forward this hypothesis, then, we can now look at what we know about the man whom Jane intimates might have killed the second victim.

The interviewer, Mrs Frazer, asks Jane whether the man connected to this woman was, 'the person who now lived there [at the mill house]'. Jane argues not, and then goes on to describe him:

> ... he looks very fierce, his eyes flash like a tom-cat's, like a tiger's; he has a white dress on like a surplice. Oh, how angry he is! He is so indignant at being disturbed. He does not want the gentleman to find out what he is there for. It is the man who makes the noises in the house. He goes stamping about. We did not like the woman, but the man is far worse. Oh, how angry he is! What a commotion there is in the cellar! They have not made the hole large enough. It is not close enough to the wall. They must make a wide, deep hole close to the wall, and they should take down the wall.

Apart from his violent disposition and vile temper, the most intriguing thing to note about the man is that he wore a priestly surplice. If the victim was indeed the witch of Willington, and her murderer was a priest, then it is not stretching things to suggest that the priest may be the very same one who refused to give her confession when she was dying. We know that the ghost of the priest was seen on numerous occasions at Willington Mill long after the witch had died.

There is one difficulty with the above hypothesis, however; Jane clearly implies that the victim's body was to be found in the cellar of the house, but we know that the Willington witch died long before the mill house was even constructed. There are two possible solutions to this problem.

Firstly, we know that the witch's cottage was built on the very same site later occupied by the mill. If the witch was murdered, her profane religious beliefs would have prevented her from being buried on consecrated ground and it is possible that she was simply buried next to her dwelling. Perhaps her body was simply covered with an unmarked stone slab. There is some circumstantial evidence that William Brown built a small mill upon the site after the witch's cottage was demolished. When the mill came to be constructed, there may have been a great deal of superstitious consternation about moving the corpse in case it precipitated some sort of demonic payback. Perhaps, then, the mill was simply built over the top of the witch's grave. Later, when Joseph Procter, Joseph Unthank and William Brown built their larger steam-operated mill, it was situated on the same spot as the older mill. We can't be sure about the finer details, but it may well be that through a mixture of fate and circumstance the grave of the witch came to be located beneath the floor of the mill house. This would explain why Joseph Procter had to bring in a team of excavators to dig down and find the slab which covered the witch's final resting place.

The ghost of the priest, we know from Jane's testimony, was extremely disturbed at the idea that someone might uncover the body buried in the cellar: 'Oh, how indignant he is that the gentleman is digging in the cellar!'

Suspect 3: The third apparition discussed by Jane wore dark, expensive clothing and jewellery. This lady was seemingly of foreign extraction, possibly Spanish, and was of a foul, bad-tempered disposition. She was, said Jane, 'as dark as the devil' and, 'just like a devil'. There is nothing in Jane's testimony that suggests directly that this woman was the victim of foul play. However, it seems odd that she should be lumped in with two other ghosts who very probably were. The description given of the woman's garb does not fit that of the mid-seventeenth century, but would not have been out of place in early nineteenth century Europe. Victim 1 may have been having an illicit affair with her killer and was murdered to keep her quiet. Did the same thing happen to the potential third victim? Indeed, could she have been killed by the same man? We simply don't know. In the final analysis, all we can say is that there may have been up to three murders committed on that site over the years, and that the same person might have been responsible for two of them.

When one reads through Jane's testimony it takes some time to separate the numerous characters she saw. Particularly with the female apparitions, she talks in such a way that it is easy to confuse just which one she is relating to at any given time. Sometimes she seems to be talking about the same person, and it is only when one scrutinises the text that it becomes clear they are two distinct personages.

Despite the difficulties, there is a real possibility that Philip Solomon may well have been right when he suggested that a 'serial killer' could have been at work at Willington Quay. To the authors' knowledge this has never been suggested before, and it was only after Philip raised the possibility that Darren and Mike reviewed the historical evidence and found that his proposition was not at all contrary to the known facts.

What Philip Solomon had to say in the rest of his e-mail was also interesting: 'I also picked up something to do with large barrels and something to do with a workhouse'. This statement would obviously fit comfortably with what we know about the Willington Mill. Philip then mentions several names, all of which have mill connections:

'The names of John …' This could be referring to either John Richardson or possibly Dr John Trotter who interviewed Jane.

'Mary …' This could well be Mary Thompson (*née* Young), the mother of Robert Davidson.

'David or Davis …' Philip seemed to be uncertain about this name, and at first the authors wondered if it was connected with the Davidsons, Mary, Thomas and Robert. Another possibility was that it was connected with the farmer called Davison who was friends with Edward Drury. However, in his diary Joseph Procter stated, '6 mo., 1st. [1 June 1841] The two maids, Davis and E. Mann, report they were unable to sleep before 2 a.m. from constant noises, particularly the apparent treading of bare feet backwards and forwards at the foot of their bed, the noise several times awaking the youngest child; some times the tread seemed to pass out on the landing and run up and down stairs. The nursery door was of course bolted'.

It seems likely, then, that the 'Davis' Philip referred to was indeed one of the maids at the mill house.

Like Tony Stockwell, Philip Solomon has played a remarkable part in the outworking of the Willington Mill mystery and, through both psychic and spiritual means, helped us gain a much clearer picture of a remarkable tableau of events.

Twenty-Five

CONCLUSIONS

The Willington Mill story is an incredibly complex one, and at this juncture the authors would like to sum up what they believe was the likely sequence of events over a period in excess of three centuries. They are fully conscious that much of what they have suggested is speculation, but this is unavoidable. Some parts of the historical record are terribly sketchy, and a number of persons involved in the affair made great efforts to conceal the truth. Written records, such as the Procter diary, were deliberately distorted to hide certain facts and to protect the reputations of individuals concerned. Further, much of what has been written about Willington Mill over the years has been inaccurate. Nevertheless, the authors feel that they have uncovered enough information to make a reasonable hypothesis which incorporates everything now known about one of the world's most amazing hauntings.

1665: A Newcastle midwife called Mrs Pepper is accused of witchcraft, but subsequently cleared of the charge. Mrs Pepper seems to practise a strange mixture of Roman Catholicism and Wicca. As far as the authors can determine, after her trial Mrs Pepper disappears from the historical record. At around the same time, a builder at Willington Quay called Oxon constructs a cottage for his mother-in-law to live in. The woman is known locally as 'a notorious witch', and the land around her dwelling is said to be haunted and/or cursed. It is possible that after her trial Mrs Pepper relocates to Willington Quay, and that she and the Willington Witch are actually one and the same person.

We know that Mr Oxon's mother-in-law, the witch, was in poor health. On her deathbed she allegedly asked a local priest to give her confession, but was refused. Her body may have been buried on the site of her cottage, which was subsequently demolished.

c. **1665–1780:** A female spectre is seen in the Burns Closes area near the mill. This may or may not have been the ghost of the Willington Witch.

c. **1780:** A man named William Brown has a mill built on the site of the old witch's cottage.

1782: A local writer called Anthony Hails has an article published in the *Umanian Magazine*, which in some way dealt with the Willington Mill mystery. As the steam-mill at Willington Quay has not yet been constructed, we know that the article must be in some way connected with the legends concerning the old witch of Willington.

1800: William Brown is joined in a business partnership by Joseph Procter and Joseph Unthank. The old mill is demolished and a new steam-mill erected in its place. William Brown and his family move into the house which was constructed as part of the mill complex. Shortly afterwards, someone connected to the mill house – possibly a resident there – commits a murder. We know that the victim was female and in some way connected to a 'gentleman' who lived on the premises with his family. The victim, however, was not the gentleman's wife. At around the same time, rumours start to circulate that a murder has been committed, although no victim seems to have been identified and no perpetrator apprehended. Rumours also start to circulate that the mill house is haunted.

1800-1806: A second murder occurs at the mill house. The female victim is of foreign appearance, well-dressed but bad-tempered. The perpetrator may have been the same person responsible for the previous killing.

1806: William Brown leaves the mill house with his family and relocates elsewhere. Joseph Unthank and his family move into the premises, and almost immediately are confronted with a range of paranormal phenomena.

1807: The partnership between William Brown, Joseph Unthank and Joseph Procter is terminated. Brown opens two mills of his own in Sunderland and North Shields.

1813: Joseph Procter dies and his place in the business is taken by his son, Joseph Procter Jr.

1829: Joseph Procter Jr. moves onto the site at Willington Mill and occupies one of the smaller residences there.

1831: The Unthank family leaves the mill house. Joseph Procter marries and moves into the mill house with his new bride.

1835: Joseph Procter begins to keep his diary of supernatural events occurring at the mill house. George Unthank tells Procter that during his own tenancy nothing supernatural occurred.

1840: Dr Edward Drury and Thomas Hudson carry out their vigil at the mill house. Drury sees the ghost of a woman. This female spectre was probably the Witch of Willington Mill.

1842: Joseph Unthank passes away and his place in the business is taken by his son George Unthank.

1847: The Procter family leave the mill house.

1853: Dr John Trotter of Durham hypnotises a highly clairvoyant patient called Jane. Jane has a series of visions in which she sees the ghosts of the Willington Witch and two subsequent possible murder victims. She also sees the two potential perpetrators of the murders. One of the murderers may have been responsible for killing two of the victims. One of the potential perpetrators is a priest who may have been responsible for killing the Willington Witch.

c. 1902: Catherine 'Kitty' Devore is tragically killed in an accident at the mill, which is now a rope factory. Her ghost is subsequently seen by numerous witnesses.

2009: Medium Tony Stockwell receives information from spiritual and/or psychic sources that confirm murder was carried out at the premises. He also presents many other details that not only support the known facts, but also the information given by Jane whilst hypnotised.

Medium Philip Solomon receives information from spiritual and/or psychic sources that confirm murder was carried out at the premises. He also presents many other details that not only support the known facts, but also the information given by Jane whilst hypnotised. Solomon also suggests for the first time that one of the perpetrators of murder at the mill may have killed more than one person.

Perhaps the fundamental question that needs to be addressed here is just why Willington Mill was subjected to such an intense cacophony of paranormal activity.

We know that in the days of the Willington Witch the area around her home was said to be haunted and/or cursed. There is also the possibility that the bizarre animals seen at the location long after were 'familiars' that the witch had created and which survived after her death. Another possibility is that witnesses were in some way catching a glimpse of the area's prehistoric past and seeing creatures that became extinct aeons ago. Tony Stockwell stated during the reading of the mill house photograph, 'Even though the place is demolished now there's still a presence there. It's not just the building, it's the whole place. There's a bad aura around it'.

We now have independent testimony from two sources that the whole area around the mill was psychically disturbed in some way.

Over the decades numerous ghosts were seen at Willington Mill. Powerful circumstantial evidence suggests that several of these ghosts were identical to those seen by Jane during her hypnotic trances. There is also circumstantial evidence to suggest that three of these ghosts may have been murder victims and that an additional two may have been the perpetrators. It seems almost clichéd, but could it be that the ghosts of the victims were crying out for justice, and that the ghosts of the perpetrators were unable to rest easy in the afterlife because of their actions? The ghost – probably the Willington Witch – who appeared to Dr Drury, pointed towards the floor, indicating perhaps that she was buried beneath the mill house and was distinctly unhappy about it. Jane had a vision of the priest becoming deeply disturbed at the thought of the cellar being excavated. Why? Could it have been because he knew that such an excavation would have uncovered the truth about something terrible he'd done, probably murdering the Willington Witch?

Tony Stockwell said that a man in the afterlife – likely William Brown – 'was closely connected with the place, and it's as if he has a story to tell about something and he's desperate for it to be heard. He's in the world of spirit now, but he definitely wants people to know the truth about something … about something that went on there'.

What did the man, if it was Brown, want to impart to the living? Did he wish to unburden his conscience about something he'd done, or simply known about and guiltily kept as a secret? Or did he wish us to know what others had done, and, from beyond the grave, see justice done for their victims?

It seems to the authors that both the place and the people who once inhabited it have dovetailed together and stimulated a haunting of phenomenal proportions, probably more protracted and intense than any other they are aware of. Profoundly mediumistic people such as Jane, Tony Stockwell and Philip Solomon have, it seems, been destined to play a part in unravelling the Willington Mill mystery and, after the passing of centuries, bring a great deal of closure to it. Others, like Edward Drury, Thomas Hudson and the authors, also seem to have been destined to play a part in the affair; not by exercising spiritual or psychic abilities but, by research and experiment, uncovering the real truth behind the enigma.

The authors are conscious that they have sometimes pointed a finger of accusation – tentative or robust – at several individuals connected with the mill. As far as the authors can determine from the historical evidence, the principle characters in the drama were devout, goodly people who only exhibited relatively minor flaws under the most excruciating pressure. George Unthank struggled to cope with the supernatural occurrences in his home and, in a moment of weakness, lied by suggesting that neither he nor anyone in his family had witnessed paranormal phenomena at the mill house. Once the untruth was set in motion, both he and his cousin Joseph Procter were inevitably forced to perpetuate it. This does not make them bad people. They were good people who simply displayed the flaws that attach themselves to us all.

It is highly likely that there was at least one murder carried out at the site, and possibly three. It is a pity that we cannot as yet identify the perpetrators, for had the authors been able to it would have removed the shadow of suspicion from those who do not deserve to be overcast by it. In the absence of conclusive proof, the authors cannot condemn any of the principle Willington characters as murderers. All they can say is that, hypothetically, some may have had a hand in the demise of the victims. Until further proof is obtained, they must be viewed as innocent without qualification.

Researching the Willington Mill affair was, for the authors, an exhausting process. They do not, however, regret the part they have played in uncovering the truth. There are still many questions to be answered, but at last much of the Willington Mill mystery has been laid bare. Hopefully, others may yet step forward and fill in the remaining gaps in our knowledge. The authors think it likely that those in the afterlife may yet step forward too and do essentially the same thing.

Apart from the solving of most of the historical enigmas surrounding Willington Mill, the authors believe that a far greater service has been performed. They believe that a rational examination of the facts points inescapably to one conclusion; the events at Willington Mill demonstrate powerfully that there is indeed life after this earthly habitation. The dead – as Jane, Tony Stockwell and Philip Solomon already know – still speak to the living. If Willington Mill teaches us anything, it is that we do not truly die at all, and that, at some point, we must all answer for our actions.

In the great scheme of things the haunting of Willington Mill is not really a ghost story at all, but more of a parable. The greatest lessons we can learn from it are to do with human nature and how it reacts to things we cannot fathom.

We cannot say that the spectres of Willington Mill are able to rest just yet, but perhaps with the publication of this book they can at least rest easier.

BIBLIOGRAPHY

Anon, *Ghosts and Legends of Northumbria* (Sandhill Press, 1996)

Anon, *The Parish of Willington, Northumberland* (North Tyneside Libraries & Arts Dept, 1986)

Anon, *The Willington Quay Ghost* (Privately published, *c.* 1972).

Anon, *The World's Greatest Unsolved Mysteries* (Chancellor Press, 2001)

Bath, Jo, *Dancing With the Devil and Other True Tales of Northern Witchcraft* (Tyne Bridge Publishing, 2002)

Boyce, Anne Ogden, *Records of a Quaker Family: The Richardsons of Cleveland* (Thomas Harris & Co., 1889)

Cohen, Daniel, *The Encyclopaedia of Ghosts* (Avon Books, 1991)

Crowe, Catherine, *Ghosts and Family Legends* (T.C. Newby 1858)

Crowe, Catherine, *The Night Side of Nature, or, Ghosts and Ghost Seers, Vol. II* (T.C. Newby, 1848).

Crowe, Catherine, *The Night Side of Nature* [ed. Colin Wilson, fr. The Colin Wilson Library of the Paranormal] (Aquarian Press, 1986)

Davidson, Robert, *The True Story of the Willington Ghost* (Robert Davidson, *c.* 1886)

Gauld, Alan & Cornell, Tony, *Poltergeists* (Routledge & Kegan Paul, 1979)

Hallowell, Michael J., *Ales & Spirits – The Haunted Pubs & Inns of South Tyneside* (Peoples Press, 2001)

Hallowell, Michael J., *Christmas Ghost Stories* (Amberley Publishing, 2008)

Hallowell, Michael J., & Ritson, Darren W., *The South Shields Poltergeist* (The History Press, 2008)

Hapgood, Sarah, *500 British Ghosts & Hauntings* (Foulsham, 1993)

Howitt, William, *Visits to Remarkable Places; Old Walls, Battle Fields, and Scenes Illustrative of Striking Passages in English History and Poetry* (Longman, Orme, Brown, Green & Longman, 1840)

Kristen, Clive, *More Ghost Trails of Northumbria* (Casdec, 1993)

Latimer, John, *Local Records or Historical Register of Remarkable Events* (Newcastle, The Chronicle Office, 1857)

Liddell, Tony, *Otherworld North East: Ghosts and Hauntings Explored* (Tyne Bridge Publishing, 2004)

Playfair, Guy Lyon, *This House is Haunted* (Souvenir Press, 1980)

Poole, Keith B., *Britain's Haunted Heritage* (Guild Publishing, 1988)

Price, Harry, *Poltergeists Over England* (Country Life Ltd 1945)

Puttick, Betty, *Supernatural England* (Countryside Books, 2002)

Richardson, Moses Aaron, *The Local Historian's Table Book Vol. VI* (M.A. Richardson, 1847)

Richardson, William, *The History of the Parish of Wallsend* (Northumberland Press, 1923)

Ritson, Darren W. & Hallowell, Michael J., *Ghost Taverns – An Illustrated Gazetteer of Haunted Pubs in the North East of England* (Amberley Publishing, 2009)

Ritson, Darren W., *Haunted Newcastle* (The History press, 2009)

Ritson, Darren W., *Supernatural North* (Amberley Publishing, 2009)

Robson, Alan, *Nightmare on Your Street* (Virgin, 1993)

Routledge (Creator), *A Historical Dictionary of British Women* (Routledge, 2003)

Solomon, Philip, *The A-Z Spiritualism Dictionary* (Apex Publishing, 2008)

Solomon, Philip, *Guided by the Light: The Autobiography of a Born Medium* (Apex Publishing, 2008)

Spencer, John & Anne, *The Encyclopaedia of Ghosts & Spirits* (BCA, 1992)

Stead, William T., *More Ghost Stories* (London, 1922)

Stead, William T., *Real Ghost Stories* (Grant Richards, 1897)

Stockwell, Tony, *Walking With Angels* (Hodder & Stoughton, 2010)

Summers, Montague, *The Geography of Witchcraft* (London, 1926)

Summers, Montague, *Victorian Ghost Stories* (Simpkin, Marshall Ltd, 1936)

Tegner, Henry, *Ghosts of the North Country* (Butler Publishing, 1991)

Tomlinson, William Weaver, *A Comprehensive Guide to the County of Northumberland* (Walter Scott, 1909)

Underwood, Peter, *The A-Z of British Ghosts* (Chancellor Press, 1971)

Wilson, Colin, *The Supernatural – Unlock the Earth's Hidden Mysteries* (Parragon, 1995)

Wilson, Colin & Wilson, Damon, *The Mammoth Book of the Supernatural* (Robinson Publishing, 1991).